my **revisi⏻n** notes

OCR GCSE (9–1)

HISTORY B
SCHOOLS HISTORY PROJECT

Richard Kennett
Carmel Bones
Sally Clifford
Katie Duce
Martyn Ellis
Alex Ford

HODDER
EDUCATION
AN HACHETTE UK COMPANY

The Schools History Project

Set up in 1972 to bring new life to history for school students, the Schools History Project has been based at Leeds Trinity University since 1978. SHP continues to play an innovatory role in history education based on its six principles:

- Making history meaningful for young people
- Engaging in historical enquiry
- Developing broad and deep knowledge
- Studying the historic environment
- Promoting diversity and inclusion
- Supporting rigorous and enjoyable learning

These principles are embedded in the resources which SHP produces in partnership with Hodder Education to support history at Key Stage 3, GCSE (SHP OCR B) and A level. The Schools History Project contributes to national debate about school history. It strives to challenge, support and inspire teachers through its published resources, conferences and website: **www.schoolshistoryproject.co.uk**

Although every effort has been made to ensure that website addresses are correct at time of going to press, Hodder Education cannot be held responsible for the content of any website mentioned in this book. It is sometimes possible to find a relocated web page by typing in the address of the home page for a website in the URL window of your browser.

Hachette UK's policy is to use papers that are natural, renewable and recyclable products and made from wood grown in sustainable forests. The logging and manufacturing processes are expected to conform to the environmental regulations of the country of origin.

Orders: please contact Bookpoint Ltd, 130 Milton Park, Abingdon, Oxon OX14 4SE. Telephone: +44 (0)1235 827720. Fax: +44 (0)1235 400454. Email education@bookpoint.co.uk Lines are open from 9 a.m. to 5 p.m., Monday to Saturday, with a 24-hour message answering service. You can also order through our website: www.hoddereducation.co.uk

ISBN: 978 1 5104 0406 9

© Richard Kennett, Carmel Bones, Sally Clifford, Katie Duce, Martyn Ellis, Alex Ford 2018

First published in 2018 by
Hodder Education,
An Hachette UK Company
Carmelite House
50 Victoria Embankment
London EC4Y 0DZ

www.hoddereducation.co.uk

Impression number   10 9 8 7 6 5 4 3 2
Year   2022 2021 2020 2019 2018

Cover photo © Shutterstock/Militarist
Produced and typeset in Bembo by Gray Publishing, Tunbridge Wells
Printed in Spain

A catalogue record for this title is available from the British Library.

How to use this book

Features

Each topic from the specification is covered in a double-page spread with the following features:

Progress tracker

Tick this box to track your progress:
- One tick when you have revised and understood the content.
- Two ticks when you have tackled the revision tasks and/or practice questions.

Key point

If you forget everything else, remember this.

Key term

- Key terms are **highlighted purple** the first time they appear.
- Glossaries can be found online giving explanations for these terms. Find them at: www.hoddereducation. co.uk/myrevisionnotesdownloads
- As you work through this book, highlight other key ideas and add your own notes. Make this your book!

Tip

Throughout the book there are regular tips that explain how you can write better answers and boost your final grade.

Revision point

Instead of headings the content is divided into revision points. These are worth learning in their own right. They summarise the three to five key points about each topic. Take the revision points together and you have the course covered.

Revision task

These tasks develop your exam skills. Sometime you write in the book, sometimes you write in your notebook.
Our advice is to work through each chapter twice:
- The first time learning the content.
- The second time using the revision tasks and practice questions.

Answers to revision tasks are provided online.

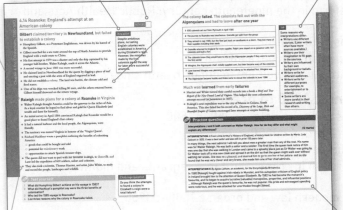

Practice question

- All the main question types are practised either as part of a revision task or as practice questions.
- Model answers to the practice questions are available online: www.hoddereducation.co.uk/ myrevisionnotes.

Bullet point

This is the detailed knowledge you need to back up the revision point. The GCSE course emphasises the use of relevant, precise and detailed knowledge. Think of the revision point as the headline and the bullets the detail you can use in your answer.
- Learn this your own way – make mnemonics, use highlights.
- Mark this up. Use your pen. This should look like your book once you have finished.
- Sometimes we have used tables and charts to make it easier to remember. A good way to revise is to turn a table into bullets or turn the bullets into tables. Whenever you change the format of the knowledge your brain has to process it.

Test yourself

- As you revise the content the first time use these to check your knowledge and recall.
- Try answering them without looking at the bullets. See how you get on.
- Usually the answers are obvious but in case they are not there are answers at www.hoddereducation.co.uk/myrevisionnotes.
- Don't worry about these questions second time through. Focus on the revision tasks instead.
- If you want to revise on the move, there are also self-marking knowledge quizzes on each topic here: www.hoddereducation.co.uk/ myrevisionnotes. These can to be used on your phone or computer.

Answers online

At www.hoddereducation.co.uk/myrevisionnotes we have provided model answers for all tasks and exam-style questions. However, just because you write something different from us it does not mean yours is wrong! Often history does not have right and wrong answers. As long as you can explain your point clearly and support your argument with evidence you can say many different things.

My Revision Planner

CONTENT   TASKS

The Thematic Study

This part of the GCSE tests your knowledge of the history of Britain from 1250 to the present day in one theme: People's Health, Crime and Punishment, or Migration. It is worth twenty per cent of your total GCSE. You must be able to:

Describe the features of different time periods: medieval (1250–1500), early modern (1500–1750), industrial (1750–1900) and since 1900, and how these affected your chosen theme.

Try to be able to list eight key features of each period.

Explain how **three issues** within each theme change or stay the same.

This is the really important one. You must know the specific details of each issue in each of the main periods.

Explain how **five factors** influenced changes and continuities in the theme.

Not all these factors will influence every period, for example in the medieval period there was very little science affecting people's health.

What do I need to do in the Thematic Study exam?

- The Thematic Study exam is taken together with the British Depth study. The exam paper in total is 1 hour 45 minutes and worth 80 marks.
- There are **40 marks** available for the Thematic Study half of the paper and you have just over **50 minutes** to complete it.
- There is a total of **five questions, of which you must answer four**.

For Question 1, give a **one-word or short-phrase answer**.
- Be really **specific**. Avoid vague terms
- 2 minutes in total!

Answer Questions 1 (a–c), 2 and 3.

1. (a) Give **one** example ...   [1]
   (b) Name **one** way in which … during the period ....   [1]
   (c) Name **one** … in the period ….   [1]

2. Write a clear and organised summary that analyses ….
   Support your summary with examples.   [9]

3. Why did … in the period … have limited impact?
   Support your answer with examples.   [10]

For Question 2, write a clear and organised summary that analyses a situation or chain of events.
- Using precise knowledge is key
- You should use one or more second-order concepts in your analysis
- 12 minutes in total

For Question 3, write a clear and detailed explanation.
- Each part of your explanation could be a separate paragraph
- Make sure you use precise knowledge in your explanation
- Base your explanation on a second-order concept
- 13 minutes in total

Answer **either** Question 4 **or** Question 5.

4.* How far do you agree that …? Give reasons for your answer.   [18]

5.* '[statement] How far do you agree with this statement? Give reasons for your answer.   [18]

Answer only Question 4 or Question 5. In your answer you should make your own judgement, explaining how far you agree or disagree with the view in the question.
- Start by making a clear statement of your overall judgement then support this with some detailed paragraphs.
- Give reasons for agreeing and disagreeing (you could write a paragraph on each) but don't feel these have to be balanced.
- Finish with your strongest reason for agreeing or disagreeing, or with a conclusion summarising the main reasons for your judgement.
- 24 minutes in total.

Second-order concepts

In your GCSE history course, you will have developed your understanding of a wide range of 'first-order concepts' such as Parliament, peasants, Protestantism, industrialisation, democracy and many more.

You will also have used different 'second-order concepts'. These are the things that historians use to make sense of the past. They include: cause, consequence, change, continuity, significance and diversity.

These are the main second-order concepts that you will probably use in the Thematic Study:

- **Cause** – why events and developments happened.
- **Consequence** – what the results of events and developments were.
- **Change and continuity** – how things changed or stayed the same over time.

In the exam you will gain marks by using second-order concepts in your answers, but don't feel that you always have to name the second-order concept that you are using. Here are some useful phrases that you can build into your answers:

Cause	'the main **cause** of this event was …'
	'this was **caused** by …'
	'the most important **cause** of the XXXX was …'
	'the underlying **cause** of … was …'
	'the short-term **cause** of … was …'
	'there were several economic **causes** for this …'
Consequence	'the **consequence** of this was disastrous because …'
	'the **consequences** of this event varied for different groups of people …'
	'the **impact** of this was mainly economic …'
	'the short-term **consequences** were … the long-term **consequences** were…'
Change and continuity	'the main **change** was in …'
	'in [give date] there was a sudden **change** in …'
	'Over the period [give dates] there were gradual **changes** in …'
	'… was a turning point in …'
	'There was little **change** in …'
	'There was remarkable **continuity** in …over the period [give dates]'

Chapter 1 The People's Health, c.1250 to present

1.1 Living conditions in medieval Britain, c.1250–c.1500 REVISED ☐

Farming and food
Most medieval people were peasants who did hard physical work on the land. Bad harvests could lead to starvation for peasants and their families

Towns
Medieval towns were small, but they were busy places containing many different crafts and trades. They became especially busy on market days

Limited technology
Technology was limited and most things were made by hand. Water mills and windmills were the most powerful machinery. Printing presses only appeared in the 1470s. The microscope had not yet been invented

Features of medieval Britain

Religion
Almost everyone was a Christian and a member of the Roman Catholic Church. Every parish had its own church and there were also many cathedrals and monasteries

Government
Medieval people were ruled by kings. Kings taxed their people, but the money was mainly used for the king's court and to fight wars. Medieval government did far less for people than we expect today

> **Key point**
>
> Ninety per cent of people lived in the countryside. The quality of life was dependent on a person's place in society, housing and access to clean water and good food.

Quality of housing depended on where you lived and your wealth, which affected your health

Housing in the countryside	<ul><li>The lord of the manor usually lived in a large manor house</li><li>Peasants' houses varied in size, but most lived in small huts made of woven sticks covered in mud</li><li>Animals were valuable so they were sometimes brought inside the houses at night</li><li>Open fires burned in the houses. Smoke escaped through the thatched roof</li><li>Windows were very small with wooden shutters, not glass</li></ul>
Housing in the towns	<ul><li>Houses were built close together in the centre of towns and only the wealthy had gardens</li><li>The workshops of craftsmen and tradesmen were often part of their houses</li><li>People were supposed to clean the drains and street near their houses, but not everyone bothered</li></ul>

Water and waste were a significant hazard to health but this varied depending on where you lived

	Town	Country
Water	<ul><li>**Conduits** were lead pipes which brought spring water to some towns</li><li>Water sellers sold water from leather sacks</li></ul>	<ul><li>Fresh water from springs or wells</li><li>Springs sometimes shared with animals so water not always completely clean</li></ul>
Waste	<ul><li>Public **latrines** (toilets) were often erected in market squares</li><li>Rakers removed waste from towns</li><li>Cesspits were used and then cleared by **gongfermors** (people who removed waste from pits), who took it outside the town walls to be used on the fields, or tipped it into streams</li></ul>	<ul><li>**Midden** (waste heap) in the garden</li><li>Some cesspits constructed near village houses</li><li>Waste used for fertiliser</li></ul>

People's diet depended on their wealth

Bread: nothing mattered more for people's daily lives than a good harvest and a plentiful supply of bread. The poor ate bread made of rye which could contain a fungus that led to illness and death

Meat and fish: people who could afford it ate a wide variety of meat. The Church did not allow people to eat meat on Fridays so fish was eaten instead. Wealthier people also ate cheese, eggs, nuts and fruit. They used honey as a sweetener

Pottage: a thick vegetable soup was widely eaten by medieval peasants. The diet of ordinary people was limited. Meat, fish, eggs and cheese were luxuries

Medieval diet

Ale and cider: ale was made by boiling water (which killed germs) and barley (full of nutrients). Cider was made in a similar way using apples. These drinks were healthier than the water in the towns

Improve the answer

Below is an extract from an answer to the question:

Write a clear and organised summary that analyses people's living conditions in the medieval period. Support your summary with examples.

(9 marks)

Annotate the answer to make it stronger:

- improve the structure
- correct any errors or simplifications
- include more precise knowledge
- improve the analysis by using one or more second-order concepts.

Medieval people lived in houses which had a high roof. There were no windows and the smoke cooked meat that was hanging from the ceiling. There were animals all over and they slept in the houses. People got germs because they could not get rid of waste. Poor people and rich people lived horrible, disgusting lives.

People in medieval times ate meat and vegetables. Poor people drank ale which was made by boiling water and adding barley. Some drank cider too.

People went to the toilet in their garden in things called middens. This was pretty horrible and shows how filthy they must have been but midden privies lasted for many years to come.

Test yourself

1 Why were good harvests so important to the health of medieval people?
2 What was a gongfermor?
3 Describe the different types of housing available to medieval people.

> **TIP**
>
> You need to consider the impact of living conditions on people's health throughout your study of this topic.

1.2 Responses to the Black Death, c.1250–c.1500

The Black Death (1348) spread quickly

- Epidemics such as typhoid and dysentery were common in the Middle Ages, but none of these compared to the most dreadful killer disease: plague.
- The Black Death (plague) began in Asia and spread to Europe along **trade routes**.
- It spread quickly throughout Britain. By the end of 1349 it had reached the far north of England, Wales and Ireland.
- The plague was mainly spread by fleas living on rats, but medieval people did not know this.

> **Key point**
>
> Medieval people may not have fully understood the causes of the Black Death, but they did come up with some ideas about how to prevent it from spreading further, such as avoiding the dead and the dying who were contagious.

We now think that the Black Death took three different forms:

Type	Symptoms
Bubonic plague	• **Buboes** (swellings in the armpits and groin) • Fever: high temperatures • Blisters: fluid filled • Death in a few days
Septicaemic plague	• Bleeding • Diarrhoea and vomiting • Fingers, toes and nose turn black
Pneumonic plague	• Coughing up blood • Chest pains and trouble breathing • Death in two days

There were **different ideas** about the **causes of the plague**

- God was punishing the people for their sins.
- Unusual movements of the planets.
- Miasma, an invisible poison in the air, was to blame.
- People were vulnerable to plague if their humours were out of balance.

There were **different treatments** but **none was successful**

- Tying live toads or chickens to the buboes to draw out the disease.
- **Blood letting** (removing blood) to balance the humours.

People used a range of **measures to protect** themselves

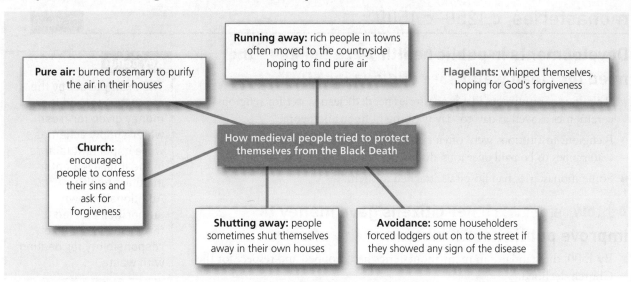

Running away: rich people in towns often moved to the countryside hoping to find pure air

Pure air: burned rosemary to purify the air in their houses

Flagellants: whipped themselves, hoping for God's forgiveness

Church: encouraged people to confess their sins and ask for forgiveness

How medieval people tried to protect themselves from the Black Death

Shutting away: people sometimes shut themselves away in their own houses

Avoidance: some householders forced lodgers out on to the street if they showed any sign of the disease

Test yourself

1 What did medieval people think were the main causes of the Black Death?
2 What was a flagellant?
3 Name one way in which medieval people tried to treat someone who was suffering from plague.

Challenge question

What caused the greater concern to those dying of the Black Death: the painful symptoms or the fear of not being able to confess their sins?

Eliminate irrelevance

Below is an extract from an answer to the question:

Write a clear and organised summary that analyses medieval people's responses to the Black Death. Support your summary with examples. (9 marks)

The answer contains some irrelevance. Identify and delete the irrelevant parts of the answer. Then explain your reasoning in the margin.

Medieval people lived during the years 1066 to around 1500. During this time they faced many issues which affected them. One of these was the Black Death which hit England in 1348. They thought that there were lots of causes of the Black Death. For example, bad air, the planets moving, God's punishment and the work of the Devil. This was because they did not understand germs.

Medieval people responded to the Black Death in different ways. One of the ways they responded was through religion. This was because people believed that the disease was a result of God punishing them. God was very important in the lives of medieval people. They did not understand science so they believed in heaven and hell. As a result of this strong religious belief, medieval people listened to the advice of the Church when it came to the Black Death. Priests encouraged people to confess all their sins and ask for forgiveness. Some people became flagellants. This meant that they went on pilgrimages from town to town. They stopped in market squares and whipped themselves. They felt pain, hoping that God would see this and remove the Black Death from their lives. This response was typical because of the belief that the plague was a result of God's anger.

1.3 Public health in late medieval towns and monasteries, c.1250–c.1500

Developments in public health were linked to the need for clean water for religious institutions

- Religious communities like monasteries needed clean water for religious ceremonies as well as day-to-day washing of linen and people.
- Religious institutions were often rich and powerful. They could pay for water pipes to be paid over long distances.
- Some monasteries had hospitals attached to them.

As towns grew, richer citizens gave money to improve public health instead of the Church

- By 1500, the standards in many monasteries had dropped and respect for the Church declined.
- Towns grew as respect for the Church was in decline. As a result, some wealthy townsmen began to fund the development of new conduits and public privies (toilets).

> **Key point**
>
> The example set by the monasteries, and the money given for fresh water supply schemes, were important factors in the improvements in public health. Additionally, town authorities started to force citizens to take responsibility for dealing with waste.

Town authorities tried to improve the urban environment

Problem	Solution and examples	Effects
• Filthy roads and market places	• Paving market places, paid for by taxation. This happened in Shrewsbury in 1301	• Better trade • Idea spread to other towns
• Dung heaps	• Move to the edge of the towns. This happened in Bristol and York as well as other towns	• Less chance of bacteria spreading
• Dumping waste	• Name and shame waste dumpers. This happened in Norwich in 1287–89	• Purer water supply
• Poor-quality meat	• Guilds (associations) of food producers set standards and fined producers who did not adhere to them. This happened in Winchester in 1329	• Safer meat and other foods

Between 1348 and 1500, London led the way in public healthcare in England

Year	Action
1385	A warden was appointed to check whether London's streets and the banks of the Thames were clear of 'filth and dunghills'
1415	The Mayor of London ordered the rebuilding of a latrine at Moorgate because it had been flooding neighbouring properties with sewage
1430s	The Mayor of London organised the extension of the pipes that supplied London with clean spring water. He and other rich citizens left money in their wills to improve water supplies and build new public latrines

Complete the paragraphs

Below are two incomplete paragraphs from an answer to the question:

Write a clear and organised summary that analyses the strategies used by towns to improve public health in the medieval period. Support your summary with examples. (9 marks)

Paragraph 1 has the opening point missing and Paragraph 2 has some supporting detail missing. Read the paragraphs and complete them by adding the missing information.

PARAGRAPH 1

___. For example, people were made responsible for getting rid of their household waste. They could not simply throw it into the street or river without expecting some sort of consequence. In Norwich, medieval fly-tippers were named and shamed. This was clearly a major step forward in the town authorities taking a role in improving public health.

PARAGRAPH 2

Monasteries were critically important in helping to improve public health. For example, ___ This happened because of the need to ensure that water was available for baptisms and washing. Over time, technology ___.

 Test yourself

1   Why did monasteries need clean water?
2   Give three examples of improvements to public health in towns.

Challenge question

What limited improvement to public health in the Middle Ages?

TIP

Clear and organised summaries mean just that! Organise your thoughts to show a clear line of development.

1.4 Living conditions in early modern Britain, c.1500–c.1750

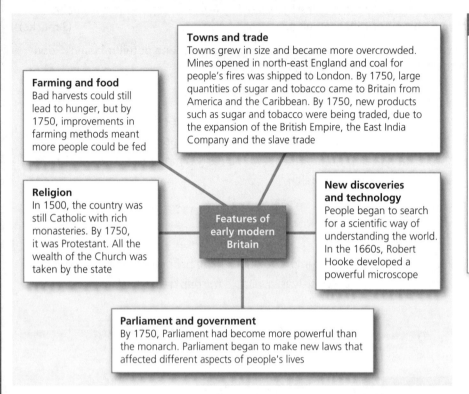

Towns and trade
Towns grew in size and became more overcrowded. Mines opened in north-east England and coal for people's fires was shipped to London. By 1750, large quantities of sugar and tobacco came to Britain from America and the Caribbean. By 1750, new products such as sugar and tobacco were being traded, due to the expansion of the British Empire, the East India Company and the slave trade

Farming and food
Bad harvests could still lead to hunger, but by 1750, improvements in farming methods meant more people could be fed

Religion
In 1500, the country was still Catholic with rich monasteries. By 1750, it was Protestant. All the wealth of the Church was taken by the state

Features of early modern Britain

New discoveries and technology
People began to search for a scientific way of understanding the world. In the 1660s, Robert Hooke developed a powerful microscope

Parliament and government
By 1750, Parliament had become more powerful than the monarch. Parliament began to make new laws that affected different aspects of people's lives

Key point
The early modern period saw some progress in people's living conditions. For many people the quality of housing improved. Bad harvests still caused hunger, but food became more varied, particularly for the rich. Water supply and waste management remained problems, but town and city authorities began to develop solutions.

Bad harvests still caused hunger, but food became more varied for the rich

Social status	Diet	Effects
Rich	• Large quantities and variety of meat and fish • Enjoyed new foods from overseas trade • White bread • Small amount of fruit and vegetables • Wine and ale were drunk more than water	• This was a diet which was about 80 per cent protein so this led to some digestive problems. The rich also suffered from **gout** (severe joint pain)
Poor	• Bread • Vegetables • Occasional: eggs, cheese, fish, meat • Pottage (thick soup)	• This was a healthier diet but lacked vitamin C and iron. Also, there were periods of hunger and starvation for the very poor

There were hidden health dangers

● Meat was often sold from market stalls, but would rot quickly.

● Animals roamed the streets leaving their excrement, which spread bacteria.

● Streets were often unpaved and became muddy tracks when it rained. Animal waste would mix with the mud and rainwater.

● **Respiratory diseases** (lung diseases) were caused by burning wood and coal in open fires. All houses had an open fire which created soot, dust and smoke which people breathed in as they walked the streets.

● Accommodation was crowded and damp, leading to lung problems.

Water = luxury! Getting water was **difficult**

Hygiene	Rich people	Poor people
Water supply	• In some towns companies piped water to houses but this was expensive • Water could be bought from a water seller	• Collected water from free public water fountains called conduits • Bought water from a water seller if they could afford to
Keeping clean	• Servants took care of washing clothes • Bathtubs were used, using water heated by a fire • Soap was made from olive oil for use on skin	• Bathed in a river • Used brushes on their skin, called dry washing

The growth of towns created a **waste management problem**

Problem	Solution	Effectiveness
Household waste	• Scavengers or rakers collected ash, food waste and sweepings from houses once or twice a week • Dunghills outside the towns	• Household waste was effectively dealt with and rakers sold the waste to market gardeners
Urine and excrement	• The flushing toilet was invented in 1596 but only became popular towards the end of the period • Privies (toilets in sheds) emptied into rivers if built nearby • Most privies emptied into a **cesspit** (pit dug under the privy) which could overflow	• The flushing toilet was expensive and only for the very rich who had access to water and drains • Privies and cesspits polluted rivers and wells. Piles of excrement could build up in gardens, yards and alleyways, spreading disease

Spot the mistakes

This paragraph attempts to answer the question:

Why did the living conditions of early modern people cause health problems? Support your answer with examples.   **(10 marks)**

However, there are mistakes. Find them and correct them.

> What people ate affected their health. People who lived at the time ate a lot of meat. There were various meats eaten such as beef, pork, turkey, liver, duck, goose and pheasant. These meats were generally very healthy and were rich in vitamins. Poor people and rich people enjoyed this food. Sometimes people would vomit to make room for more food. This was very unhealthy. Poor people had a healthy diet but lacked some essential vitamins and there were sometimes periods of famine.

Test yourself

1 What were the main differences between the diets of the rich and poor during this period?
2 What caused respiratory diseases in this period?
3 When was the flushing toilet invented?

Challenge question

How far had town authorities made progress with waste disposal since medieval times?

1.5 Responses to the outbreaks of plague in early modern Britain, c.1500–c.1750

REVISED

People continued to live in **fear of plague** until 1667

- There were many serious outbreaks of plague in the period 1500–1667.
- The most serious outbreak of plague was the Great Plague of 1665.
- Plague was terrifying because it was so frequent, the symptoms were terrible, so many people died and nobody understood what caused it.

> **Key point**
>
> Outbreaks of plague continued in the early modern period, culminating in the Great Plague of 1665. Responses by national and local governments show that more actions were taken to prevent the spread of the disease. However, people still clung to their old explanations of its causes.

There was some **continuity** in people's beliefs about the causes of plague

- People still believed that disease was God's punishment for sin.
- The 'bad air' theory was still accepted, although by the end of the period scientists began to think that close contact with an infected person may be a cause of the disease spreading.

New national laws showed changing knowledge and attitudes

Year	New rules	Effectiveness
1518	• Isolate plague victims in their own houses and identify them: straw was hung outside infected houses; anyone leaving the house had to carry a white stick • Isolate people in **pesthouses** outside the city walls	Limited effectiveness as the orders were not enforced everywhere
1578	• Plague orders: seventeen orders including recording the spread of the disease, financial help for the sick, and burning of victims' clothing and bedding • Plague sufferers and the healthy who lived in the same house were **quarantined** (isolated away from others) for at least six weeks • Special prayers were said to ask for God's forgiveness	Effective in reducing the spread of the disease, although it isolated the healthy with the sick and caused criticism at the time The connection between dirt and disease was being made
1604	• The Plague Act increased financial help for the families of the sick • City and town watchmen could use harsh punishments to enforce the policy of isolation • There were harsher **sanctions** (punishments) imposed if a victim left isolation. A plague victim who left their house and mingled with other people could be hanged	The punishments, including death, for those leaving isolation reduced the spread of the disease because people stayed in isolation, but people still did not know that plague was spread by fleas and rats

Some local government reactions were more effective than others

- In Yarmouth, the **local authorities** (people appointed to govern the towns) banned pigs, dogs and cats from infected streets.
- The village of Eyam quarantined itself in 1665 to stop the disease spreading to nearby Sheffield. Sheffield was saved but 75 per cent of Eyam died.
- Some towns like Cambridge only allowed strangers into the city if they had a certificate of health.
- Many towns produced 'Bills of Mortality' – detailed weekly records of plague deaths.

Individuals responded to the plague in different ways

Response	Explanation
People went to church	As in the Middle Ages, nearly everyone believed in God so people prayed that God would take away the plague
People ran away or stayed	Only the rich could leave an infected town. Most people had to stay and deal with the disease as best they could
People tried to find a cure	There was no shortage of people claiming to have invented a cure Plague doctors used sweet-smelling posies to fight against the miasma Smoking tobacco became more popular as people felt that the smoke stopped miasma
People avoided the sick	It became a sensible option to avoid people who were contaminated Sometimes foreign immigrants were blamed
People stuck together	People did not usually abandon their families; they stayed together and prayed that they would survive

 Support or challenge?

Below are a sample exam-style 18-mark question and a table showing various points, which could support or challenge the statement given. For each one, decide whether it supports or challenges the overall statement, then add three more points.

'Responses to plague in the early modern period were not really that much different from responses in the medieval period.' How far do you agree with this statement? Give reasons for your answer. (18 marks)

Points	Supports	Challenges
Isolating victims in their homes		
Miasma was regarded as a major cause of the illness		
Laws were passed which provided help for the victims and their families		
Various methods of treatment were used which were ineffective		
People turned to prayer		

 Test yourself

1 What were pesthouses?
2 Why was Sheffield saved from plague in 1665?
3 What were plague doctors?

Challenge question

What was the most effective response to the plague during the early modern period?

1.6 Impact of local and national government on public health, c.1500–c.1750

The authorities in towns tried to improve the urban environment

- Local government officials were aware that clean streets would help to improve public health.
- People in York were told to clean the area outside their houses and not to put waste for scavengers outside until after 7 p.m.
- A fines system was imposed in York for any household which threw human waste into the street at night. People were encouraged to have their cesspits emptied regularly.

Plague outbreaks stopped after 1670. Towns were still improved but mainly for the rich

- In London, water companies brought piped water into people's homes. However, only rich people could afford this luxury.
- In the period 1670–1750, local authorities made big improvements to the centres of their towns. Large houses were built for the wealthy and streets were lit with lamps.
- In some areas streets were paved.
- Conditions did not improve in the poorer areas of towns.
- Privies and cesspits, and the problems associated with them, were still a typical feature of life.

In the eighteenth century, alcohol became a health problem with stronger and cheaper drinks

- Rum was a **by-product** (not the main product made) of the slave trade and became popular in Britain; sailors were given a **tot of rum** (daily ration).
- Porter's ales and Guinness were very popular by the mid-eighteenth century. These ales were darker and stronger than the traditional ale, but soon became popular. Drinking large quantities had an impact on health.

Between 1720 and 1751, the gin craze was a serious issue

- The craze for gin started because it was cheap. Advertising from the time proclaimed *'Drunk for a penny, dead drunk for two pence.'*
- Gin was a cheap buzz which allowed the consumer to escape from the dreadful drudgery of life at the time.
- Gin drinking led to an increase in crime, the ruin of many families and a big increase in the death rate.
- Many women as well as men became addicted to gin. Some women drank while pregnant, which led to babies being born deformed. Gin became known as 'mother's ruin'.
- One famous incident in 1734 illustrates the danger that gin posed. A woman called Judith Defour killed her two-year-old daughter, Mary, so she could sell her clothes to buy gin.

> **Key point**
>
> During the period 1500–1750, both national and local governments put many more measures in place to tackle public health problems than they had done in the medieval period. Plague was eradicated but governments had to deal with new public health problems such as the gin craze.

The **national government** introduced **measures** to stop the gin craze

Government action	How effective?
Alehouses had to have a licence	Only limited effect as there were many smaller alehouses which were not regulated
Gin Act 1729 introduced a £20 licence fee for sellers and a 5 shilling (25p) tax per gallon for producers	The 1729 Act was impossible to enforce because of the number of small gin shops
Gin Act 1736 increased the licence fee to £50 and the producers' tax to 20 shillings (£1)	The 1736 Act failed because of similar reasons to the 1729 Act. There was rioting against this law. Many people started **distilling** (making) gin in their homes illegally
Gin Act 1751 imposed harsh punishments on anyone selling illegal gin	The 1751 Act worked: **consumption** (the amount drunk) fell

 Which is better?

Here are two answers to an explanation question about the gin craze. Choose the better answer and explain why.

Why did the 'gin craze' cause so many problems for the government? Support your answer with examples.

(10 marks)

ANSWER A

The gin craze was one of those periods of time when people turned to alcohol to solve their problems. The government tried to tackle it by passing laws like the Gin Acts of 1729, 1736 and 1751. These new laws imposed new regulations for gin production and selling. The Gin Act of 1729 introduced a licence fee. The 1736 Act introduced a licence fee of £50. Only when the 1751 Act was introduced did the people realise that they had to stop drinking gin. The government finally solved the problem with this Act.

ANSWER B

The gin craze caused problems for the government because it found it very difficult to solve. The gin craze worried the government because it was causing serious health problems. Gin was cheap and easily accessible. As a result, it was very popular among poorer sections of society who used it to help them to forget about their dreadful lives. For the government, trying to eliminate this problem would be unpopular.

The gin craze caused problems for the government because the laws passed to solve the problem were not effective. Various licences and taxes were introduced in the period 1729–51 but were almost impossible to enforce because there were so many gin houses. After the passing of the Gin Act of 1736 there were serious riots in Spitalfields which led to the government backing down.

 Test yourself

1   What were scavengers?
2   Why was gin known as 'mother's ruin'?
3   Identify one feature of town life which had not changed from the medieval period.

> **TIP**
>
> When explaining, it is important to come up with points that you can relate directly to the question. Then use supporting evidence to back up your points.

1.7 Living conditions in industrial Britain, c.1750–c.1900

Britain in 1900 was very different from 1750

Movement of people, from
- The countryside to the towns, in search of work
- Britain to the colonies of the British Empire, in search of a new life
- Town to town, by the railways which provided cheap transport for all

Work
- People stopped working from home and worked in factories
- Machinery in the countryside made supply of food easier

Democracy
- More and more men were given the right to vote in 1832, 1867 and 1884
- Governments had to take more notice of the needs of the poorer people

Features of industrial Britain

People's ideas changed
- The theory of evolution was accepted
- Religion declined
- Scientists discovered that germs caused disease

Society
- The middle classes had grown in number and power
- The working classes were ignored as their living conditions worsened
- In 1870, children under ten were given free education

Transport and technology
- Railways with steam trains transported goods nationwide
- Steam ships sailed with goods to and from the British Empire

Key point

Living and working conditions during the industrial period were terrible for the urban poor. People who had moved from the countryside to the towns found themselves in crowded, poorly built slum houses, and disease was rife, mainly caused by dirty water. Despite this, by the end of the period, the growth of democracy and trade unionism showed the government that poorer people needed help.

Appalling living conditions harmed people's health

Feature of urban life	What caused this feature?	What effect did this have on public health?
Industrial towns and cities were overcrowded	• **Migration** (movement of people) from the countryside of people looking for work • Housing quality was poor and rents were high; families often lived in one room	• There weren't enough privies so human waste flowed on to the streets, causing disease • Diseases like **tuberculosis** (killer lung disease) were common because of the damp walls in the poorly built houses
There wasn't any help for people who were poor	• Richer people who ran the town councils did not want to see **rates** (taxes) increase to pay for water and waste facilities • Governments believed in an idea called *laissez faire* (leave alone) which said that they should not interfere in people's lives	• Working-class men were only given the vote in 1867 • There was no free healthcare. Doctors and medicines had to be paid for. The poor could not afford this so their health got worse
Disease was common	• Until 1861, people did not know about germs • Many people had to drink dirty water • The six biggest killers of the industrial age were: tuberculosis, influenza, diphtheria, typhoid, typhus and cholera • People lived close together	• Disease spread quickly; people could not understand why • Life expectancy was low • Infant **mortality** (death) was high • In the later part of the period, scientists researched health issues and made breakthroughs by observing city life

The quality of accommodation was related to income

- The cheapest accommodation was a rented cellar space which was damp and not ventilated.
- Back-to-back housing was cheap and poorly constructed. A family often had just one room downstairs and another upstairs.
- The effect on health was significant as the lack of fresh air led to chest infections and lung-related diseases.

Private water companies were unregulated and waste remained a problem

- Water companies sourced their water from ponds, rivers and streams.
- The water was often dirty and unhealthy; typhoid and cholera were prevalent.
- In the early part of the period, people still did not understand that dirty water caused disease.
- In most areas of cheap industrial housing the sewers could not cope with the amount of human waste.

- Privies collected waste which built up until it was emptied or it overflowed. In a typical street of industrial housing, over ten families shared one privy.
- There were some developments during the period but they often created more problems. For example, where better sewers were built, the waste emptied into the rivers where water companies got their 'fresh' water from.

The industrial working class's poor diet caused malnutrition and a weakened immune system

- The diet of the industrial working class was basic: potatoes, bread, butter, beer and tea. Beer was cheaper than tea!
- In the towns and cities it was often difficult to obtain fruit and vegetables. This contributed to **malnutrition** (a lack of the right nutrients).
- The diet was high in carbohydrates (needed for the long hours of labour).

- Until the end of the nineteenth century, there was no government **regulation** (checking quality) of food so working-class families often ate food which had been mixed with other products. This is called adulteration.
- Cheap meat was sometimes available to the **underprivileged** (poor) but the quality of the meat was very poor, sometimes from diseased animals.

Make revision cards

In your exam you will need to use precise, relevant and detailed information in your answers. Revision cards can help to make the details stick. When making revision cards, write a topic heading on the front and then put up to five key words/phrases on the back. Use the words to explain your knowledge on the topic. Once you have made your cards you should test yourself, or work with a friend to test each other. An example revision card is shown below.

Overcrowded cities	• Rural to urban migration • Fast built, poor-quality housing, high rents • Unhealthy conditions = diseases like TB

Here are some headings for you to make revision cards for this part of the course.

- housing
- water
- waste
- diet.

Test yourself

1 What is meant by rural to urban migration?
2 What was a back-to-back style house?
3 Identify two diseases which became very prevalent during this period.

Challenge question

How far do you agree that the industrial age represented progress for the majority?

Practice question

Why were the new industrial towns and cities so unhealthy? Support your answer with examples. (10 marks)

1.8 Responses to cholera epidemics

Cholera spread quickly and affected the poor

- Cholera was brought to Britain in 1831 by sailors who arrived in British ports from India.
- Water became infected by the excrement of people who carried the disease (most towns and cities did not have a proper sewerage system).
- There were cholera **epidemics** (widespread outbreaks) in 1831–32, 1848, 1854 and 1865–66. Overall, it killed over 100,000 people.

> **Key point**
>
> There were four significant cholera epidemics in Britain between 1831 and 1866. Advances in scientific research forced changes in government attitudes towards improving public health by making sure that people had clean water and a hygienic waste management system.

Beliefs and government responses changed over time

Date	Beliefs about disease and change over time	Government responses and change over time	
		National	**Local**
1830s	People still believed in the miasma theory which said that the disease was spread by poisoned air The Church said that cholera came from God as a punishment for sin Connections were made between dirt and disease	The Central Board of Health was set up to study the disease in other countries A national day of fasting, humiliation and prayer on 2 March 1832	Burning tar in the street to purify the air Clearing rubbish from the streets to stop the stench Quarantines which stopped poor people entering towns Separate hospitals and graveyards to stop contamination Health boards to give advice and to monitor the spread of cholera
1848	Edwin Chadwick produced his 'Sanitary Report'. It contained shocking details of the public health crisis	The Public Health Act of 1848 set up the General Board of Health and encouraged local councils to set up health boards to clean up towns	Limited progress because the 1848 Public Health Act did not force change Town leaders thought that change would be too expensive Local ratepayers resented an increase in taxation to pay for the Act
1854	Dr John Snow proved that cholera was spread by infected water. He found evidence that a water pump near his surgery was the cause of the disease in that area	A *laissez faire* attitude continued The General Board of Health was abolished!	
1866	The ideas of Snow were widely accepted In 1861, Louis Pasteur had proved that germs cause disease	Sanitary Act 1866 made local councils responsible for sewers, water supply and street cleaning. Good sewers limited the impact of the 1866 cholera epidemic	In 1865, Joseph Bazalgette's new London sewerage system was opened. This **revolutionised** (made a huge change to) public health

New developments like **germ theory** helped to change beliefs

- Knowledge about how disease spread improved through the work of scientists like John Snow and Louis Pasteur. By the time of the 1866 cholera outbreak, the government was starting to abandon its *laissez faire* attitude and introduced new laws to clean up the towns and cities.

- The miasma theory was replaced by the germ theory. This made dealing with the causes of diseases like cholera much easier as the importance of cleanliness became accepted as a way to prevent disease.

- The research into how disease spread led to a local and national government focus on providing clean water and good waste management systems such as the replacement of the **midden privy** (toilet with a pit dug underneath) with a **pail privy** (toilet with a removable bucket).

- In 1875, a new Public Health Act replaced the 1848 Act. This new law forced local councils to take responsibility for cleaning up their towns, which included the appointment of health inspectors.

There were no further cholera epidemics in Britain after 1866. It had taken four major epidemics and changes in scientific thought to bring about a change in the way that government dealt with diseases such as cholera.

 Spot the second-order concept

Second-order concepts are the things that historians use to make sense of the past. They include: cause, consequence, change, continuity, significance and diversity. In the exam you will gain marks by using second-order concepts in your answers, but don't feel that you have to name the second-order concepts that you are using.

This extract from an exam answer contains several examples of second-order concepts. Highlight where they occur and note the second-order concept in the margin.

Why were there different responses to the cholera outbreaks in the industrial period? Support your answer with examples. **(10 marks)**

> Responses to the four major outbreaks of cholera differed. Historians can explain these different responses by looking at the times in which they occurred. For example, during the first major outbreak of cholera in 1831, people still accepted the miasma theory. This idea was centuries old and demonstrates that there had been very limited progress in understanding the causes and spread of diseases like cholera. By the 1848 outbreak, there had been advances in scientific understanding, most notably the work of Snow. However, beliefs and attitudes had not changed and his work was ignored. There was a turning point in 1854 when Snow proved his theories by his investigation of the Broad Street water pump. This development had a long-term impact on how both national and local government dealt with improving public health.

 Test yourself

1 Give the dates of two cholera epidemics in Britain.
2 Why did cholera spread so quickly?
3 Why did the 1848 Public Health Act have limited effect?

Challenge question

Why did it take so long for the miasma theory to become outdated?

1.9 Public health reform in the nineteenth century: Public Health Acts and local initiatives

Events included: **Chadwick's report, changes to central government** and the **1848 cholera** epidemic

- Edwin Chadwick's 1842 report on *The Sanitary Conditions of the Labouring Population of Britain* challenged the government to introduce reform to address the appalling poverty that many industrial workers lived in.
- Chadwick suggested that a national public health authority be set up which would force local councils to act to improve the public health by providing clean water and a sewerage system.
- *Laissez faire* was being challenged.
- Water company bosses objected to Chadwick's proposals because they thought they might affect their profits.
- **Ratepayers** (local taxpayers) objected to Chadwick's proposals because they did not want to pay more in tax.
- The cholera epidemic triggered the 1848 Public Health Act.

Key point

There was a change in the attitudes of both central and local government towards public health. As a result, several pieces of legislation were passed which represented significant progress, particularly the 1875 Public Health Act.

The **1848 Public Health Act** was a **limited step forward**

Evidence of progress	Limitations
• The Act created the General Board of Health • The government could force local councils to make public health improvements • Councils were encouraged to have a medical officer who would oversee local health issues • The *laissez faire* approach was challenged	• The government could only force local councils to make improvements if the death rate was higher than 23 per 1000 • By 1853, there were only 163 places with a local board of health • The General Board of Health was abolished in 1854 so there was limited long-term impact • London was excluded • Still no government minister for public health

Make revision cards

Make revision cards with one for each significant event and law:

- 1848 Public Health Act
- The Adulteration of Food Act 1860
- Sanitary Act 1866
- Sale of Food and Drugs Act 1875
- Public Health Act 1875.

Test yourself

1 Why was Edwin Chadwick significant in this period?
2 What does adulteration of food mean?
3 Identify one example of local action which led to improvements in health.

Different reasons helped to speed up reforms

	Form	Reason for reform	Progress and limitations
1860	The Adulteration of Food Act	There were no laws to protect people from eating unhealthy food. For example, bread was often made with a combination of flour and substitutes like **alum** (potassium sulphate)	**Progress** • The first law to try to prevent the contamination of food • Provided for the appointment of food analysts • Another blow to *laissez faire* **Limitations** • Only seven analysts were appointed • There were no compulsory inspections of food • The Act was soon ignored, revised in 1872 and eventually replaced by the 1875 Sale of Food and Drugs Act
1865	Opening of Bazalgette's new London sewerage system	London sewers flowed into the central part of the River Thames, causing the 'Great Stink' in 1858, and the miasma theory was still accepted	**Progress** • 1300 miles of sewers were created in London • Low-level sewers built behind embankments (man-made banks) took waste to a treatment plant • The spread of **waterborne** (can survive and travel in water) diseases was prevented
1866	Sanitary Act	A cholera outbreak and the need to make local authorities responsible for public health led to this development	**Progress** • Forced local authorities to take action to provide fresh water, and sewage and waste disposal • All houses had to be connected to a mains sewer • It defined 'overcrowding' • If local authorities did not carry out the work they were billed by central government, who did it for them • Another blow to *laissez faire* **Limitation** • The Act was clumsily worded and was slow to be put into operation
1875	Sale of Food and Drugs Act	There were still some basic food quality problems which needed solving. Harsher punishments were needed for those who continued to break the law	**Progress** • Improved the quality of basic foods • Introduced harsh sanctions for food adulteration • Local authorities were given the power to seize unhealthy food
1875	Public Health Act (replaced 1848 Act)	The 1867 Reform Act meant that working-class men were now voters and so their views had to be listened to	**Progress** • Local councils were forced to clean up towns, and provide clean water and proper drains and sewers • A medical officer had to be appointed by local councils • Sanitary inspectors had to be appointed • This led to improvements in public health
1894	Opening of Thirlmere Dam, Manchester	Cities likes Manchester found providing fresh water difficult. Developments in engineering helped projects like this to happen	**Progress** • Fresh water was carried from a new reservoir to Manchester • Hugely successful feat of engineering • Encouraged other towns and cities to fund similar schemes **Limitation** • Took over fifteen years from approval to completion
1891	Slum clearance in Spitalfields	There was a need to clear out the overcrowded, unhealthy slum dwellings	**Progress** • Newly established London County Council ordered the clearance of the overcrowded Old Nichol slum • New modern three-roomed tenements were built

1.10 Living conditions in Britain since c.1900

Feature	Britain in 1900	Britain in 2000
Society	Lots of work in heavy industry Majority working class No welfare state Leisure hours = exercise Most people went to church Women could not vote Life expectancy = 50	Lots of service industry jobs Majority middle class Comprehensive welfare state Leisure hours = inside homes Less than ten per cent go to church Everyone aged eighteen and over can vote Life expectancy = 77
Technology	A few cars for the very rich No aeroplanes Radio telegraph system sent messages internationally Electricity was becoming popular	Cars are a normal feature Air travel is a normal feature Telephones and internet have led to instant communication Electricity exists in almost all homes

Key point

The twentieth century was one of great change. In Britain, it was the century in which the welfare state was born and developed. The impact of war and various governments led to improvements in health, yet by the end of the century people's poor diet and inactivity caused new health issues.

Public housing and food issues had an impact on public health

Turning point	Impact on housing
The First World War	**Positive:** • Government took responsibility for public housing • 50 per cent of promised 500,000 homes were built • 1930 Housing Act led to final slum clearances **Negative:** • Slow progress by government
The Second World War	**Positive:** • Cheap high-rise accommodation with gas and electricity **Negative:** • High-rises destroyed the **community spirit** (friendly close neighbours) of back-to-back housing
The government of Thatcher	**Positive:** • People were encouraged to buy their council houses **Negative:** • Local councils could not replace houses sold; this encouraged more private landlords, some of whom rented poor-quality accommodation which affected health

Factor	Impact on food
War	During the Second World War, **imports** (products coming in to a country) fell and so food was **rationed** (restricted). People were encouraged to grow food and keep animals. **Rationing** (controlling the amount of food) improved people's health
Technology	Refrigeration and **canning** (preserving food in cans or tins) improved supply and made food cheaper Home refrigerators allowed people to keep foods longer and microwave ovens led to convenience foods becoming popular
Wealth	After 1950, people became richer and could afford the new technology The impact of immigration meant that Indian and Chinese food became popular
Fears	The disease **BSE** (mad cow disease) affected cattle and spread into the human food chain. This created a fear about modern farming methods Fears about artificial ingredients led to a demand for fresh local produce instead

Changing living conditions have created new health problems

- In the first part of the twentieth century, **smog** (smoke and fog) in the big industrial cities from factories caused conditions such as pneumonia.
- The Clean Air Act 1956 made people burn smokeless fuel such as charcoal. This created smoke-free zones which helped to solve the problem of killer smog.
- Since 1980, the huge increase in car ownership and other forms of transport has caused increased air pollution.
- During the Second World War, people became healthier and did more physical activity as fuel supplies were rationed.
- Labour-saving devices, cars, televisions and computers have all led people to become more inactive.
- Since the 1980s, Britain has faced a series of health scares about its food. The amount of sugar consumed by children is causing new health problems.

 You're the examiner

Below is an extract from an answer to the question:

Why were there improvements in public housing during the period 1900–2000? Support your answer with examples. (10 marks)

Annotate the answer to make it stronger:

- improve the structure
- correct any errors or simplifications
- include more precise knowledge
- improve the analysis by including more reasons and explaining how they are connected.

There were lots of reasons why there were improvements in housing. One reason is that WW2 destroyed lots of homes which then had to be rebuilt. Another reason was WW1 because soldiers were promised new homes but they were not all built. Mrs Thatcher got people to buy their council houses. The homes which were built after the bombing raids in WW2 were tower blocks. These had modern features like gas and electricity. The government used the opportunity to clear some of the Victorian slums which still existed. Modern homes were not always popular because there was no community spirit any more and people missed this.

 Test yourself

1 Identify one turning point in the history of housing since 1900.
2 What was meant by 'homes fit for heroes'?
3 What provisions were made by the 1956 Clean Air Act?

1.11 Responses to Spanish influenza and AIDS

The **Spanish flu epidemic (1918–19)** was **devastating**

Between 1918 and 1919, Spanish influenza (flu) killed almost three times as many people worldwide as the First World War had done in the years 1914–18.

The symptoms of Spanish flu were terrifying:

- The flu started with cold- or flu-like symptoms: high temperature, aches and pains, coughs and sneezing.
- The symptoms developed into **pneumonia** (a lung disease). The skin went blue and there was bleeding from the nose, ears or stomach.

We know now that it was a bird flu which also infected humans. The reactions to Spanish flu had mainly positive effects:

- face masks prevented contamination
- newspapers, films and posters gave advice on how to prevent contamination.

> **Key point**
>
> Epidemics like Spanish flu and AIDS surprised the governments of the time. Reactions were swift and generally effective. The media was used to get information out to citizens as quickly as possible as communications technology advanced.

The **response to HIV/AIDS** in **Britain** has **changed**

AIDS (acquired immune deficiency syndrome) is not a disease but a medical condition: the virus which causes AIDS is called HIV (human immunodeficiency virus). It is spread through blood or bodily fluids. There are five distinct phases of reaction to AIDS in the UK.

When?	Response to HIV/AIDS in Britain
1970s–1983	Raised awareness of the disease but negative reaction. People affected were **stigmatised** (having the disease was seen as shameful)
1984–85	Alarm and fear that AIDS could be spread easily through the slightest contact with a victim
1986–87	Better understanding of AIDS: • Diana, Princess of Wales, shook hands with and hugged AIDS victims, showing that the disease was not spread by touch • Publicity campaigns helped to educate the public
1988–95	Understanding and acceptance of HIV/AIDS: • TV and the media embraced the need to publicise the disease and the need for a supporting attitude • Support for charities and research, including the Freddie Mercury tribute concert
1996 onwards	A worrying decline in awareness of HIV/AIDS: • Educational campaigns about HIV/AIDS stopped • HIV and sexually transmitted infection cases on the rise again

Develop the detail

Each of the following statements could be used to support points made in an exam answer to the question:

Write a clear and organised summary that analyses responses to the AIDS epidemic in Britain since 1900. Support your summary with examples. **(9 marks)**

However, the statements are vague and general. Add specific details to show that you understand the general point being made. One example has been done for you. This will help with most questions as it is important throughout your exam to use 'detailed, accurate and relevant knowledge'.

Vague statement	Detail and explanation
TV soaps had characters who had HIV/AIDS	As part of the strategy to get the British public to be more supportive of HIV/AIDS victims, the TV soap 'EastEnders' had a character who had HIV/AIDS. As the character was heterosexual, this caused a wide audience to change their views about the disease being a 'gay plague'
Princess Diana changed people's attitudes	
AIDS was blamed on gay men	

 Sort the similarities and differences

Sort the information in these two pages into the table below.

Similarities in the reactions to Spanish flu and HIV/AIDS	Differences in the reactions to Spanish flu and HIV/AIDS

Challenge question

How far do the examples of reactions to Spanish flu and AIDS prove that modern governments cared much more about their people than those from earlier periods?

 Test yourself

1 What was Spanish flu?
2 Identify one method of mass communication used by those fighting Spanish flu.
3 Identify one way in which attitudes to AIDS changed between 1984 and 1995.

1.12 Growing government involvement in public health since c.1900

Laws have had a significant impact on public health

These laws saw the government having a more 'hands on' attitude to improving public health.

> **Key point**
>
> In 1900 the Conservative government had no plans to review welfare provision. The 1906 Liberal government changed this attitude and introduced a series of reforms. From that time, governments have passed laws to improve public health with varying degrees of success.

When?	Law	How significant?
1902	The Midwives Act	**Short term**: regulated **midwives** (nurses who specialise in the birth and care of babies) by requiring them have a certificate **Long term**: the Central Midwives Board set up by the Act lasted until 1951
1906	Free School Meals	**Short term**: provided a hot meal for some poor children as it was the responsibility of local councils to choose whether to fund them or not **Long term**: the principle of giving poor children a free meal was made compulsory in 1914. The school milk scheme began in 1934
1907	Medical inspections in schools	**Short term**: it had an immediate impact as it examined all children but it did not treat the problems found **Long term**: school clinics were set up in 1912 to treat children. Medical inspections continued and by the 1930s most local councils had provisions to treat minor ailments
1908	Old-Age Pensions	**Short term**: it saved many of the aged poor from the **workhouse** (places where the poor went if they were homeless and penniless) **Long term**: the principle of providing help for the elderly still exists today
1911	National Insurance	**Short term**: it protected against unemployment and sickness by providing money to live on **Long term**: the principle of helping working people still exists today
1919	The Housing Act	**Short term**: the Act promised 500,000 homes 'fit for heroes' but economic problems meant that less than half were built **Long term**: a series of Housing Acts over time led to slum clearances, council housing and government recognition that housing was a social responsibility
1929	The Local Government Act	**Short term**: the workhouse system ended. Local councils took responsibility for running local hospitals **Long term**: old workhouses became new hospitals and these were eventually taken over by the National Health Service in 1948
1940	Immunisations	**Short term**: mass immunisation programmes against diphtheria in 1940 and tuberculosis in 1948 **Long term**: vaccinations became routine under the National Health Service
1948	National Health Service	**Short term**: free medical care for all UK citizens **Long term**: healthcare was no longer a luxury that only a few could afford
1956	Clean Air Act	**Short term**: various measures introduced to control air pollution **Long term**: the first of a series of laws which are designed to protect the environment
1974	Health and Safety at Work Act	**Short term**: regulations put in place to ensure the health and safety of workers **Long term**: it is still in force today

Smoking is a good example of effective government action ...

- In 1962, the link between smoking and cancer was accepted so the government began to introduce measures to encourage people to stop smoking.

- Between 1964 and 2016, the government took steps to tackle smoking. These included banning cigarette advertising (1964–86), promoting nicotine-replacement products (1998), banning smoking in public places (2007) and finally making all cigarette packaging blank (2016).

- The government has started to tackle the problem of obesity, which is a major cause of heart disease. Campaigns to eat less and move more are helping to combat this problem.

... Although the government was also criticised

It has been seen as:

- being too slow to act, probably because of the loss in tax revenue from selling cigarettes, and the loss of donations from tobacco companies

- being interfering or a 'nanny state'. Some think that people should be free to buy what they want even if it harms them.

> **Challenge question**
>
> To what extent do you agree with the view that by improving the public health, successive twentieth-century governments have made people too dependent on the state and unwilling to help themselves?

Eliminate irrelevance

Below is an extract from an answer to the question:

'Government action has always been the most important factor in improving public health in Britain.' How far do you agree with this statement? Give reasons for your answer. (18 marks)

The answer contains some irrelevance. Identify and delete the irrelevant parts of the answer. Then explain your reasoning in the margin.

Government action in the twentieth century has really improved public health. For example, the Liberal government of Asquith and Lloyd George from 1906 introduced a series of measures which had a hugely positive impact on public health; medical inspections, for example. But the Liberal government had to tackle the issue of women's suffrage too which stopped them doing more. Women in Britain had campaigned for the vote for years and the NUWSS and the WSPU carried out various strategies, some of them violent, like smashing windows. At the same time, the government introduced school clinics in 1912, at the height of the suffragette militancy.

The National Health Service was also a really important government strategy which improved public health. The Labour government introduced this after the Second World War. If Churchill had won the 1945 election this may not have happened, but the voters rejected him as they did not feel that he would be an effective peacetime leader.

Test yourself

1 What is a midwife?
2 Which law ended the workhouse system?
3 Identify one measure that was introduced to improve the health of children.

2.1 Medieval crimes and criminals, c.1250–c.1500

REVISED

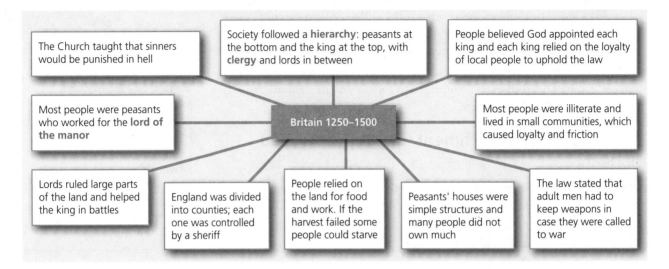

The Church taught that sinners would be punished in hell

Society followed a **hierarchy**: peasants at the bottom and the king at the top, with **clergy** and lords in between

People believed God appointed each king and each king relied on the loyalty of local people to uphold the law

Most people were peasants who worked for the **lord of the manor**

Britain 1250–1500

Most people were illiterate and lived in small communities, which caused loyalty and friction

Lords ruled large parts of the land and helped the king in battles

England was divided into counties; each one was controlled by a sheriff

People relied on the land for food and work. If the harvest failed some people could starve

Peasants' houses were simple structures and many people did not own much

The law stated that adult men had to keep weapons in case they were called to war

Medieval **criminals committed serious and petty crimes**

- **Felonies** (serious crimes), such as murder and stealing expensive goods (worth more than 12d), would lead to severe punishment such as **hanging**.
- People most feared gangs of robbers, generally **outlaws** (people who were on the run to escape the law), who would **ambush** travellers and burgle houses.
- **Petty crimes** (small and not very significant) included getting into debt and doing limited harm to a person or property. Occasionally laws were passed against **dice** and football as the Church argued that they encouraged idleness.
- The majority of crimes were non-violent and theft was by far the most common crime.
- Later on in the fifteenth century, crime grew as rebellious rich landowners used their **retainers** (private armies) to control their local area. This kind of problem grew worse during the **Wars of the Roses** (1455–85).
- There was terrible **famine** across England in the fourteenth century when harvests failed. Hunger and debt increased the crime rate.

Homicide **rates were high**

- Sudden deaths had to be reported to a **coroner**. A few months after this, the homicide case went to trial. Homicide included justifiable homicide, homicide in self-defence, accidental homicide, suicide and murder.
- Suicide was considered a serious crime because the Church taught that only God could decide when a person's life should end.
- Records suggest over half of medieval homicides stemmed from arguments.
- **Strip farming** involved people working very close to each other, with heavy tools to hand and no real medical care, which helps to explain the high homicide rates. Arguments were worse during harvests.

> **Key point**
>
> The teachings of the Church, the rigid structure of society and the people's reliance on farming to make ends meet all contributed to both the types of crime committed and rates of crime during the medieval period.

In the medieval period, **new crimes** emerged as attitudes and circumstances changed

- **Vagrancy** (when people wander from place to place in search of work) became a problem after the Black Death of 1348 killed over half of the population. The resulting shortage of workers led to cases of debt and theft.
- In 1351, Parliament passed a law that required all able-bodied men to swear that they would stay and work in their home village. In 1388, it became illegal for a labourer to leave their **hundred** (a way in which counties were divided) without written permission.
- Medieval **manors** (villages) were free to devise their own laws and punishments. After 1350, **scolding** (the crime of using offensive or abusive speech in public) appeared. It spread steadily after this date and was applied mainly to women.
- In 1351, **treason** (the crime of plotting against your monarch or country) was clearly defined. It included a woman killing her husband, as men were thought to be the head of a family. **Counterfeiting** coins was also considered to be treason.
- **Heresy** (spreading beliefs not allowed by the Church) became a major crime after 1500. The Church feared that people such as the **Lollards** might go to hell if they were free to interpret Christ's teachings.

Test yourself

1. What was considered to be a serious crime in the medieval period?
2. Name two types of new crimes that emerged during this time.
3. Who were the most feared criminals during the medieval period?
4. Who were the Lollards?

Practice questions

1. Name one type of crime committed during the medieval period. (1 mark)
2. Name one type of crime that was considered to be homicide in the medieval period. (1 mark)
3. Name one reason why homicide rates were high in the medieval period. (1 mark)

Spot the second-order concept

Second-order concepts are the things that historians use to make sense of the past. They include: cause, consequence, change, continuity, significance and diversity. In the exam you will gain marks by using second-order concepts in your answers, but don't feel that you have to name the second-order concepts that you are using.

This extract from an exam answer contains several examples of causation (why something happened). Highlight the extract to show where they occur.

Write a clear and organised summary that analyses the types of crimes committed between 1250 and 1500. Support your answer with examples. (9 marks)

During the medieval period, a number of different crimes were committed. However, homicide rates were particularly high because this crime included a range of offences such as suicide, homicide in self-defence as well as murder. In addition, the medieval system of strip farming sometimes led to increased hostilities between people as it meant they worked closely alongside each other. The situation was further worsened when harvests failed, as they did in 1315–16, as this led to famine and desperation. It was such situations that led to arguments and rising crime rates.

As attitudes and circumstances changed during this period, new crimes appeared. For example, the Black Death struck England in 1348 and killed over half of the population. This led to a shortage of workers, which in turn led to vagrancy becoming a problem as some people wandered the country looking for work. As a result, in 1351, Parliament passed a new act that stated all able-bodied men had to swear they would stay and work in their home village.

2.2 Enforcing law and order, c.1250–c.1500

With no paid police force, **law enforcement** was carried out by **sheriffs, constables** and **ordinary people**

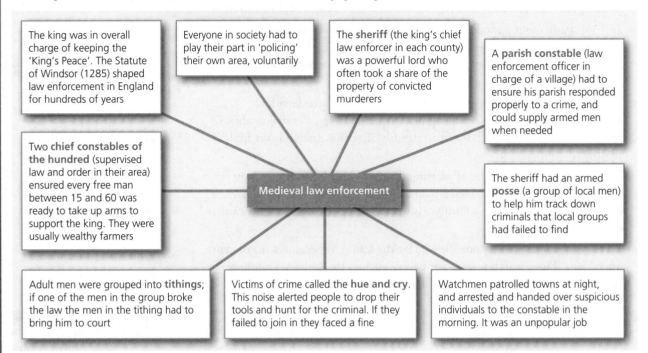

The king was in overall charge of keeping the 'King's Peace'. The Statute of Windsor (1285) shaped law enforcement in England for hundreds of years

Everyone in society had to play their part in 'policing' their own area, voluntarily

The **sheriff** (the king's chief law enforcer in each county) was a powerful lord who often took a share of the property of convicted murderers

A **parish constable** (law enforcement officer in charge of a village) had to ensure his parish responded properly to a crime, and could supply armed men when needed

Two **chief constables of the hundred** (supervised law and order in their area) ensured every free man between 15 and 60 was ready to take up arms to support the king. They were usually wealthy farmers

Medieval law enforcement

The sheriff had an armed **posse** (a group of local men) to help him track down criminals that local groups had failed to find

Adult men were grouped into **tithings**; if one of the men in the group broke the law the men in the tithing had to bring him to court

Victims of crime called the **hue and cry**. This noise alerted people to drop their tools and hunt for the criminal. If they failed to join in they faced a fine

Watchmen patrolled towns at night, and arrested and handed over suspicious individuals to the constable in the morning. It was an unpopular job

A **system of courts** was established to deal with **serious and petty crimes**

- Royal courts heard the most serious criminal cases and were overseen by a paid judge. Jurors were drawn from the criminal's local area.
- From 1293, royal judges visited each county two or three times a year to try cases of serious crime in the county assizes.
- From 1361 **Justices of the Peace (JPs)** took over **hundred courts** (courts run by a county sheriff) by judging people in their own courts. After 1388, they did this four times a year at the **quarter sessions**.
- Manor courts dealt with most crimes in England, including offences by the lord's **villeins** and, from 1250, all petty crimes that affected the local community, such as thefts and fights. The court was run by the lord and wealthy villagers made up the jury.
- Towns had borough courts, which had a similar role to hundred courts.
- Church courts dealt with crimes that were considered to be un-Christian, such as priests having sex, homosexuality and failure to attend church. There were no juries and priests heard the evidence and passed judgement.

Medieval juries were often unwilling to convict

- Jurors used their knowledge of the accused's background to reach their verdict.
- Jurors had to know as much as possible about a case before it went to court.
- The judge accepted the jurors' verdict and few court cases lasted longer than twenty minutes.
- Medieval juries were quite lenient in serious offences as punishments were harsh.

> **Key point**
>
> Although the king was in overall charge of keeping the peace, his work was carried out by a range of different law enforcement officers and courts. The local community was key both in helping to maintain peace and in passing judgement on crimes committed.

Complete the paragraph

Below is an incomplete paragraph from an answer to the question:

Write a clear and organised summary that analyses how law and order was enforced in the period 1250–1500. Support your summary with examples. (9 marks)

Read the paragraph and complete it, adding in the missing information.

> Law and order was enforced in many different ways between 1250 and 1500. Although the king was in overall charge of police keeping he had a range of people to help him keep the peace within local areas. In addition to these law enforcement officers, there was a complex system of courts where criminal cases were heard. The royal courts heard the most serious crimes; however, Church courts dealt with crimes relating to religion. Medieval juries were made up of local people but they were often unwilling to convict criminals of serious crimes.

 ## Eliminate irrelevance

Below is an extract from an answer to the question:

What caused the medieval system of law enforcement? Support your answer with examples. (10 marks)

The answer contains some irrelevance. Identify and delete the irrelevant parts of the answer. Then explain your reasoning in the margin.

> Medieval England was a very Christian country that followed Roman Catholic teachings. Most people were Christians; however, there were some examples of people who did not believe in the Catholic faith. They were known as Lollards. From the fourteenth century, this group challenged the teachings of the Roman Catholic Church and demanded to be allowed to read the Bible in English. Because religion was so important the Church was in charge of Church courts. People who were accused of offences that were un-Christian, such as failing to attend church or homosexuality, were tried in these courts. There were no juries in these courts and the priests heard the evidence and convicted the accused.

 ## Test yourself

1   What was the role of a sheriff?
2   What sort of crimes were tried at royal courts?
3   How often did quarter sessions meet?
4   Name two features of medieval juries.

 ## Practice question

'In the period 1250–1500, law and order was the responsibility of wealthy individuals.' How far do you agree with this statement? Give reasons for your answer. (18 marks)

2.3 Medieval punishments, c.1250–c.1500

Fines, public humiliation and prison were used for petty crimes

- The king received fines paid at the hundred court and the quarter sessions, and the lords received fines from the manor courts.
- Mayors and town leaders took the fines imposed by borough courts, and the Church kept fines for sins such as gambling.
- Public humiliation included forcing women accused of scolding to sit in public on a **cucking stool** (a sort of wooden toilet).
- Public humiliation also included putting traders in the **stocks** or the **pillory** for cheating customers by selling faulty goods.
- Prisons were used to keep those waiting for trial or to punish **debtors** (people who owed money), forgers, or those who had falsely accused someone at trial.
- Prisoners had to pay the **gaoler** (person in charge of the prison) for bedding, food and drink. Rich prisoners stayed in luxury rooms in castles. Poor prisoners were often found begging, chained up outside a gaol.

> **Key point**
>
> A range of punishments were used to make criminals suffer and to deter others from committing similar crimes. However, a number of factors impacted on the severity of punishment a person might have received, such as their wealth and whether or not they knew the jury who were convicting them.

Serious crimes were punishable by death, carried out to show the public that justice had been done

- Hanging involved slow strangulation. It was used for crimes such as murder and burglary and robbery (even if nothing was stolen).
- After 1275, hanging was also used for rape and theft of goods worth more than 12d. Before 1350, there were local variations on hanging, such as being thrown from the cliffs at Dover.
- **Hanging, drawing and quartering** was used to punish common people committing **high treason** (plotting to kill the king) and counterfeiting coins.
- Being burned alive was used to punish **petty treason** (such as a wife killing her husband) and heresy, such as the beliefs of the Lollards.
- For all cases of serious crime, the criminal's property was passed to the king. Innocent victims or their families never regained their valuables.

People did all they could to avoid these punishments. Here are ten ways they used to cheat death

1 Criminals could run away to avoid a trial and join an outlaw gang.

2 Criminals could stay in a church or cathedral to avoid a trial: these places offered sanctuary. Staying there for 40 days and nights meant they could confess and then **abjure the realm** (leave England forever).

3 If a criminal had powerful friends, such as a member of the jury at the manor courts, or the local lord, this could help them to avoid a trial.

4 Sometimes prisoners refused to plead guilty or not guilty. They were sent back to gaol to live on rotten bread and dirty water. This way, they avoided the king getting their property, but would be likely to die a long, unpleasant death.

5 Jurors at assize courts often knew the criminal on trial and would try to help. Strangers were more likely to be hanged than local people.

6 To avoid being executed even when found guilty, criminals could buy a pardon from the king, although this was only helpful for the wealthy.

7 Kings often pardoned criminals in times of war if they agreed to join the king's army.

8 A death sentence was often changed to a fine for pregnant women, even if they had been found guilty.

9 Criminals could also claim the **benefit of clergy** (priests were given this option as only the Church could try them and the Church did not execute people). This involved reading a verse from the Bible aloud while begging God for mercy. Illiterate criminals would learn the verse by memory. This did not benefit women, as they could not become priests.

10 Criminals could become a king's approver, which involved providing the court with evidence against other criminals. If they were found guilty, the accuser would be let off their own sentence.

 Develop the detail

Each of the following statements could be used to support points made in an exam answer to the question:

Write a clear and organised summary that analyses the types of punishments used in the period 1250–1500. Support your summary with examples. (9 marks)

However, the statements are vague and general. Add specific details to show that you understand the general point being made. This will help with most questions as it is important throughout your exam to use 'detailed, accurate and relevant knowledge'.

Statements	Specific details
Punishments for petty crimes included fines, which were often payable to the rich, such as the lord	
In the Middle Ages, land was the basis of all wealth and most people were poor	
More violent crimes, such as murder and theft, were punished using a range of harsh methods. These methods included hanging, drawing and quartering, and burning alive	
In the early Middle Ages, there were variations on hangings	
However, despite the harshness of these crimes, there were a number of ways in which criminals could be let off or could escape trial. They could seek sanctuary or they could work for the king by giving details of other criminals	

 Test yourself

1 What was a cucking stool used for?

2 What were medieval prisons like?

3 What was the benefit of clergy?

4 What was a king's approver?

2.4 Early modern growth in crime: Puritans, vagrants and highway robbers, c.1500–c.1750

There were some continuities and new changes in crime and punishment

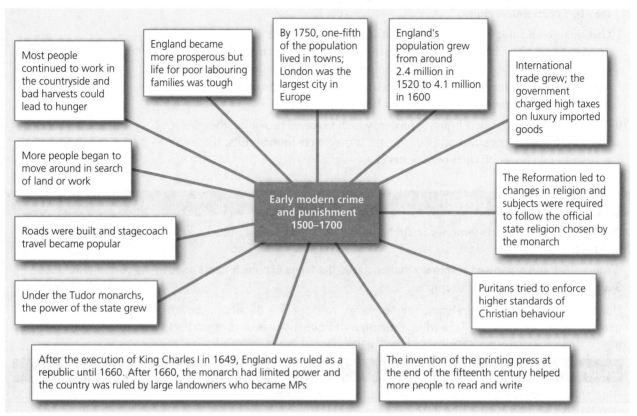

Most people continued to work in the countryside and bad harvests could lead to hunger

England became more prosperous but life for poor labouring families was tough

By 1750, one-fifth of the population lived in towns; London was the largest city in Europe

England's population grew from around 2.4 million in 1520 to 4.1 million in 1600

International trade grew; the government charged high taxes on luxury imported goods

More people began to move around in search of land or work

The Reformation led to changes in religion and subjects were required to follow the official state religion chosen by the monarch

Roads were built and stagecoach travel became popular

Early modern crime and punishment 1500–1700

Under the Tudor monarchs, the power of the state grew

Puritans tried to enforce higher standards of Christian behaviour

After the execution of King Charles I in 1649, England was ruled as a republic until 1660. After 1660, the monarch had limited power and the country was ruled by large landowners who became MPs

The invention of the printing press at the end of the fifteenth century helped more people to read and write

Population growth and poverty led to a new type of crime: vagrancy

- There was a dramatic increase in crime from the mid-sixteenth century until the mid-seventeenth century, due to the huge increase in population, falling wages and rising prices.

- When harvests failed because of bad weather, or if there was a decrease in demand for English woollen cloth, people had no choice but to leave their village and become vagrants.

- In Elizabethan England, printed pamphlets and books sensationalised gangs of vagrants committing thefts, assaults and murders.

- Thomas Harman's book of 1568 warned of dangerous 'rogues' and 'vagabonds' roaming the land.

- In reality, few vagrants were criminals. They travelled alone or in twos or threes in their desperate search for work.

> **Key point**
>
> While the types of crimes committed by ordinary people in the early modern period were similar to the medieval period, vagrancy, witchcraft, smuggling and highway robbery emerged as new, significant crimes.

Test yourself

1 What was a vagrant?
2 Which religion led to an increase in 'moral crimes'?
3 What was a 'familiar'?
4 What was a venturer's role in a smuggling gang?

Religion and people's beliefs influenced their perception of crimes, and crime rates

- Growing Puritan beliefs in the late sixteenth century led to more punishment of moral crimes such as drinking, swearing, not attending church, scolding in public and **sexual immorality** (sexual activity outside of marriage).
- Between 1500 and 1650, there was widespread belief in magic and the Devil, which led to concern about witchcraft.
- People believed the Devil gave witches power through **familiars** (spirits in the form of small animals which fed on the witch's blood).
- Accusations of witchcraft often began as a quarrel between a rich villager and a poor, elderly woman who had made a nuisance of herself.
- Witchcraft trials increased during the famine of the 1580s/1590s and during the chaos of the English Civil War.
- The emergence of scientific ideas about the world in the early eighteenth century led to a decrease in witchcraft trials.

By the **eighteenth century, organised crime** such as **smuggling** emerged

- The government's dependence on **import duties** (taxes paid by the merchants who imported the goods) for its revenue led to smugglers secretly bringing goods into the country without paying the duty.
- Tobacco was a popular product to smuggle, and from 1720 brandy, silk and tea attracted smugglers after their import duties were raised by 30 per cent.
- Smuggling gangs were made up of a venturer to provide the money to buy goods in France or Holland, a ship's captain and crew to bring them across the Channel, and landers to bring the goods ashore on small boats.
- Smugglers included respectable people who disliked the duties, and poor people who could earn as much through smuggling as by doing a week's honest work.

Highway robbery, another type of organised crime, also emerged

- During the seventeenth and eighteenth centuries, roads were built and travelling increased, which led to growing concern about **highway robbers** (gangs of robbers on horseback) attacking them.
- Roads were remote and badly lit, and people travelling carried their money and jewellery with them (there were no banks).
- While highway robbers were later portrayed in a romantic way as gentlemen thieves, in reality they were often brutal thugs.

 Spot the second-order concept

This extract from an exam answer contains several examples of causation (why something happened). Highlight where they occur.

What led to the development of new types of crime in the early modern period? Support your answer with examples. (10 marks)

In the late sixteenth century, the population of England grew from 2.4 million people in 1520 to 4.1 million in 1600, which led to a rise in prices and therefore increased rates of poverty. The problem was worsened when harvests failed because of bad weather or when there was a downturn in demand for English woollen cloth. As a result, many people had no choice but to leave their villages in search of work, begging and sometimes stealing to survive. These individuals were known as vagrants, who became of great concern to people in Elizabethan England. In addition to this, people's beliefs in the early modern period influenced what they considered to be a crime. For example, because people at that time believed in magic and the Devil, there were increasing numbers of witchcraft trials. People believed that the Devil gave the witch powers through familiars, which were often animals which fed on the witch's blood. In addition, the growth in Puritanism led many people to see immoral behaviour, such as sexual immorality, drinking and swearing, as crimes. In the seventeenth and eighteenth centuries, organised crimes became the major concerns.

2.5 Enforcing early modern law and order, c.1500–c.1750

There was **both continuity and change** in **law enforcement** in the early modern period

Continuity from the medieval period	Change from the medieval period
• There was no police force so local communities continued to police themselves • Individual victims of crime made the decision to prosecute someone • The constable raised the hue and cry and people were expected to join in • Law enforcement was administered by unpaid and **amateur** (not officially trained) officials, such as JPs, constables and churchwardens	• As towns grew, some started to employ more **watchmen** to patrol the streets and arrest drunks, vagabonds and other criminals • The most important change was the extended role of JPs. From the seventeenth century, more criminals were dealt with at petty sessions • As a result, the office of sheriff became less important, and manorial courts and Church courts declined

A **range of courts**, similar to the medieval courts, dealt with **serious and petty crimes**

- The **assizes** were the country's main courts for serious crimes.
- They dealt with 'capital offences' such as murder, manslaughter, **grand larceny** (stealing goods worth more than 12d), witchcraft and rape. Punishment could result in a death sentence.
- JPs met in the quarter sessions four times a year to try less serious crimes, including petty theft (goods worth less than 12d). During Elizabeth I's reign, 1558–1603, JPs were given extra powers such as licensing ale houses, regulating local sports games and arresting vagrants.
- In the seventeenth century, small groups of JPs began to meet in their local areas to cope with the amount of work. They also dealt with petty crimes such as drunkenness.
- Manorial courts dealt with crimes committed by people on individual manors such as letting animals stray. These court duties were soon taken over by the petty sessions in the seventeenth century.
- Church courts concerned themselves with keeping up church attendance and Christian behaviour, although they declined after 1660.

Test yourself

1. What types of crime were dealt with in the assizes?
2. Which courts dealt with petty crimes?
3. What new duties did JPs acquire in during the Elizabethan period?
4. Which courts began to take over the role of manorial courts?

Around **90 per cent** of the population **lived in villages and small towns.** Individual communities **laid down the law**

With no police force, local wealthy men were appointed for one or two years as unpaid and untrained churchwardens, constables and overseers of the poor

The local officials were sometimes criminals or troublemakers themselves

Law enforcement was flexible as the law enforcers often knew the criminals, which meant most people only appeared before the courts once

Community

Local people were relied on to help, for example, in providing evidence against the accused in witchcraft trials

The process of investigating a crime was often started by the victims, or people who were offended by a neighbour's behaviour

It became more common in the early modern period for wealthier people to make accusations against their poorer neighbours

 Complete the paragraph

Below is an incomplete paragraph from an answer to the question:

Write a clear and organised summary that analyses how law and order was enforced in the period 1500–1750. Support your summary with examples.

(9 marks)

Read the paragraph and complete it, adding any missing information.

Many of the medieval systems of law and order continued during the early modern period. There was still no police force so the major aspects of law enforcement fell to the citizens. These citizens were very important in the early modern period as they were often called on to help in other ways. The constable still raised the hue and cry. Law enforcement officers were often rich and they had to do the job unpaid and untrained for one or two years. There was still a range of different courts to deal with different types of crime. For example, the assizes dealt with serious offences. These crimes were considered to be very serious and therefore they were punished very harshly by death. JPs dealt with more petty crimes in the quarter sessions. However, changes did occur. In the early modern period, the role of JPs increased to include more everyday duties. As the seventeenth century progressed, these JPs began to meet more regularly in petty sessions in their local areas. In addition, Church courts and local manor courts declined in influence as the petty sessions developed.

 Sorting into a table

Look carefully at the headings in the table below. Use the information on these two pages to fill in as much detail as you can about each heading. Aim for at least three facts per heading.

Law enforcement officials	
Role of the community	
The assizes	
Quarter sessions	
Petty sessions	
Manorial courts	
Church courts	

2.6 Early modern punishments, c.1500–c.1750

Humiliation and physical punishments became widespread as crimes such as vagrancy increased

- Public penance was used for crimes such as **fornication** (having sex outside of marriage). The accused would stand up in front of a church and confess to their sins.
- The pillory was used for those who traded unfairly or committed sexual offences. Offenders' heads and arms were put in a frame where they were pelted with rotten food, stones and excrement.
- Disorderly women, scolds (women accused of scolding) and dishonest tradesmen were paraded around on a cucking stool.
- Another punishment for scolds was the **scold's bridle** (a heavy iron frame locked on to the woman's head with a projecting spike pressing down on her tongue).
- A harsher punishment was a ducking stool, which saw the offender tied to a chair with an iron band and repeatedly lowered into a river or pond.
- Stocks were heavy pieces of wood to keep offenders locked in position, often in a public place, so people could spit on, insult or kick them.
- Vagrancy led to an increase in whipping, branding and humiliation. From 1572, vagabonds over the age of fourteen were whipped and burned through the ear.

Using prisons for punishment became less common as bridewells were introduced

- As in the medieval period, prisons were mainly used to hold those in debt or those awaiting execution or another form of punishment.
- Castles, town gates and bridges continued to be used as prisons. Some new prisons were built after the 1531 Gaol Act, which forced JPs to build prisons where they were needed.
- **Bridewells** (also called 'houses of correction') were a new form of punishment where prisoners were forced to work or punished if they refused to do so.
- Bridewells were introduced as a response to the problem of vagrancy.
- In 1609, the Vagabond Act forced JPs in every county to build bridewells.

The new Bloody Code system (1688) increased capital offences. People were hanged for minor crimes

- Capital offences other than treason were punished by hanging, which took place in public. There was no sudden drop so the condemned person faced a slow and agonising death.
- The Bloody Code was introduced in 1688 and lasted until 1820. MPs used the threat of **capital punishment** (the execution of offenders) to scare people into obeying the law.
- In 1723, the Black Act made poaching deer, rabbit and fish into a capital offence.
- By 1820, there were 200 capital offences, compared to 50 in 1688, and most of them were for crimes against property.
- However, the number of hangings decreased from the middle of the seventeenth century as assize judges and juries were often unwilling to pass a sentence of hanging for minor crimes.

Key point

While there was some continuity in the use of punishments between the medieval and early modern periods, some types of punishment became more widespread. New types of punishment were introduced to deal with the changing nature of crime and the lack of a police force.

 Test yourself

1 What types of crimes were punished with the pillory?
2 How were women accused of scolding punished?
3 Why were bridewells introduced?
4 What was the Bloody Code?

TIP

If you think you have finished an answer to an exam question, make sure you take time to read back through it to see if you can develop your explanation further.

Support or challenge?

Below are a sample exam-style 18-mark question and a table showing various points that could support or challenge the statement given. For each one, decide whether it supports or challenges the overall statement, then add three more points.

'In the period between 1500 and 1750 there were big changes in punishment.' How far do you agree with this statement? Give reasons for your answer. **(18 marks)**

Points	Supports the statement	Challenges the statement
The Bloody Code		
Vagrancy		
The pillory		
Hanging, drawing and quartering		
The cucking stool		
Bridewells		

Spot the second-order concept

This extract from an exam answer contains several examples of change and continuity. Highlight where they occur.

'In the period between 1500 and 1750 there were big changes in punishment.' How far do you agree with this statement? Give reasons for your answer. **(18 marks)**

Although prisons continued to be used for debtors and those awaiting other forms of punishment, bridewells were a totally new form of punishment introduced in the early modern period as a response to the new crime of vagrancy. The accused were forced to work as punishment for their crimes, or, if they refused, they faced a physical punishment. In 1609, the Vagabond Act forced JPs in every county to build bridewells, which shows how their numbers increased in this period. In addition to this, from the late seventeenth century the government introduced the Bloody Code, which showed a big change in punishment. This was a series of laws that meant the number of offences which people could be hanged for significantly rose, and by 1820, 200 crimes were considered to be capital offences. These minor crimes included the poaching of deer, rabbit and fish. The reason why these crimes were treated in such a harsh way was because there was still no police force in early modern England, so wealthy landowners had to take drastic steps to protect their wealth and property; they hoped through introducing the Bloody Code that potential criminals would be frightened into becoming law-abiding citizens.

2.7 Crimes and criminals, c.1750–c.1900

The **Industrial Revolution**, between **1750 and 1850**, caused or contributed to **major changes**

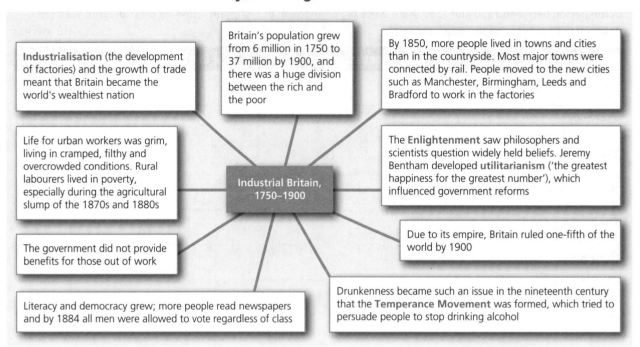

Industrialisation (the development of factories) and the growth of trade meant that Britain became the world's wealthiest nation

Britain's population grew from 6 million in 1750 to 37 million by 1900, and there was a huge division between the rich and the poor

By 1850, more people lived in towns and cities than in the countryside. Most major towns were connected by rail. People moved to the new cities such as Manchester, Birmingham, Leeds and Bradford to work in the factories

Life for urban workers was grim, living in cramped, filthy and overcrowded conditions. Rural labourers lived in poverty, especially during the agricultural slump of the 1870s and 1880s

Industrial Britain, 1750–1900

The **Enlightenment** saw philosophers and scientists question widely held beliefs. Jeremy Bentham developed **utilitarianism** ('the greatest happiness for the greatest number'), which influenced government reforms

The government did not provide benefits for those out of work

Due to its empire, Britain ruled one-fifth of the world by 1900

Literacy and democracy grew; more people read newspapers and by 1884 all men were allowed to vote regardless of class

Drunkenness became such an issue in the nineteenth century that the **Temperance Movement** was formed, which tried to persuade people to stop drinking alcohol

The **Industrial Revolution** had a **huge impact** on **types of crimes, many** of which were **new**

- Petty theft was the most common type of crime, with factories and warehouses full of goods, middle-class homes stuffed with possessions, and banks opening in towns and cities.
- New crimes included fare-dodging and vandalism on railways, failing to send children to school, stealing water from standpipes, as well as 'white-collar crimes' such as businessmen embezzling their investors.
- Only ten per cent of crimes involved violence and the murder rate was low.
- Most crime was **opportunistic** (unplanned) and committed by first-time offenders.
- About three in four of all offenders were men; the most common offence for women was prostitution.

Overall, **crime increased** from **1750 to 1850**, followed by a **fall** in the **late nineteenth century**

- An increase in population, growth in trade and the environment of growing towns and cities led to a rise in crime after 1750.
- Overcrowded lodging houses packed with people's possessions, and crowded alleyways, contributed to increasing crime rates.
- There was a very sharp increase in crime after 1815, when the Napoleonic Wars finished – thousands of soldiers returned home to face rising prices, falling wages and a deepening economic **recession** (decline).
- Poverty and times of high unemployment also contributed to steep rises in crime rates.

> **Key point**
>
> Although crime rates fluctuated, the general increase in crime from 1750 to 1850 was a consequence of the huge changes brought about by the Industrial Revolution.

New ideas emerged about causes of crime, such as poverty, bad moral habits or physical features

- 'Radical thinkers' such as John Glyde made the link between crime and poverty, arguing that the poor environment in which working-class children grew up was the cause of crime.

- Those with more **conservative** (traditional) views blamed crime on the bad moral habits of the poor, especially drunkenness.

- A growing number of people joined the Temperance Movement. The movement argued that pubs left poor people without money, and led to gambling, prostitution and violence.

- Some thought that poor people made a deliberate choice to be criminals. They believed that children born into this 'criminal class' inherited criminal tendencies from their parents.

- Others argued that criminals could be identified by their physical features, such as the shape of the skull or the hands.

- People in the nineteenth century were very interested in crime, enjoying the **penny dreadfuls** (cheap illustrated newspapers detailing the most shocking crimes) and Charles Dickens' novels.

 Mind map

Mind maps are a useful tool to help you to organise information. You can use them to structure your notes, and also to plan answers to a particular question. The mind map below has a number of headings. For each one you need to add supporting detail from this spread.

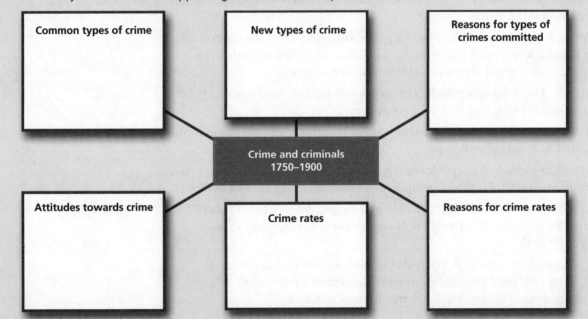

- Common types of crime
- New types of crime
- Reasons for types of crimes committed
- Attitudes towards crime
- Crime rates
- Reasons for crime rates

Crime and criminals 1750–1900

 Test yourself

1 What was the most common type of crime in this period?
2 Why did crime rates suddenly increase after 1815?
3 Who was John Glyde?
4 What was the Temperance Movement?

 Practice questions

1 Name one type of new crime that emerged between 1750 and 1900. (1 mark)
2 Give one example of a nineteenth-century attitude towards rising crime rates. (1 mark)

2.8 Changes in law enforcement, c.1750–c.1900

A more **professional police force** was established in **London** as crime rates increased

- In 1750, parish constables worked part-time and were unpaid. They were sometimes supported by watchmen, who patrolled the streets at night, and thief-catchers.
- The first experiments in professional policing were in London in the 1750s, with John Fielding's **Bow Street Runners**.
- These part-time constables were paid to patrol London's streets each evening until midnight.
- There were 68 Bow Street Runners by 1800.
- In 1773, Fielding also published *The Hue and Cry* – a weekly newspaper that detailed criminals and stolen property. The government supported it with £400 a year.
- After 1775, Fielding suggested extending the Bow Street Runners to the rest of the country, but his ideas were considered too radical at the time and would not influence attitudes until after 1780.

Sir Robert Peel set up the **Metropolitan Police**, beginning the age of 'modern' policing

- Due to rising crime rates at the beginning of the nineteenth century, London's Bow Street Runners, constables and watchmen were struggling to enforce law and order.
- People were opposed to the idea of a police force paid for by the government as they felt it was not the government's job, it would cost too much and it might lead to brutal **suppression** putting an end to protest.
- In 1829, Home Secretary Sir Robert Peel set up the first Metropolitan Police force of 3000 men paid for by the government.
- 'Peelers' or 'bobbies' were armed only with a truncheon and wore a uniform of dark blue tall hat and coat.
- The 1835 Municipal Corporations Act allowed towns across the country to set up a police force, although attitudes were slow to change because of money.
- The 1839 Rural Constabulary Act allowed magistrates to set up a police force for their county, although only two-thirds of counties had a police force by 1855.
- The County and Borough Police Act of 1856 was the first step towards creating a **national** (under the control of the central government) police force as it ensured that local forces met national standards.

> **Key point**
>
> There were significant changes to policing with a centralised police force that was paid for by the government.

Test yourself

1. Who set up the Bow Street Runners?
2. What was the name of the Home Secretary who introduced the Metropolitan Police force?
3. In what year was the CID introduced?
4. When was telegraph first used to speed up police communication?

> **TIP**
>
> Make sure you read the questions carefully before you begin answering them – don't include irrelevant information.

It is **likely** that the **new police force contributed** to **falling crime** in the second half of the 1800s

- The most important role of these new police officers was in preventing crime. They were responsible for removing drunks, prostitutes and vagrants from the streets, and also for dealing with pubs that allowed Sunday drinking, gambling and illegal sports.
- Police officers' main function was the prevention of theft and violence.
- Some important developments in crime detection included the first use of detectives by the Metropolitan Police in 1842 and the introduction of the CID (Criminal Investigation Department) in 1878.
- By the mid-1880s, there were 800 detectives.
- New technology began to aid crime detection, including photographing crime scenes from the 1880s, the use of the telegraph in 1867 and the use of fingerprinting in 1897.
- Courts developed little during this period; however, it became more common for lawyers to act for the prosecution and for the defence, and trials became longer and more formal.

 Getting from A to B

The development of professional policing is a complex story. It will help you to remember the story if you are clear about the main events.

You have been given the start and the end of a story. Complete the blank boxes to show how policing developed in industrial Britain.

| **A** Policing in 1750: constables, watchmen and thief takers | → | | → | | → | | → | **B** Policing in the 1880s: detectives took photos of crime scenes |

 Complete the paragraph

Below is an incomplete paragraph from an answer to the question:

Write a clear and organised summary that analyses how law and order was enforced in the period 1750–1900. Support your summary with examples. (9 marks)

Read the paragraph and complete it, adding any missing information.

> At the start of the period, law and order was enforced as in the medieval and early modern methods. However, as towns and cities grew as a result of the changes brought about by the Industrial Revolution, crime rates also grew, and it became clear that a more centralised system was needed. Early experiments with a paid police force were made by Sir Henry Fielding. However, people at the time were still not supportive of a larger police force that would be run and paid for by the government. Nevertheless, as crime rates continued to grow, Sir Robert Peel decided to introduce the Metropolitan Police force. It was the responsibility of these officers to prevent crime. Although the greatest changes in crime detection would not occur until the twentieth century, these police officers were helped by some important developments.

2.9 Changes in punishment, c.1750–c.1900

New changes in capital punishment led to **more humane forms** of **hanging** and **fewer executions**

- In the 1780s, executions were brought inside prison walls as the government grew concerned about the rowdy behaviour of the 'lower classes' on 'hanging days', but they were often held on a roof so people could still witness them.

- In the 1780s, a more humane form of hanging was introduced called the **new drop**, which meant the condemned person fell through a trapdoor and died more quickly.

- **Humanitarian** (caring) views from the Enlightenment contributed to a fall in executions, dropping from 871 between 1800 and 1809 to 297

between 1830 and 1839. More people thought execution for minor crimes was morally wrong.

- Between 1832 and 1837, Sir Robert Peel's government reduced the number of capital crimes; after 1837, only murder and attempted murder were punished by hanging. In 1868, public executions were made illegal.

- In 1872, the more humane **long drop** was introduced, which calculated how much rope was needed to break the neck instantly, leading to a quick and painless death.

> **Key point**
>
> The humanitarian attitudes of the Enlightenment led to significant changes in punishments, eventually creating a more humane system in which prisoners were encouraged to reflect on their crimes.

The punishment of **transportation**, of prisoners to America, then Australia, took place **from 1750 onwards**

- From 1750, prisoners who had committed crimes that did not carry the death penalty were transported to America to work on plantations.

- Initially, the government stored its prisoners on **hulks** (old, rotting warships situated on the River Thames). Conditions were overcrowded and terrible and diseases such as typhus led to many deaths.

- After America's declaration of independence in 1776, Britain was forced to find a new destination.

- During the 1780s, the government decided to send its prisoners to south-eastern Australia, after the country had been mapped and claimed for Britain by Captain Cook in the 1770s.

- Australia was chosen because it was unknown and therefore might deter criminals, it might reduce crime in Britain by removing people from the 'criminal classes' and the convicts would provide the labour needed to build Britain's new territory in Australia.

Transportation peaked in the **1830s**, with 5000 convicts a year sent to Australia, but **ended in 1868**

- The first fleet left Britain in May 1787, carrying 736 convicts. It took eight months to get there, during which time 48 convicts died.

- The majority of convicts had committed theft and some of them were political prisoners, such as the Tolpuddle Martyrs, who were accused of forming a **trade union** (workers' organisation to protect workers' rights).

- All convicts faced either seven years, fourteen years or a lifetime of hard labour.

- Conditions were harsh. Prisoners often carried out hard physical labour with iron chains around their ankles.

- Most prisoners who had served their sentence then worked for one of the free settlers; few could afford the cost of the return journey home.

- By the 1830s, transportation came under criticism for the inhumane conditions of the journey and the penal colony, from ratepayers who had to support the families of transported men, from those who thought it was a 'soft option' and from the authorities in Australia who did not want convicts dumped on them.

After **campaigns for change**, our **modern prison system** was formed

Prisons in 1750 were overcrowded and insanitary. Prisoners were expected to pay for everything, including bedding, candles, food and coal

↓

After 1770, people such as John Howard and Elizabeth Fry began to campaign for reform. Their actions went on to have a much wider influence

↓

John Howard's *The State of the Prisons* (1777) recommended that gaolers should be paid a salary, and each prisoner should have their own cell

↓

Elizabeth Fry, a **Quaker** (a member of a Christian movement), brought reforms to the overcrowded and unsanitary women's section of Newgate Prison

↓

Millbank was the first national prison to be built in 1811, but only opened in 1816. Discipline was a massive problem and the prison failed

→

The government then introduced the 1823 Gaols Act to regulate local prisons. This meant that each prisoner was to have a separate cell. JPs had to visit their gaols and report on their conditions

↓

Following the decline of transportation in the 1840s, the government began to build national prisons, including Pentonville in 1842. By 1877, 90 prisons had been built or rebuilt

↓

Many of these new prisons used the separate system in which prisoners were kept apart from each other to reflect on their crimes. This often led to loneliness and mental breakdowns

↓

From the 1850s, the **silent system** was used instead: prisoners were allowed to work alongside each other but they were not allowed to speak to one another

↓

As a response to the **garrotting panic** of the early 1860s, prisons were made harsher, with the 1865 Prisons Act emphasising 'hard labour, hard fare and hard board'. This brutal system stayed in place for 30 years

---

Getting from A to B

You have been given the start and the end of a story. Complete the blank boxes to show how prisons changed between 1750 and 1900.

A In the late eighteenth century, prisons were mainly used for debtors and were unsanitary places. Therefore, Britain had been transporting its prisoners whose crimes did not deserve the death penalty at first to America and then to Australia from the 1780s.

➤

➤

➤

➤

B Further change to prisons was also brought about when the silent system replaced the separate system, because prisoners under the silent system were becoming mentally ill through lack of contact.

Test yourself

1 What was the new drop and what was the long drop?
2 Why were prisoners transported to Australia?
3 What was the name of John Howard's book?
4 What was the silent system?

Practice question

What caused the changes to punishment in the period between 1750 and 1900? Support your answer with examples.   (10 marks)

2.10 Crime and criminals since c.1900

The **twentieth century** saw many wide-ranging economic, social and political changes in Britain

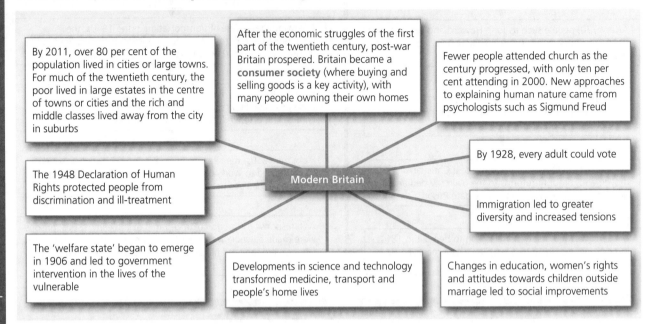

By 2011, over 80 per cent of the population lived in cities or large towns. For much of the twentieth century, the poor lived in large estates in the centre of towns or cities and the rich and middle classes lived away from the city in suburbs

After the economic struggles of the first part of the twentieth century, post-war Britain prospered. Britain became a **consumer society** (where buying and selling goods is a key activity), with many people owning their own homes

Fewer people attended church as the century progressed, with only ten per cent attending in 2000. New approaches to explaining human nature came from psychologists such as Sigmund Freud

The 1948 Declaration of Human Rights protected people from discrimination and ill-treatment

Modern Britain

By 1928, every adult could vote

Immigration led to greater diversity and increased tensions

The 'welfare state' began to emerge in 1906 and led to government intervention in the lives of the vulnerable

Developments in science and technology transformed medicine, transport and people's home lives

Changes in education, women's rights and attitudes towards children outside marriage led to social improvements

From the **late 1920s to 1955**, there were **severe economic problems** and **increasing crime**

- There are problems with crime statistics in this period, as in others: some crimes were not reported while some crimes were reported more than others.
- Additionally, some offences were no longer crimes, some new crimes were created and the systems for recording crime changed.
- We do know that economic problems in the 1920s and 1930s led to increased crime rates.
- Crime rates also rose steeply during the Second World War, during air raids, when criminals looted from homes, shops and even dead bodies. Stolen goods were often sold on the **black market** (illegal trade).

> **Key point**
>
> Since 1900, Britain's government has been challenged with how to deal with new types of crimes, experiencing success in some areas but further problems in others.

Crime rates increased from **1955**, but the introduction of **new laws** helped to **control** these

- On 28 January 1896, Mr Arnold became the first person to be caught driving over the speed limit after he passed a policeman while going at 8 mph when the limit was 2 mph.
- Subsequent laws included a limit on the amount of alcohol allowed in a driver's bloodstream (1967), the compulsory wearing of seatbelts (1991) and the introduction of fixed roadside cameras to capture speeding (1992).
- Road deaths have fallen since the 1960s and car thefts have reduced since the 1990s, with improved car security.
- Football hooliganism reached a peak in the 1970s and 1980s, which led to changes in security at matches.
- The introduction of CCTV in the late 1980s, crowd control and high ticket prices have led to a reduction in football-related violence in and around stadiums.

Further changes in society led to the introduction of new types of crime

- Increased immigration to Britain after the Second World War led to clashes and violence between different groups.
- Drug taking became a problem in the 1960s.
- In 1998 and 2003, a new category of offence known as 'hate crime' was introduced, which gave greater protection to victims of crime based on their race, gender, religion or disability.
- The emergence of the internet in the 1990s led to new types of crime including illegal downloading, **phishing** (emails that trick people into sharing their credit card details) and cyber criminals hacking big businesses.
- In 2015, cyber crime was included in Britain's national crime statistics for the first time, which meant the crime rate doubled on the previous year.

The government has tried to reduce these crimes, with varying success

- The government introduced new laws to tackle discrimination, such as the Race Relations Acts of 1965, 1968 and 1976.
- The case of Stephen Lawrence, murdered in Eltham on 22 April 1993, led to changes in Britain's approach to race-related crimes, although it took nineteen years for such changes to happen.
- Despite Parliament's attempt to deal with the problem in 1971 by listing illegal drugs according to categories (A, B and C) and ensuring class A drugs carried the harshest penalties, the 'war on drugs' has continued.
- Governments today struggle to keep up with the invention of new chemical mixtures known as 'legal highs'.

Test yourself

1. Give one reason why crime figures can be misleading.
2. Why did crime rates increase during the Second World War?
3. In what decade was CCTV introduced to football stadiums?
4. What were the terms of the 2005 law passed in response to the Stephen Lawrence murder?

Practice questions

1. Name one type of new crime that has emerged between 1900 and the present day. (1 mark)
2. Give one reason for the decrease in football-related violence in and around stadiums. (1 mark)
3. Name one way in which cyber crime can occur. (1 mark)

The Thematic Study

Mind map

The mind map below has a number of headings. For each one, you need to add supporting detail from this spread.

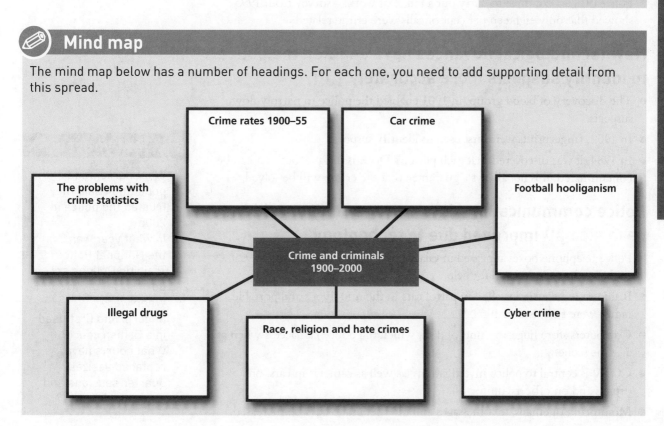

2.11 Enforcing the law since c.1900

The twentieth century saw changing views of the police

- From 1955 to 1976, the TV drama *Dixon of Dock Green* reflected public affection for the police.
- Yet in 2005, only 58 per cent of the population said they trusted the police.
- Changing attitudes could be the result of fewer police on foot, as officers today have a larger area to cover.
- Some resent the police for punishing them for what they see as petty driving offences such as speeding.
- Police are also criticised for their use of force when controlling large crowds.
- Police corruption, such as in the Hillsborough football disaster (1989), also caused people to distrust the police.

> **Key point**
>
> Policing and the courts system have become more centralised and better equipped to deal with the new types of crime that have emerged since 1900.

There were also new, significant developments in the police force

- In 1900, officers were poor, working-class men with little training or education. Today, male and female officers receive starter training from the National Police Training College (set up in 1947).
- Since 1900, forensic science, predicting and investigating terrorist attacks and investigating complex 'white collar' fraud are all included in police work.
- From 1964, the 200 separate police forces of Britain were merged. There are now only 43. Since 2013, Scotland has just one national police force.
- The modern police force keeps the community aspect of policing alive by visiting schools and encouraging neighbourhood watch schemes.
- The policeman's truncheon is now aided by pepper sprays and tasers; only about five per cent of officers are qualified to use firearms.
- Police officers continue to carry out a range of work: a survey from 1993 showed that only eighteen per cent of calls were crime related.

New technological advances have enabled the police to identify suspects more accurately

- The discovery of blood groups in 1901 enabled the police to narrow down suspects.
- In 1902, fingerprints were first used to identify suspects.
- In 1984, it was discovered that each person's DNA is unique, but as it can be contaminated, it is not always a guarantee that the crime will be solved.

Police communication, data storage and surveillance have also all improved due to technology

- Police telephone boxes appeared in Glasgow in 1891 and London in 1929, enabling the police to call for help.
- Radio systems were installed in patrol cars in the mid-1960s and portable radios were first used in 1969.
- Computers store huge amounts of data, which the police can access when at a crime scene.
- CCTV is central to police investigations (as well as cameras in cars, on drones and on officers' uniforms).
- Monitoring of emails, text messages and internet usage has also increased.

 Test yourself

1 What percentage of the population said they trusted the police in 2005?
2 In what year was the National Police Training College set up?
3 When were fingerprints first used in a British court?
4 What courts have replaced assizes, quarter sessions and other local courts?

Changes to the **court system from 1971** have led to a **more national system** covering **England and Wales**

- The Courts Act (1971) replaced the assizes, the quarter sessions and other ancient local courts with the new Crown Court, where judges hear the most serious cases.

- Less serious cases are tried in magistrates' courts.

- The workings of all the courts are organised by the government under the Ministry of Justice, as the system of local courts has become more of a national system.

- However, this only covers England and Wales; Scotland and Northern Ireland have different systems.

- From 1986, the Crown Prosecution Service took on the responsibility of bringing trials to court. This had previously been done by the police.

There were other **important changes** in terms of the **roles of women**, **juries** and **juvenile courts**

- Following the Sex Disqualification Removal Act (1919), women took their place on juries.

- In 1920, Ada Summers became the first JP (or magistrate, as they are called today).

- Psychologists argued that the best way to improve society was to improve care for young people. Juvenile courts were introduced in 1908 to try children aged seven to sixteen.

- Juries now reflect the breadth of British society as since 1974 there have been no property restrictions on who can sit on a jury.

- Recently, the government has tried to reduce the number of trials by jury as they are expensive.

- The internet can cause problems in trials by jury if jurors are tempted to look up the case online.

 Eliminate irrelevance

Below is an extract from an answer to the question:

Write a clear and organised summary that analyses how law and order has been enforced in the period since 1900. Support your summary with examples. (9 marks)

The answer contains some irrelevance. Identify and delete the irrelevant parts of the answer. Then explain your reasoning in the margin.

> Since 1900, police officers have continued to patrol neighbourhoods in an effort to prevent and investigate crime; however, officers today are more likely to patrol in cars than on foot because they have far larger areas to cover than in the past. Police officers today are not really respected like they used to be. For example, from the mid-1950s to the mid-1970s a television show called 'Dixon of Dock Green' showed how people felt great affection towards the police, and yet in 2005 only 58 per cent of the public said they trusted police officers. There are many reasons why people today are less trusting of the police, including the worry that fewer officer patrol the streets on foot and that some police officers have used violence when controlling huge crowds. Officers today still carry a truncheon, as they did in 1900; however, they are more likely to now also carry pepper spray and tasers as a result of technological advancements. However, firearms are still only used by a minority of officers, with only five per cent of officers today being qualified to use them, which shows some continuity since 1900. Similarly, as in 1900, officers today continue to carry out a range of work. A survey carried out in 1993 showed that only eighteen per cent of calls to the police were crime related, and that much of a police officer's time includes carrying out work such as teaching the public and helping people who are locked out of their houses.

2.12 Punishment since c.1900

Corporal punishment continued alongside the introduction of prisons, but was eventually abolished

- In 1900, **corporal punishment** (whipping and beating) was widely used: many argued that it was quick, cheap and an effective deterrent; more liberal-minded people argued that it was preferable to a brutal prison sentence.

- There were also special restraining birching benches, which had been introduced to hold the offender in place during whipping.

- However, corporal punishment ended for young offenders in 1933, ended as a punishment for all offenders in 1948, and ended as a punishment for prisoners who misbehaved in 1962.

> **Key point**
>
> Since 1900, prisons have undergone significant changes, leading to a greater emphasis on education, rehabilitation and alternative forms of punishment. Despite these changes, problems in the system still remain.

Capital punishment was abolished as ideas became more liberal

- Capital punishment was ended in stages, beginning in 1908 with the abolition of execution for anyone aged under sixteen.

- In 1953, there was a public outcry after the hanging of Derek Bentley, a nineteen year old who had a mental age of ten.

- This led to the Abolition of the Death Penalty Act in 1965, followed by the permanent abolition of the death penalty for all murderers in 1969.

- Arguments for the death penalty include: it is a powerful deterrent, it brings peace to the victims' families, and the British justice system can be trusted to convict the right criminal.

- Arguments against the death penalty include that most murders are committed in the heat of the moment and therefore deterrents will not work.

- In 2012, it was found that over 60 per cent of the British public favour the reintroduction of hanging, but MPs do not want it bought back.

By 1900, reformers believed rehabilitation and education were the keys to improving society

- **Rehabilitation** (restoring a criminal to a non-offending member of society) became a more popular way to deal with criminals in the twentieth century.

- In 1902, the first **borstal** was opened: this was a separate prison for offenders under the age of 21, where they were educated and trained in skills.

- In 1988, borstals were replaced by **young offender institutions** for offenders between eighteen and twenty. Offenders between ten and seventeen are kept in secure children's homes, where they also receive education and support.

- In 1908, children aged seven and above were held to be accountable for committing a crime. Nowadays, this age is ten years and above.

- Between 1979 and 1990, young offenders were subjected to a 'short, sharp shock' treatment to stop them reoffending. Since then, the focus has been on education.

- In 1896, Broadmoor Hospital was set up as a separate prison for mentally ill offenders.

Prison reforms did not eliminate prison problems

- Alexander Paterson was responsible for changes between 1922 and 1947, including a relaxation of the silent system and more meaningful, paid prison work.

- Paterson included a clause in the Criminal Justice Act (1948) which stated that a prisoner could be kept for longer than their original sentence if they posed a danger to the public.

- There has been a rise in prison populations since 1940: many more prisoners receive short sentences; some criminals cannot pay the fines so have to go to prison; people awaiting trial spend months in prison.

- Prisons are now very overcrowded: in 1990, a 25-day riot in Strangeways Prison (in response to overcrowding) led to two deaths.

- The government built 25 new prisons between 1985 and 2006 and allowed low-risk prisons to be run by private firms to cut costs.

Alternative forms of punishment were introduced

- In 1907, the government introduced the probation service for minor offenders deemed trustworthy enough to take responsibility for their behaviour.

- In 1967, a parole system was introduced to supervise prisoners released early for good behaviour.

- Since 1990, some offenders wear digital tags to locate them and since 1972 some offenders have taken part in **community service** (undertaking unpaid work for the community).

- Most prisoners reoffend and imprisonment is expensive. A study in 2007 estimated that it cost about £27,000 each year to keep someone locked up.

Since 1990, the government introduced direct support for victims

- The Victim's Charter (later the Victims' Code) sets out victim's rights on what support they should receive.

- Victims could choose to write a Victim's Personal Statement (VPS), explaining how the crime affected them, that was read out to the guilty party once a verdict had been reached.

- However, some victims, whether due to police corruption, lack of support or incompetence, never received the support they needed.

 Support or challenge?

Below are a sample exam-style 18-mark question and a table showing various points. For each one, decide whether it supports or challenges the overall statement, then add three more examples.

How far do you agree that the most important changes in the punishment of offenders took place in the twentieth century? Give reasons for your answer. (18 marks)

You may want to go back over pages 44–47 to gather evidence from other periods.

Key events and examples	Supports the statement	Challenges the statement
The Bloody Code		
Community service		
John Howard		
Alexander Paterson		
Transportation		

 Test yourself

1 What was the name of the bench introduced to administer corporal punishment in prisons?
2 In what year was the Abolition of the Death Penalty Act introduced?
3 Who was responsible for prison reforms between 1922 and 1947?

The British Depth Study

This part of the GCSE focuses on a short period of time when Britain faced pressure due to invasion or the threat of invasion. It is worth twenty per cent of your total GCSE. You must be able to:

Understand the interplay of **politics, religion, economy, society and culture**. This means how each of these factors affected the others.	The interplay part is important here. To help you with this, write these words randomly across a big piece of paper and then draw links between them if they affect each other. Along the line explain why they are linked.
Identify and describe the **main features of England** at the time.	This point is linked with the one above about interplay. To truly know the features of England at this time you must know what the politics, religion, economy, society and culture were like. Try to think how these features changed during this period.
Understand **how and why different interpretations have been constructed** of this period of time: • **The Norman Conquest, 1065–1087**. In particular, what lies behind the myth of '**the Norman Yoke**' and the extent to which the myth is accurate. • **The Elizabethans, 1580–1603**. In particular, the ways in which this has been interpreted as a '**golden age**' and why this interpretation has been challenged.	This is important. For each interpretation ensure you know what it is and that you have evidence to support or challenge it. This could be the main focus of the longer questions in the exam.

What do I need to do in the British Depth Study exam?

- **The British Depth Study exam is taken together with the Thematic Study unit.** The paper in total is 1 hour 45 minutes and worth 80 marks.
- There are **40 marks** available for the British Depth Study half of the paper and you have **52.5 minutes** to complete it.
- There is a total of **five questions, of which you must answer four**. On the next page is a guide to how to do this.

For Question 6a you need to identify and explain how an artist or a writer has reached a specific interpretation.
- The best way to do this is to explain **why they have used a particular word or part of a picture** to convey their message
- 3 minutes in total

For Question 6b you are asked you to suggest a line of enquiry based on the interpretation.
- Think about the second-order concepts (cause, consequence, similarity or difference) to help you
- Include some of your own knowledge
- 6 minutes in total

Answer Questions 6 (a–b) and 7.

6. (a) In Interpretation A the historian ... Identify and explain **one** way in which the historian does this. [3]
   (b) If you were asked to do further research on one aspect of Interpretation A, what would you choose to investigate? Explain how this would help us to analyse and understand ... [5]

7. Interpretations B and C are both ... How far do they differ and what might explain any differences? [12]

Answer **either** Question 8 **or** Question 9.

8. In ... the historian ... argued that ... How far do you agree with this view? [20]

9. According to ... How far do you agree with this view? [20]

For Question 7 explain how similar or different two interpretations are. To help you do this, think about the overall message, details, points of emphasis and overall style and tone.
- To explain any differences, think about why each interpretation was produced
- 16 minutes in total

You must only answer Question 8 or 9. The question asks you how far you agree with a quotation. In your answer, you should make your own judgement, explaining how far you agree with the quotation in the question.
- Start by making a clear statement of your overall judgement then support this with some detailed paragraphs.
- Give reasons for agreeing and disagreeing (you could write a paragraph on each) but don't feel these have to be balanced.
- Finish with your strongest reason for agreeing or disagreeing, or with a conclusion summarising the main reasons for your judgement.
- 26 minutes in total.

Key skill: dealing with interpretations

As you will have seen, many of the questions for the British Depth Study deal with **interpretations**.

Interpretations are accounts of the past produced some time later. When you analyse any interpretations (whether it is in the exam or in class), think about the following things.

Message	What is the interpretation trying to suggest overall? Is it positive or negative about the situation, person or event?
Details	What specific points are included in the interpretation? What, exactly, does the writer focus on? What details does the artist include?
Purpose	What is this interpretation trying to achieve? Is it trying to educate or entertain? Who is the target audience for this interpretation?
Style	How is it written or drawn? What language does the writer use? How does the artist paint the scene?
Date	When was the interpretation made? Is this after or before historians have revised their opinion about a situation, person or event?

3.1 Anglo-Saxon society in 1065

REVISED

In the eleventh century, **England** was one of the **wealthiest** and **best-governed countries** in Europe

- In 1065, the kingdom of England had only existed for just over 100 years. Before that, each region had been separate, with several different rulers.
- This meant that people had strong regional differences: Anglo-Saxons in the Midlands, descendants of Viking settlers in the north, and ancient Britons in Cornwall.
- In 954, the rulers of Wessex led the other Anglo-Saxon kings to defeat the Vikings in the north and east of England. England became a single kingdom for the first time.
- English kings had strong, central control over their realm. England was divided into **shires** (counties), which made it easier to administer.
- Most shires had several royal **burhs** (fortified towns) where local people could go for safety. Markets were held in burhs, and they became centres of trade as well as government.
- English kings set up **mints** (machinery that makes coins), producing good-quality coins which were trusted. This encouraged trade and made taxation easier.

> **Key point**
>
> In 1065, England was wealthy and well run. The king had strong central control and an efficient tax system. However, English society was very divided with a strong hierarchy.

> **TIP**
>
> In your exam, you may be asked to compare English society before and after the Conquest. Make sure you look through your notes and revise some examples of similarities and differences!

England was ruled by the **king**, advised by **earls**, and **most** of England's population were **peasants**

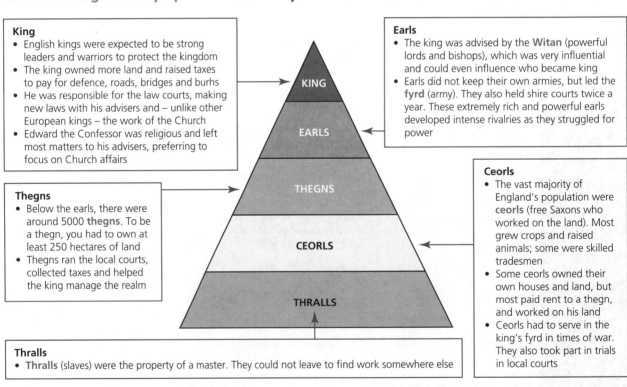

King
- English kings were expected to be strong leaders and warriors to protect the kingdom
- The king owned more land and raised taxes to pay for defence, roads, bridges and burhs
- He was responsible for the law courts, making new laws with his advisers and – unlike other European kings – the work of the Church
- Edward the Confessor was religious and left most matters to his advisers, preferring to focus on Church affairs

Earls
- The king was advised by the **Witan** (powerful lords and bishops), which was very influential and could even influence who became king
- Earls did not keep their own armies, but led the **fyrd** (army). They also held shire courts twice a year. These extremely rich and powerful earls developed intense rivalries as they struggled for power

Thegns
- Below the earls, there were around 5000 **thegns**. To be a thegn, you had to own at least 250 hectares of land
- Thegns ran the local courts, collected taxes and helped the king manage the realm

Ceorls
- The vast majority of England's population were **ceorls** (free Saxons who worked on the land). Most grew crops and raised animals; some were skilled tradesmen
- Some ceorls owned their own houses and land, but most paid rent to a thegn, and worked on his land
- Ceorls had to serve in the king's fyrd in times of war. They also took part in trials in local courts

Thralls
- **Thralls** (slaves) were the property of a master. They could not leave to find work somewhere else

Pyramid levels (top to bottom): KING, EARLS, THEGNS, CEORLS, THRALLS

Under **Anglo-Saxon law**, every person's **life** was given a cash **value** based on their **rank**: the 'wergild'

- If someone was killed in Anglo-Saxon England, the person responsible had to pay the person's **wergild**. If they could not pay, they were executed.

- The wergild was set in **shillings** – one shilling was about the value of a cow. Thralls had no value, but the life of a ceorl was worth 160 shillings, and a thegn 1200 shillings.

- Killing an earl was an expensive business – his wergild was 4800 shillings.

- A prince's life was valued at 9000 shillings, and a king's wergild was 18,000 shillings. That's a lot of cows!

- A woman's wergild was the same as a man's of the same rank. It increased by 50 per cent if she was pregnant.

 Eliminate irrelevance

Questions 7 and 8 in the depth study exam are worth most marks. You only answer one of these questions. They always ask you how far you agree with a quotation.

Below is an extract from an answer to the question:

In 2013, the historian Peter Sawyer described England in 1065 as 'an exceptionally wealthy, highly urbanized kingdom, with a large, well controlled coinage of high quality'. How far do you agree with this view? (20 marks)

The answer contains some irrelevance. Identify and delete the irrelevant parts of the answer. Then explain your reasoning in the margin.

> In 1065, England had only been a single kingdom for about 100 years. In the tenth century, the leaders of Wessex, one of the kingdoms, had led wars to end Viking rule. By AD954, the last Viking ruler had been defeated. Unlike France, where local lords ran their regions like small kingdoms, England's king had strong central control. The country was divided into shires, which made collecting tax easier. Most shires had fortified towns called burhs that kept the community safe and acted as trading centres. They also had mints making high-quality coins. This combination of control and trade made the English kings powerful and gave them a source of income.
>
> The king was advised by the Witan, which was a mix of earls and leading bishops. The Witan was very influential and could even choose the next king when the old king died. Unfortunately, King Edward was not very interested in anything except the Church, so left running the country to the earls. The earls had lots of land and were very rich and powerful. Sometimes they competed for power, which made the country unstable. Below the earls were the thegns, who ran the local courts and collected taxes. They did not have castles like knights in France.
>
> Most people were ceorls, who farmed the land. They sometimes owned their own land but usually paid rent to a lord. They were expected to serve in the king's 'fyrd' (army) – unlike Normandy, England did not have many dedicated fighting men.

Challenge question

Why do you think some historians have described Anglo-Saxon England as a 'golden age'? Do you think this is accurate?

 Test yourself

1. When did England become a single kingdom?
2. List three features that made England strong in 1065.
3. What was the wergild?

3.2 Anglo-Saxon religion

The **English Church** had an **independent identity**

- The Church in England had many influences, so by the eleventh century, it had developed a unique character.
- The Roman Catholic Church came to England in AD597 and the pagan Anglo-Saxons gradually converted to Christianity.
- However, missionaries from Ireland had come to the north of England and had spread different ideas, and forms of worship and art.
- Unlike the Church in Europe, which followed Rome's insistence that only Latin should be used, the English Church often used English during Mass.

Key point

The Anglo-Saxon Church was unique – it had been influenced by many beliefs and had developed a distinct identity. However, by 1065, the Church in England was seen as backward and corrupt.

The **English** did **not always follow** the **Church's rules**

- The individual character of the Church, with its Roman Catholic and Celtic influences, was reflected in the religion of the people.
- Many **pagan** (pre-Christian) beliefs and customs influenced their beliefs, as shown below.

Some villages don't have a church. They worship around a stone cross

I can't read. Very few people can. So Bibles are only for the priests, even if they're in English

The priests are always making sermons saying that we eat and drink too much and that we're sexually immoral

We have lots of local, English saints. The Pope doesn't like it – he thinks only he can make people saints

Lots of people believe in elves and goblins and use charms and spells, even though the Church doesn't like it

The **tenth-century Church** was **reformed** by **St Dunstan**

- Dunstan was a monk who became Archbishop of Canterbury in AD960. He was a pious man (and a skilled artist and musician) who devoted himself to the Church. A rich woman left Dunstan a fortune, and he spent it on improving monasteries.
- Dunstan set high standards for the Church by:
  - ending corruption among Church leaders
  - improving the education of monks, nuns and priests
  - forbidding priests to marry
  - rebuilding churches, abbeys and monasteries.
- After Dunstan died in 988, English Church leaders made him a saint, but his reforms were not continued because the Vikings began their raids on England again. In 1011, much of Canterbury was destroyed.
- This disruption ended the reform of the Anglo-Saxon Church. Although the Danish kings who ruled England from 1014 to 1042 were Christian, the Church did not recover.

TIP

Remember that time is limited in an exam, so you need to make sure that every sentence you write counts. The longest answers don't always get the highest marks! As you practise answering exam questions, ask yourself how each point you make relates to the question you have been asked.

By the **eleventh century**, the **Church** was **accused** of **corruption** and **backwardness**

1 Edward the Confessor was a devout Christian. When he became king, he brought Norman priests to England.

2 One of these was Robert of Jumièges, who became Archbishop of Canterbury in 1051. He tried to reform the Church, but English priests did not want change.

3 During 1051–52, Harold Godwinson resented the power of Edward's foreign friends and forced him to replace Robert with a new archbishop, called Stigand.

4 Stigand was a skilled administrator, but was not particularly religious. He concentrated on advising the king rather than reforming the Church.

5 He broke several Church rules: he held two Church positions at once (**pluralism**) and sold off Church posts for money (**simony**), but kept his position because Harold Godwinson supported him. Stigand became very rich.

6 The Pope was unhappy as he thought that the English Church was backward and that Stigand was corrupt. He insisted Stigand give up one of his posts. Stigand took no notice.

7 Compared to priests elsewhere in Europe, English clergy were poorly educated and, much to the Pope's disapproval, were still allowed to marry.

Test yourself

1 What were the main influences on Anglo-Saxon religion?
2 List three ways St Dunstan reformed the English Church.
3 Who became Archbishop of Canterbury in 1051?

Challenge question

Do you think the independent nature of the English Church was a strength or a weakness? Why?

Structure the detail

In the exam, you will be asked to write clear and concise answers, which means you will need to be able to structure your information effectively. An effective answer will include evidence to support your points, and explain why they are relevant.

Nicholas Orme, a history professor, described the Anglo-Saxon period as the 'birthtime' of the Church of England. How far do you agree with this view?   (20 marks)

Read the sentences and use them to structure an answer to the question. Mark the key points with a P, and the evidence with an E.

- Edward the Confessor was a very pious man, and wanted to improve standards in the English Church.
- In the tenth century, St Dunstan had reformed the English Church, rebuilding churches, starting monasteries and improving the education of monks and priests.
- The English Church had been influenced by Roman Christianity and Celtic Christianity.
- The Pope was unhappy with the English Church and saw it as backwards.
- King Edward appointed a Norman, Robert of Jumièges, as Archbishop of Canterbury in 1051. Robert wanted to reform the Church.

- The Viking invasion in 1011 ended the reform of the Church begun by Dunstan.
- The English Church had an independent identity.
- The Pope insisted that the Church should use Latin, but the Anglo-Saxon Church used English.
- Harold Godwinson persuaded Edward to replace Robert as Archbishop of Canterbury and appoint an Englishman called Stigand.
- English people worshipped local saints.
- Pagan beliefs were still common in England.
- As Archbishop of Canterbury, Dunstan worked hard to eradicate corruption from the Church.
- Stigand was accused of corruption, including selling Church offices.

3.3 Anglo-Saxon culture

Anglo-Saxon England produced high-quality art, especially engravings, often with jewels

- The few works of art that survive from Anglo-Saxon England show that the Anglo-Saxons were skilled artists – some historians argue that this is evidence of a 'golden age'.
- Many of these artworks were made with precious metals and jewels.
- Some of the finest examples we have involve **engraving** (cutting a design into a hard surface such as metal, bone or stone).
- The Alfred Jewel (probably made in AD890 on the orders of Alfred the Great) is perhaps the finest surviving example of Anglo-Saxon art, featuring high-quality enamel, surrounded by intricate metalwork in gold.

> **Key point**
>
> Anglo-Saxon England produced a wide variety of arts, crafts and literature. The examples we have show that English metalwork and enamelling, in particular, were very fine. Evidence of a broad range of literature also survives.

Anglo-Saxon literature was rich and varied, including Beowulf and the Anglo-Saxon Chronicle

- We know that there was a huge variety in the literature produced by the Anglo-Saxons. As well as religious books produced in monasteries, there were other books.
- There are many surviving examples from the period, including:
  - calendars
  - maps and descriptions of far-off places
  - poems, riddles and sermons
  - information about astronomy, grammar and medicine.
- The most famous Anglo-Saxon work of fiction is *Beowulf*, which is set in Scandinavia. It was written down in the early Anglo-Saxon period, but was still very popular in the eleventh century.
  - Like most stories from the period, it would have been read aloud. *Beowulf* is still read today, and new versions are still being written.
- One of our best sources from the period is the *Anglo-Saxon Chronicle*, a history of England starting with the Roman invasion. Copies were sent to monasteries throughout England.
  - The monks updated the chronicle until the twelfth century. It isn't perfect – it's very one-sided and incomplete – but it tells us a great deal about the Anglo-Saxons, their lives and attitudes.

> **TIP**
>
> The idea of an Anglo-Saxon 'golden age' is central to the concept of the 'Norman Yoke' that is a key part of the specification – the argument for the Norman Yoke is based on the claim that Anglo-Saxon England was more free and that the Normans ended that freedom. Make sure you can explain the concept of the golden age and discuss to what extent it was true.

Test yourself

1. Why do so few artworks survive from the Anglo-Saxon period?
2. What is the name of the best-known Anglo-Saxon story?
3. What was the purpose of the burhs?

Quick quizzes and answers at **www.hoddereducation.co.uk/myrevisionnotesdownloads**

Most Anglo-Saxon buildings were wooden houses, although there were some churches built from stone

- Anglo-Saxons built most of their buildings with wood, clay and straw. This means that they were at risk of fire, and those that did not burn down have now rotted away.

- Archaeologists can work out the shape of the buildings by looking at the soil where upright timbers once stood. This shows us that most Anglo-Saxons lived in rectangular one-storey houses with thatched roofs. Thegns lived in bigger houses with two floors.

- Written descriptions tell us that some Anglo-Saxon buildings were beautifully decorated, with carved woodwork, fine plasterwork and staircases and painted walls.

- The Anglo-Saxon kings built burhs (towns that were protected by walls and earthworks of ramparts and ditches). The local population could go there for safety during Viking raids.

- Winchester was the English capital, but Londenburh (or London) was the largest city and was becoming more important.

- Most stone buildings were churches, and even they were much less common in England than in the rest of Europe. Many villages still worshipped around stone crosses or in wooden churches. Church building was not an Anglo-Saxon speciality.

- The exception to this is Westminster Abbey, built for Edward the Confessor. It was built in stone and larger and grander than any other Anglo-Saxon church.

> **Challenge question**
>
> Why do you think the best examples of Anglo-Saxon art are carvings and enamel-work?

 ## Spot the mistakes

One of the key skills you will need in your exam is writing clear, focused answers, with relevant detail and clear explanation. This is not easy, as there's a lot of information to manage. Read these sentences from students' answers and identify the problem in each. Is the sentence clear? Is all the information accurate and relevant? Is all the necessary detail included? Are any statements supported with evidence?

> Most Anglo-Saxon buildings were made from wood, which means that they no longer survive. This means that we have to rely on written descriptions to find out what they looked like.
>
> The *Anglo-Saxon Chronicle* is a history of England starting with the Roman invasion. Copies were sent to monasteries throughout England and the monks continued writing it until the twelfth century. It's very biased, which means that it isn't a reliable source.
>
> The Alfred Jewel (probably made in 990 on the orders of Alfred the Great) is probably the finest example of Anglo-Saxon art we have.
>
> Many of the works of art we have from the Anglo-Saxon period are engravings and fine metalwork. Records from the period show that England was renowned for its high-quality craftsmanship. This is why the Anglo-Saxon period was a 'golden age'.
>
> One of the best-known Anglo-Saxon stories is Beowulf. It is set in Scandinavia and is the story of a hero, Beowulf, who kills the monster Grendel, and Grendel's mother.

Once you have spotted the mistakes, rewrite each answer to improve it.

3.4 Normandy in 1065

Norman society was based on the feudal system: powerful men held land for providing service

- There was no country called 'France' until the thirteenth century. The 'King of the Franks' ruled much of what is now France, but he had much less control over his kingdom than the English kings.
- Most of the land was ruled on the king's behalf by dukes or counts. They swore loyalty to the king, and promised to lend him their armies if necessary. They became the king's 'vassal' and were given land in return called a **fief**.
- This 'land for loyalty' arrangement is called the **feudal system**. At first glance, it seems similar to the system in England – the key difference was that although the earls and thegns gathered armies, they were the *king's armies* and were loyal to him.
- The French dukes and counts had their own armies, which gave them a lot of independence. They ruled their lands like small kingdoms.

Normandy was a powerful fief

- One of the strongest fiefs in France was Normandy, which had begun as a Viking colony in the early tenth century.
- The Vikings had relied on their fast ships and warriors armed with battleaxes – but once they settled in Normandy, they adopted the French form of warfare.
- The Viking leader, Rollo, became a vassal of the Frankish king in 911. Over the next 100 years, the Normans had doubled their territory through conquest and marriage alliances.
- They crushed rebellions brutally, but adopted the local language and customs of the people they ruled. By the early eleventh century, Normandy was one of the more stable parts of the Frankish kingdom.

> **Key point**
>
> Normandy was a powerful, strong and stable fief in 1065, until a crisis in 1035, when the Duke of Normandy died. William, his eight-year-old son, became Duke but had to crush revolts until he finally took power in 1047.

 Test yourself

1 What was a vassal?
2 Why were the Normans effective warriors?
3 How did William take control of Normandy in 1047?

The Normans did several things militarily and socially to remain powerful

What the Normans did	This was important because
Dukes and counts began building private armies by giving their supporters weapons and armour	This meant that they had full-time soldiers, not just troops to call on in times of war
The invention of the stirrup made **cavalry** (fighting while riding on horseback) possible	This meant that the rider could charge at their enemy, and swing their sword while still in the saddle. In French these mounted warriors were called 'chevaliers'. In English, they were **knights**
Knights became part of the feudal system – they swore loyalty to their duke or count and received land in return	This helped the ruler to control the land. However, if the knights sensed weakness in their lord, they would challenge him
Knights took as much tax and rent as they could from the people who lived on the land they controlled	Land became a source of wealth and power, and many knights treated the people on their land badly
Knights built castles – often from earth and timber, but some were replaced with stone later	Castles were a symbol of power and enabled knights to defend and control their fiefs. (See pages 76–77 to revise what castles were like and how they were built)

Normandy led the way in **Church reforms**, and was praised for its **piety, and religious art and music**

- The Viking settlers in Normandy were pagan, but when Rollo became the vassal of the Frankish king, he converted to Christianity.
- The Normans became devout supporters of the Roman Catholic Church, and were at the forefront of Church reform.
- Their monks and nuns were praised for their devotion and the quality of their teaching, as well as their religious art and music.
- Norman churches were larger and finer than those in Anglo-Saxon England. Even in small towns, the churches were usually built from stone. The Normans favoured a style called 'Romanesque', with clean lines and elegant rounded arches.

Normandy was **stable and wealthy** until an **eleventh-century crisis** led to **William becoming Duke**

- In 1035, the Duke of Normandy died. William, his eight-year-old son, became Duke, but was too young to rule.
- Norman knights sensed a chance and grabbed what land and power they could, leaving Normandy unstable.
- The lords ruling in William's place were killed – and the ones who took their place may have been responsible. William had to learn who to trust.
- In 1047, a full-scale revolt broke out. William took charge and persuaded the King of the Franks to help him crush the rebels. He was merciless and regained control of the duchy.
- William then made a very advantageous marriage to Matilda of Flanders. Flanders was a powerful neighbouring country.

> **Challenge question**
>
> Why do you think Norman rulers adopted the feudal system?

> **TIP**
>
> The Depth Study is arranged thematically but you should always be looking out for connections between the sections. For example, Norman military organisation had an impact on the Battle of Hastings (page 67), castles (pages 78–79) and the changes the Normans made to government and landownership (pages 82–84).

 Mind map

Mind maps are a useful tool to help you organise information. You can use them to structure your notes, and also to plan answers to a particular question. For this task, use information from this page to help you complete the mind map.

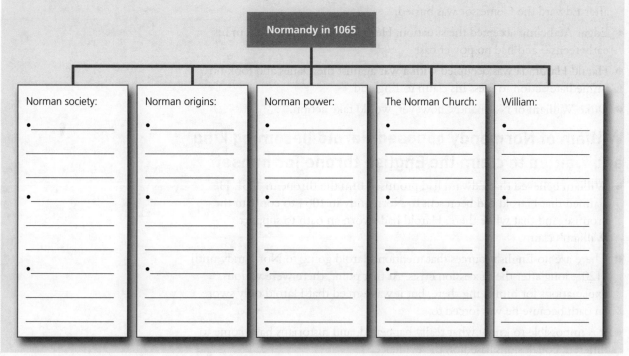

Normandy in 1065

Norman society:
- _____
- _____
- _____

Norman origins:
- _____
- _____
- _____

Norman power:
- _____
- _____
- _____

The Norman Church:
- _____
- _____
- _____

William:
- _____
- _____
- _____

3.5 The succession crisis

When **Edward the Confessor died** in **January 1066,** there were **four claimants to the throne**

- Edward had no children, so it was not clear who would be the next king. In eleventh-century England, the throne did not automatically go to the king's closest relative, but ideally it would be someone who was:
  - in the **bloodline** (a direct relative) of the previous king
  - chosen by the previous king
  - chosen by the Witan.

In 1066, there were four claimants to the throne. The table shows how the claimants measured up.

> **Key point**
>
> The succession crisis happened because Edward the Confessor had no direct heir and because two of the four claimants said that he had promised them the throne.

	Edgar Aetheling	Harold Godwinson	Harald Hardrada	William of Normandy
Direct bloodline?	Yes. As Edward's great nephew, he was the closest male relative	No	No	An indirect relationship via his great aunt
Chosen by the previous king?	No	A powerful and wealthy earl, he claimed Edward chose him on his deathbed	No, but he had inherited a claim from Cnut, the Danish king	His family had close links to Edward, and he claimed Edward promised him the throne in 1051
Chosen by the Witan?	Rejected	Accepted	Ignored	Ignored

Harold Godwinson became king. Each of the three other claimants reacted differently

- Harold Godwinson was the man on the ground, and he had the support of the Witan.
- He also won the support of the two powerful earls of Mercia and Northumbria, Edwin and Morcar, by promising to marry their sister.
- On 6 January, Harold was crowned king at Westminster Abbey – just hours after Edward the Confessor was buried.
- Edgar Aetheling accepted the situation. He was very young – only in his early teens – and had no power base.
- Harald Hardrada was occupied with a war against the Danes and took no immediate action to press his claim to England.
- Duke William of Normandy, however, would take action.

William of Normandy opposed Harold becoming king and wanted to **claim the English throne** for himself

- William believed that Edward had promised him the throne in 1051. He claimed that Harold had been sent to Normandy in 1064 to confirm the promise, and that while there, Harold had sworn an oath to support William's claim.
- There are no English sources that mention Harold going to Normandy until 1120 – long after the succession crisis. At that point, there were various explanations for him being there, but it was agreed that Harold only swore an oath because he was forced to.
- It is impossible to know what really happened, and historians have come to different conclusions based on the evidence.

William prepared to invade England and claim the throne

- William told the Pope about Edward's promise and Harold's broken vow. He also told him that Harold had been crowned by Stigand, whom the Pope loathed.

- The Pope supported William, and sent a **papal banner** to carry into battle as a sign that God was on the Normans' side.

- William's vassals had to fight for him, but the Pope's support meant other powerful rulers from across northern France supported William.

- William also promised his followers land in England as a reward.

- William began building extra ships to carry his army to England and moved armour, weapons and food to the coast.

- By the summer, a huge camp of soldiers, archers and knights had assembled at Dives-sur-Mer. In August, William's army was ready to invade England.

> **TIP**
>
> When you're explaining both sides of an argument, you might find it helpful to structure your points by using phrases like: 'On the one hand …', 'On the other hand …', 'However, this is contradicted by …' and 'Further evidence to support this point is …'.

Support or challenge?

Below are a sample exam-style 20-mark question and a table showing pieces of evidence that could support or challenge the statement given. For each one, decide whether it supports or challenges the overall statement, then add three more examples.

According to historian Jacob Deacon, 'William of Normandy had no legal claim to the English throne. Edward's deathbed bequeathal of the kingdom to Harold Godwinson superseded [replaced] his earlier promise to William.' How far do you agree with this view? **(20 marks)**

Evidence	Supports the statement	Challenges the statement
The Witan supported Harold's claim		
Harold was not a blood relative of Edward's		
Harold was a powerful man and an experienced warrior		
The Pope supported William's claim and gave him a papal banner		
Harold was crowned by Archbishop Stigand in January 1066		
Edward's wife, Queen Edith, was Harold's sister		

Test yourself

1 What does 'in the bloodline' mean?
2 How did the Witan react to Edgar Aetheling's claim to the throne?
3 When did William claim that Harold had sworn an oath of allegiance to him?

> **Challenge question**
>
> Which version of events do you think was more likely to be true, Harold's or William's? Why?

3.6 The three battles

Harald Hardrada took Harold by surprise with an invasion of York

- Harold was waiting for William's army on the south coast. His spies told him about William's plans. He quickly began to defend his kingdom.
- Harold raised more taxes than any king before him, and used the money to pay the fyrd (army) and build ships to defend the coast.
- By June 1066, thousands of soldiers were waiting for the Norman invasion. It did not arrive.
- By September, the army was running out of food, and the men were needed for the harvest. Believing that William would also need to bring in the harvest, Harold disbanded the fyrd.
- Harold's brother Tostig, angry at losing his earldom, had encouraged Harald Hardrada, the king of Norway, to take the English throne.
- Harold heard that Hardrada and Tostig's army had landed in the north of England. The northern earls, Edwin and Morcar, fought Hardrada but were driven away.

Harold then beat Hardrada at the Battle of Stamford Bridge. Both Hardrada and Tostig died

- When Harold heard about Hardrada's invasion, he gathered the remains of his army and marched north, gathering more troops on his way.
- In less than a week, Harold had reached York. Tostig and Hardrada had left the city, to a river crossing called Stamford Bridge. He marched his army straight through York and launched a surprise attack.
- The two armies clashed for several hours and thousands of men on both sides were killed, including Hardrada and Tostig. The Norwegians surrendered.

William's army went to England to meet Harold's army

- Harold did not have much time to enjoy his victory. Just days after Stamford Bridge, he heard that William's army had landed on the south coast, near Hastings.
- William's army had been delayed by bad weather and because the wind was coming from the wrong direction. The six-week wait had been difficult, but William's army was strictly disciplined.
- On 28 September 1066, William's army landed at Pevensey. William quickly built defences at Pevensey and Hastings.
- He encouraged his men to raid the surrounding area – probably as much to annoy Harold as to provide food for his army.
- Meanwhile, Harold rode south to London in four or five days and gathered a new army. Despite his haste, William was waiting for him.

Test yourself

1 Why did Tostig encourage Harald Hardrada to invade England?
2 Why did William encourage his troops to raid the land around Pevensey?
3 How did the Normans break the English shield wall?

Key point

The battles of Fulford, Stamford Bridge and Hastings took place in 1066 and were key events in the Norman Conquest.

TIP

You may be presented with an interpretation that suggests that William's strengths were the reason that the Normans won the Battle of Hastings. This is a complex question and not all historians agree on an answer! You may find it helpful to structure your revision by looking at:
- the Normans' strengths
- the English weaknesses
- how much was luck involved.

Challenge question

The only contemporary accounts of the Battle of Hastings were written by Normans. (The only contemporary English source, the *Anglo-Saxon Chronicle*, only mentions that the battle was long and that the Normans won.) Why do you think this is? How do you think this affects our understanding of what happened?

William and Harold's armies met to fight the **Battle of Hastings** on 14 October 1066

William's Norman army	Harold's Anglo-Saxon army
About 7000 men	About 7000 men. Many others were trying to join him from across the south but were still a long way away. If Harold had waited, he might have had twice as many
William's soldiers were well rested	Many of the soldiers who had fought with Harold in the north would have been tired or wounded
William's troops stood at the bottom of the hill	Harold chose a ridge near Hastings, with a forest behind it – this gave him a strong defensive line but would make retreat difficult
William's army consisted of knights on horseback, archers and infantry	Harold had no horsemen or archers. His soldiers formed a deep line, protected by a wall of shields

At the **Battle of Hastings, Harold was killed** and the **Normans won**

1 At nine o'clock, the trumpets sounded and the Battle of Hastings began. William's archers fired a hail of arrows on the English, allowing the infantry to climb the hill. Harold's army flung javelins and stones at the advancing Normans.

2 The Normans pounded the English shield wall but it held firm, even when the cavalry joined in, battering the fyrd with swords and clubs.

3 After a few hours of stalemate, a group of Norman knights turned from the battle and rode down the hill. Some English soldiers chased after them, breaking the defensive line.

4 At the same time, a rumour started that William had been killed and the Normans began to drop back. William pulled back his helmet and showed his face, calling out that he was alive.

5 William's men attacked the English who had broken away, killing them all. These retreats may have been genuine panic, but feigned retreats were a Norman tactic before 1066, so it was likely to be a deliberate trick.

6 The real turning point was the death of Harold. It is not certain how he died – whether it was an arrow in the eye as shown in the Bayeux tapestry, or whether he was cut to pieces by William's knights.

7 With Harold killed, the English tried to flee and were chased by William's knights. Thousands of English were killed, and William was victorious.

Unpicking an interpretation

INTERPRETATION A *A modern oil painting depicting the Battle of Hastings.*

Look at Interpretation A. Can you find evidence in the painting to show:

- What the battlefield was like?
- The differences in fighting style between the two sides?
- What weapons each side used?
- That lots of men were killed?
- Whether either side was winning at this point in the battle?

The artist has made the Normans look dominant. How has he done this?

3.7 The first uprisings, 1066–68

Edgar Aetheling was chosen to be king, but **William took control** and eventually **became king**

- After the Battle of Hastings, William rested his troops for two weeks, hoping that the English might surrender the kingdom to him. Instead, the Witan chose Edgar Aetheling to be king.
- William began to take control of England, first by securing the route back to the coast. Then he marched through Kent, building castles as he went.
- Then he moved through the land around London before setting up camp and waiting.
- Eventually, Edgar Aetheling came to William to surrender the kingdom.

> **Key point**
>
> Many English were reluctant to accept William as their king. Almost as soon as he was crowned, rebellions began. The first were in the south-west, and included a plot by King Harold's mother, Gytha, which William put down.

William tried to calm the country while he established his rule

- William was crowned at Westminster Abbey on Christmas Day 1066, in a tense atmosphere. Many English were angry and resentful, while the Normans were suspicious and fearful.
- In the first months of his reign, William tried to establish his authority:

William took control by ...	But he also ...
Claiming all English land as his own, and giving the land of those who had died at Hastings to his supporters	Allowed English earls and thegns to buy back their land
Giving his closest friend, William FitzOsbern, control of East Anglia, and putting his half brother, Odo of Bayeux, in charge of the south-east	Allowed English nobles to keep their positions if they formally submitted to William
Taking Edgar Aetheling and Edwin and Morcar with him to Normandy, to discourage English rebellion	Kept them in comfort and safety, rather than threatening them or having them killed
Leading an armed force through East Anglia, an area with strong links to the Danes	
Forcing the English to build motte and bailey castles for their new Norman lords	

Edric the Wild began the first uprisings against the Normans, but was not a serious threat

- The first large uprisings against Norman rule took place near Hereford in August 1067. One of the most powerful English thegns was called Edric. He lost most of his land to Norman knights.
- Edric joined with Welsh princes to raid Norman-held land and destroy Hereford itself. He lived in the open as an outlaw and became known as Edric the Wild.
- Edric's raids were never a serious threat, but he carried on for years, becoming a folk hero.

King Harold's mother, Gytha, plotted a more serious rebellion in Exeter

- William stayed in Normandy, leaving England in the hands of FitzOsbern and Odo. By the end of 1067, William's spies told him that trouble was coming.
- William came back to London. He treated the lords and bishops well, to encourage their loyalty, and sent messages to Exeter, where he knew rebellion was brewing.

- Gytha was behind the rebellion. She had fled to Exeter, where her family had land, after the Battle of Hastings. The rebels strengthened Exeter's defences.
- Gytha sent Harold's sons to Ireland to gather an army to drive out the Normans. She also contacted the Danish king, hoping he would invade from the east at the same time.
- William had to put a stop to this. He tried to win Gytha and the citizens of Exeter over, asking them to swear an oath of loyalty to him.
- They refused, adding that he would not be allowed in the city – and that they would not pay any more tax to him than they had to previous kings.

Test yourself

1 Why did William take key English nobles to Normandy?
2 Which city was destroyed by Edric the Wild?
3 How did William get the city of Exeter to promise to be loyal to him?

William fought back and Exeter surrendered

- William was not prepared to put up with such blatant rebellion. He gathered an army and marched to Exeter, where a group of citizens came to meet him and promised that he could enter the city.
- When these spokesmen returned to the city, their fellow citizens were furious and barred the city gates against William. William besieged the city, undermining the walls.
- After eighteen days, Exeter surrendered, offering William precious objects and holy books and begging for mercy. William pardoned them.

In return for their loyalty, he promised:

- not to plunder the city
- not to punish the people
- not to demand more tax
- that Exeter could keep the precious things they had offered him.

- He also seized Gytha's lands, and built a large castle in Exeter, before marching west to deal with any further rebellion, and building more castles, for example, at Barnstaple and Totnes.

TIP

Your study of the Norman Conquest will have given you a deeper understanding of first-order concepts, for example, king, Witan, rebellion, earldom. Make sure you use these terms in the exam. Strong answers will also use second-order concepts (for example, cause consequence, change, continuity, significance and diversity) to analyse events and situations in the past.

Challenge question

Why do you think William treated the Exeter rebels so leniently?

 Spot the second-order concept

Second-order concepts are the things that historians use to make sense of the past. They include: cause, consequence, change, continuity, significance and diversity. In the exam you will gain marks by using second-order concepts in your answers, but don't feel that you have to name the second-order concepts that you are using.

This extract from an exam answer about how William dealt with uprisings in England from 1066 to 1068 contains several examples of second-order concepts. Highlight where they occur and note the second-order concept in the margin.

> William returned to Normandy, leaving William FitzOsbern and Bishop Odo to run England. This shows that he believed that the realm was secure and there were no serious threats. He returned to England at the end of 1067, however, when he heard about a rebellion brewing in Exeter. King Harold's mother, Gytha, had fled to Exeter after the Battle of Hastings, and began plotting against William. She sent Harold's sons to Ireland to win support, and contacted the Danish king, hoping he would invade at the same time. At first, William tried to use persuasion, asking Gytha and the citizens of Exeter to swear an oath of loyalty. They refused, and added that he could not enter the city or increase their taxes. William changed tactics, and marched an army to Exeter, besieged the city and forced the citizens to surrender. William pardoned them, and promised not to punish them or plunder the city. This is important because it shows that punishing people was not William's main priority at this point. He did not forgive Gytha, however, and seized her lands. He also built a large castle to prevent any further rebellion.

3.8 Rebellions in the north, 1068–70

Many **English** still **distrusted** the **Normans** and **resisted** their rule

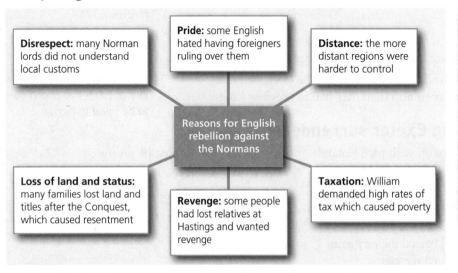

Disrespect: many Norman lords did not understand local customs

Pride: some English hated having foreigners ruling over them

Distance: the more distant regions were harder to control

Reasons for English rebellion against the Normans

Loss of land and status: many families lost land and titles after the Conquest, which caused resentment

Revenge: some people had lost relatives at Hastings and wanted revenge

Taxation: William demanded high rates of tax which caused poverty

> **Key point**
>
> By 1069, rebellion against William's rule had not stopped. After a revolt in the north of England, William began treating uprisings more harshly. The most famous example is the Harrying of the North, in which William destroyed large areas of the north.

In **1068**, William marched **north** to **defeat** the **rebels**

- In the summer of 1068, William got a letter from the people of the north of England. It told him that if he tried to enter their lands, they would fight him.
- The letter was the result of an agreement between some powerful lords, including Edgar Aetheling, Earl Edwin and Earl Morcar. They had decided to band together to rebel against William.
- William gathered an army and marched north, and built a castle at Warwick, in the middle of Edwin's lands.
- He then built another castle in Nottingham. By this point, Edwin and Morcar decided to surrender. William did not punish them, but their power and influence were damaged.
- By the time William got to York, the rebels were gone, but again, William built a castle as a show of strength. On his way home, he built castles at Lincoln, Huntingdon and Cambridge.
- Harold's sons sailed from Ireland with an army but the people of Bristol drove them off when they tried to land. This was good news for William.

Rebellion spread throughout 1069. William responded with increasing harshness

- After the rising in 1068, William appointed an experienced soldier, Robert of Comines, as Earl as Northumbria. He wanted someone who could keep the north under control.
- Robert arrived with 500 armed mercenaries, and before long had attacked rebels at Durham. His army behaved terribly, looting and killing.
- The people of Durham retaliated by attacking the soldiers, and when Robert and his men took shelter in a house, it was set on fire. Everyone was killed.
- This episode sparked another full-scale rising. Edgar Aetheling and the other rebel leaders attacked York. William soon heard about this and rode north again. After a vicious battle, he retook York.
- The rebel leaders had escaped, so William built a second castle in York, put his most trusted friend, William FitzOsbern, in charge, and returned home.
- In June 1069, Harold's sons made another attempt to invade, but were driven off again.

> **TIP**
>
> Question 7 will ask you to compare two different interpretations and explain any differences. You should aim to spend around fifteen minutes answering this question, so don't get too bogged down in the detail or in describing the interpretations. You'll get the top marks if you use your knowledge of the historical context to explain your answers.

The **Danes** took advantage of the turmoil and **invaded** England in **1069**

- William's problems were not over. In early September 1069, the Danes returned with a fleet of 250 ships. Gytha had fled to Denmark, and may have persuaded the Danish king to invade.
- The king's brother led a huge army which landed in the Humber Estuary, where they met the English rebels headed by Edgar Aetheling. They made straight for York.
- The people of York had tried to protect the city by burning timbers so that enemies could not use them to cross the moat. The fire got out of control and destroyed the city.
- The rebels and Danes plundered what was left of York and withdrew into north Lincolnshire. William marched north for the third time that year.
- Meanwhile, the rebels along the Welsh borders began to attack, and there were uprisings in the south-west and a rebellion in Stafford.

William took **several actions in 1070** to **finally discourage rebellion**

What did William do?	What impact did it have?
Paid the Danes to leave	This reduced the pressure on him and allowed him to focus on the rebellion
Sent for his crown to wear for the Christmas celebrations	This was a very symbolic act and reminded his subjects that he was God's chosen king
Sent his troops to destroy the land and root out rebels in the **Harrying of the North**	Crops, animals and food were destroyed, causing a widespread famine. It is not clear how many people died, but we know from Domesday Book that some areas of the north were depopulated

 Test yourself

1 Why did some English people lose respect for their Norman lords?
2 What happened when Harold's sons arrived from Ireland?
3 What was the Harrying of the North?

Challenge question

Do you think William was justified in the way he dealt with the rebellions against him?

 Practice question

Interpretations B and C both focus on the sort of king William was. How far do they differ and what might explain any differences?

(12 marks)

INTERPRETATION B *By Peter Ackroyd*, Foundation (The History of England, *vol. 1*), 2011.

No cultivated land was left between York and Durham, and a century later the ruins of the destruction were still to be found … Yet the north would rise against William no more. He had created a desert, and called it peace. In the Harrowing [Harrying] of the North, William had not behaved as an English king. He had behaved like a tyrant. … 10,000 Normans were attempting to control a country of 3 or 4 million natives, and the only weapons they had at their disposal were those of brute power and terror. Spies and collaborators, punishment beatings and secret murders … were indispensable.

INTERPRETATION C *By Marc Morris, 'William the Conqueror Reassessed'*, History Today *Vol. 66, No. 10, 2016.*

What was surprising about William's behaviour as king of England was not that he imprisoned his enemies for a long time, but that he bothered to imprison them at all. … Although many of the English elite had perished at Hastings or during the course of the rebellions that followed, only one high-ranking Englishman – Earl Waltheof of Northumbria – was deliberately put to death, beheaded in 1076 for his role in a plot against the king the previous year.

3.9 Rebellions in the east, 1070–71

William's **Church reforms were unpopular,** and the Church played a **key role** in the next **uprising**

- Dealing with rebellions had cost William a lot of money. He ordered monasteries to provide, or pay for, soldiers, and confiscated money and treasure that had been hidden in monasteries.
- Church leaders were very unhappy about this and William's other Church reforms, such as:
  - ○ Replacing Stigand as Archbishop of Canterbury with Lanfranc, an Italian who came from a monastery in Normandy.
  - ○ Any churchmen who had sympathised with rebels were replaced with Normans. Some were imprisoned. (See page 85 for more on William's Church reforms.)

In **1070,** the **Danes attacked England** and captured **Ely, supported by** an English thegn, **Hereward**

- At Christmas, William had paid the Danes to leave – they had taken the money but had not left. King Svein of Denmark arrived with more troops.
- In June, the Danes attacked, capturing Ely, which at the time was an island in the **fens** (an area of marshland in East Anglia).
- The local people did not resist the Danish attack. East Anglia had been a Viking stronghold, and the people there hoped that the Danes would get rid of William.
- An English thegn called Hereward attacked Peterborough Abbey, taking its treasure before the Normans could confiscate it. He gave the treasure to the Danes and joined forces with them.

William persuaded **King Svein of the Danes to leave,** but **Hereward stayed**

- William was able to persuade Svein to take his army home. The Danes who had spent a hard winter in England were hungry and tired and would not be able to fight well.
- Svein had not brought enough troops with him to take England. He decided to return to Denmark, with the treasures from Ely and Peterborough.
- With the Danes gone, Hereward was left to take on the Normans alone. William decided it was safe for him to return to Normandy.
- He left local lords, and the new Norman Abbot of Peterborough, to keep Hereward under control.

Hereward's position in Ely strengthened while William was away

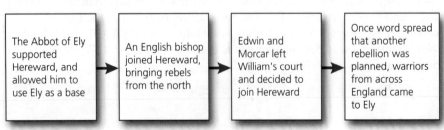

| The Abbot of Ely supported Hereward, and allowed him to use Ely as a base | → | An English bishop joined Hereward, bringing rebels from the north | → | Edwin and Morcar left William's court and decided to join Hereward | → | Once word spread that another rebellion was planned, warriors from across England came to Ely |

Key point

The final revolt against William was in East Anglia. Hereward, a local thegn, joined forces with the Danes. William persuaded the Danes to leave, but Hereward's rebellion grew, forcing William to return from Normandy to deal with it.

 ### Test yourself

1. Why did William confiscate treasure from monasteries?
2. Why did King Svein decide to leave England?
3. How did William capture Ely?

Challenge question

Why do you think Hereward was still seen as a hero in the nineteenth century?

TIP

Question 6a will show you an interpretation (which could be text or a picture) and explain what it is trying to do. To get top marks you will need to identify a feature and explain how it does this. This sounds a lot, but it's important not to get bogged down – don't write too much, and make sure you focus on the question you've been asked, not everything you know about the topic!

William besieged Ely and built a causeway to the island. The rebels surrendered

- By 1071, William could see that the local lords were not able to deal with the threatened rebellion. He gathered an army and marched to East Anglia.

- Ely was an island, so he could not just attack – he had to plan carefully. He sent ships and boats to block supplies to the rebels, and ordered his soldiers to build a causeway through the fens.

- William's army used the causeway to reach the island (some sources say that monks at the abbey betrayed the rebels and led them over another secret pathway). The English surrendered.

- Morcar and other leaders were imprisoned, and other rebels had their hands cut off or their eyes gouged out.

Hereward became a hero of English legend, but his rebellion was the last serious uprising

- Hereward escaped. He carried on resisting Norman rule, but never posed a serious a threat to William. His rebellion was the last widespread uprising against William's rule.

- We don't know what happened to Hereward – like Edric the Wild, he became a folk hero. The Victorians called him 'The Last of the English'.

- The **Norman Conquest** of England was complete.

Getting from A to B

The chain of events of what happened during the rebellion in the east is a complex story. It will help you to remember the story if you are clear about the main events. You have been given the start and the end of a story. Complete the blank boxes to show how the final rebellion against William developed.

| **A** In 1070, a Danish army attacked the east of England, and captured the town of Ely | → | | → | | → | | → | **B** Hereward's rebellion had ended – and there were no more major revolts against King William |

Practice question

In your exam, you will be shown an interpretation and asked to identify features in it based on your knowledge of the topic.

In Interpretation D, Emma Borley argues that Hereward's motivation for rebelling against the Normans was patriotism. Identify and explain one way in which the author does this. **(3 marks)**

INTERPRETATION D *By Emma Borley, from www.bbc.co.uk/legacies/myths_legends/england/ cambridgeshire/article_2.shtml*

Hereward returned to find his beloved country undermined by foreign rule. He learned of a band of resistance fighters holed out in the Isle of Ely and swiftly joined their fight. He quickly won their respect and became their leader, heading a series of damaging attacks against the Normans.

The next part of the question asks you to suggest a line of research linked to the interpretation. To gain high marks you will need to use some of your own knowledge to justify your choice. Try this example:

If you were asked to do further research on one aspect of Interpretation D, what would you choose to investigate? Explain how this would help us to analyse and understand Hereward's rebellion. **(5 marks)**

3.10 What was new about Norman castles in England?

Before the Norman Conquest, the **Anglo-Saxons** had defended enclosures called **burh-geats**

- The Anglo-Saxons did not build castles, but did have royal burhs, which were fortified towns.
- Thegns also built smaller defended sites called **burh-geats**. We know about these burh-geats from archaeological digs, for example, at Goltho in Lincolnshire.
- The burh-geats would have been important features and would have shown the status of the thegns who lived there.

> **Key point**
>
> The castles built by the Normans were very different from Anglo-Saxon fortified structures – they were designed to control the people, not protect them.

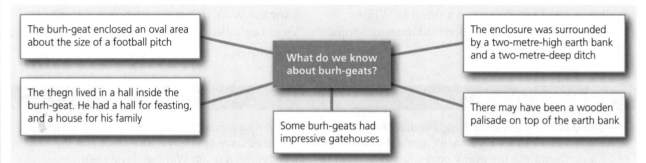

The burh-geat enclosed an oval area about the size of a football pitch

The thegn lived in a hall inside the burh-geat. He had a hall for feasting, and a house for his family

What do we know about burh-geats?

Some burh-geats had impressive gatehouses

The enclosure was surrounded by a two-metre-high earth bank and a two-metre-deep ditch

There may have been a wooden palisade on top of the earth bank

Castles were common in France, but the first mottes in England were built by Normans

- Castles were built in France around 200 years before they were introduced to England.
- The Normans adopted several French ideas about war and defence, and built castles in Normandy. See page 62 for more about castles in Normandy.
- In the *Anglo-Saxon Chronicle*, there is a mention of one of the first castles in England. Some Norman friends of Edward the Confessor built castles near the Welsh border.
- The monk who wrote about these castles in the Chronicle described the **motte** (huge earth mound) with wooden towers on top, and a wooden **palisade** (fence) around it.

Castle building was a key strategy in William's invasion and conquest of England

- Castles were vital to William's conquest of England, as they helped him to secure south-east England and capture London (see table below).
- Not all castles had mottes – at some sites the Normans built earth enclosures called 'ringworks' inside existing sites if that was more efficient.

 **Test yourself**

1 Who lived in the burh-geats?
2 True or false? The first castles in England were built by the Normans in 1066.
3 What was a 'ringwork'?

> **Challenge question**
>
> Look at Topics 3.1 and 3.4 on pages 56–57 and 62–63. What features of Anglo-Saxon and Norman society can you link to the burhs, burh-geats and castles?

Pevensey	When William landed at Pevensey in 1066 (see page 66), one of the first things he did was build a castle there. He used the remains of a Roman fort as the basis of his castle
	The fort was in ruins, but William's army quickly strengthened the remaining Roman walls and built an earth bank and palisade in one corner of the fort
Hastings	At Hastings, the Normans used the remains of an Iron Age fort as the basis of their castle – although at Hastings they also built a motte
London	When William captured London, he immediately built a castle there – on the site of what later became the Tower of London

Unpicking an interpretation

In your exam, you will be asked to look at an interpretation and pick out the key features. The question might be something like the one below.

INTERPRETATION E *A painting by Alan Sorrell, who worked throughout the 1960s and 1970s. He specialised in illustrations of historical sites.*

In interpretation E, Alan Sorrell attempts to re-create how Pevensey Castle may have looked in 1066. Identify and explain one way that has he done this.   **(3 marks)**

Study the image carefully then answer the question.

The next part of the question asks you to suggest ideas for further research.

If you were asked to do further research on one aspect of Interpretation E, what would you choose to investigate? Explain how this would help us to analyse and understand how the Normans built castles. (5 marks)

TIP

There are Norman castles all over the country. If you have the chance to visit one it could provide useful context and evidence for answering questions about Norman castle building.

3.11 Where were Norman castles built and what did they look like?

Between 1068 and 1071, William built castles to show his power. The castles were unpopular among the Anglo-Saxons

- When William left for Normandy in 1067, he put Odo of Bayeux and William FitzOsbern in charge. They immediately built more castles across the south of England.
- The *Anglo-Saxon Chronicle* records several English attacks on castle builders (see diagram).
- Between 1068 and 1071, there were serious threats to William's rule, with uprisings in the south-west, the north and East Anglia (see pages 68–73).
- William used castles to crush these revolts, and to secure the area once the threat had been dealt with.

> **Key point**
>
> Castle building was key to William's control of England. The first castles were built in key towns and to control strategic areas like rivers and roads. Later, William's lords built castles to control and manage their lands.

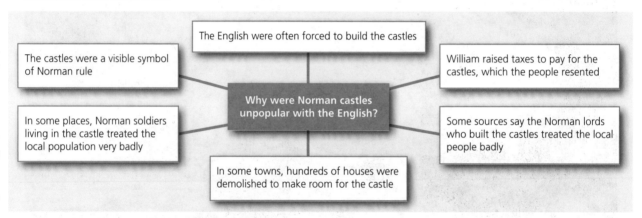

- The castles were a visible symbol of Norman rule
- The English were often forced to build the castles
- William raised taxes to pay for the castles, which the people resented
- In some places, Norman soldiers living in the castle treated the local population very badly
- **Why were Norman castles unpopular with the English?**
- Some sources say the Norman lords who built the castles treated the local people badly
- In some towns, hundreds of houses were demolished to make room for the castle

Castles were built in key towns, and to allow control over important rivers and roads

- York was an important city, so the castle there was imposing. The motte was over 60 metres wide and overlooked the rivers Ouse and Fosse. After the 1068 uprising, the castle was strengthened.
- Castles were also built to protect roads so that William could move his army across England. The royal castles at Lincoln, Cambridge and Huntingdon were vital in securing the kingdom.
- The king also relied on a small number of trusted Norman lords to establish control across the country.

> **Challenge question**
>
> Find out where the nearest Norman castle is to where you live. Why do you think the Normans chose to build a castle there?

Location	Trusted lords	Events
Southern England	The Sussex barons	Sussex was divided between six barons, who each built a castle. These castles protected the roads between London and Normandy
Western England	Robert of Mortain	Robert was William's half brother. William gave him huge amounts of land. Robert built a number of castles across the west – including one on a steep hill at Montacute
Welsh borders	William FitzOsbern	William's closest friend was William FitzOsbern. He was made Earl of Hereford and was given the job of controlling the border with Wales. By 1071, FitzOsbern had built castles at Chepstow, Berkeley, Clifford and Wigmore

After the Conquest, **William's knights** continued to build castles to **control their territories**

- By 1071, there were about 35 castles across England. Even though resistance to the Normans had passed, castle building continued.

- When William I died in 1087, there were probably around 500 castles in England and Wales. Most of these were built by Norman lords.

- William gave blocks of land to his knights, who were expected to control these territories. To do this, the barons and knights built castles.

- These castles were nearly all built in the countryside – they were used to settle and manage the land as well as for military purposes.

Most of these **early castles** were timber 'motte and bailey' castles

- The castles built by the Normans were different from Saxon defences. They were smaller, designed to house a small number of soldiers. They were taller and dominated the landscape.

- Most castles were motte and bailey castles, built from timber on an earth 'motte' or mound. The castles were not all alike – the design varied from place to place. A few castles were built from stone.

- Some castles did not have a motte – instead they had earthwork defences called 'ringworks'. Ringworks were often built on sites of existing fortresses, for example at Pevensey.

- All that remains of most rural Norman castles are overgrown earthworks, but archaeological research can tell us a lot about the castle that stood on the site.

TIP

In the exam, you will be shown an interpretation and asked to suggest further lines of enquiry or topics to investigate. The interpretation is a prompt to get you to think about the topic – your investigations should relate to the topic, not the interpretation.

 Test yourself

1 List three reasons why Norman castles were unpopular with the English.
2 How many castles had William built by 1071?
3 What was a palisade?

Feature	Definition
Ramparts	Earth banks which could be several metres high
Palisade	A tall wooden fence on top of the ramparts
Moat	A deep channel outside the ramparts, which sometimes contained water
Bailey	An enclosure inside the ramparts, usually smaller than the enclosures in the Saxon burh-geats
Gatehouse	A fortified entrance to the bailey
Motte	A mound inside the bailey which was several metres high
Tower	The centre of the castle, built on top of the motte

 Unpicking an interpretation

In Interpretation F, an archaeologist, Tim Taylor, argues that castles were built to control the local population. Identify and explain one way in which he does this.   (3 marks)

INTERPRETATION F *By Tim Taylor,* The Time Team Guide to the Archaeological Sites of Britain and Ireland, *2005.*

The motte and bailey fortress that is Norwich Castle is one of many built to subjugate [dominate] the local people, and it survives as a symbol of their military and political power. [It] was built between 1066 and 1074 by Ralph de Guader, the earl of the East and follower of William the Conqueror. The Norman keep is one of the largest in the country and was originally made up of garrison quarters, pantry, kitchens, latrines, chapel, and a private room for when the king made a visit. Parts of the original flint and Caen stone walling are visible.

To answer this question, you could make the point that Tim Taylor chooses some powerful words and phrases to describe Norwich Castle and then give some examples of this.

3.12 What were Norman castles used for?

Very few stone structures still exist from the Norman period. Those we have are very important

- At Exeter, there is a Norman gatehouse. It has some interesting features:
  - The gatehouse faces into the city. The gatehouse incorporated some features of Anglo–Saxon design.
  - The gateway originally had large wooden doors. Some historians think that this shows that the gatehouse was a status symbol, not a defensive structure.

Most early Norman castles were built from earth and wood, not stone. The earthworks survive

- Aerial photographs and ground surveys tell us about the layout of the castles.
- Ringwork castles had a ditch surrounding an enclosure. The earth from the ditch was made into a bank, which was topped with a palisade. Sometimes ringworks were built using natural features or existing structures.
- Mottes were built from soil from a ditch, or used hills or ancient burial mounds. The shape of the motte varied. The motte was surrounded with one or two baileys.

We can also learn about castles by studying the surrounding landscape

- In the 1980s, archaeologists started to study the areas around Norman castles.
- They found out that most castles were at the centre of the lord's estate, and were used for administration.
- These castles were often near a Saxon settlement or church, or on the site of a burh-geat.
- Norman lords often altered the landscape to make it more impressive, building monasteries, diverting roads or creating deer parks.

Archaeological digs are revealing, but they are expensive and take a long time

- A good example of an excavation was at Hen Domen on the Welsh border from 1960 to 1992.
- The excavation told us that there was a large tower, which would have given a good view over the roads and river crossing.
- There were double ramparts and deep ditches.
- Very few valuable items were discovered, suggesting it was occupied by soldiers.

> ### Key point
> Over the years, historians have offered different theories about why the Normans built castles. Some argue they were purely military in function, others that they were about status and power. Recent historians think that castles were built for all these reasons.

✎ Test yourself

1 What did archaeologists discover by studying the landscape around castles?
2 What was the key discovery made by Ella Armitage in 1912?
3 What was the revisionist interpretation of the purpose of Norman castles?

Historians have suggested different theories about what Norman castles were used for

Traditional theory	• Until the beginning of the twentieth century, many people thought the mottes dotted around the country were Roman or Saxon remains • In 1912, Ella Armitage published a book which showed that it was the Normans who had built the mottes • Armitage and other historians in this period argued that the castles were entirely to serve a military purpose
Revisionist theory	• In the 1960s, some historians proposed a new theory. They discovered that many Norman castles used ringworks, which were not that different from Saxon fortifications • Other historians examined the remains of stone castles and found out that some of them had defensive weaknesses • The revisionists argued that the Normans built their castles to demonstrate their status, not for military purposes
Recent theory	• Recent interpretations have come down somewhere in the middle of the argument. These historians say that although the revisionists were right to point out the status angle, the military aspects of Norman castle building cannot be ignored • They point out that the early castles were often heavily defended and housed cavalry soldiers, who could have a terrifying impact on local people • Although castles served an economic and administrative function, and served as status symbols, they were also central to the military occupation of England

✎ Suggest a line of enquiry

Question 6b in the exam will always ask you to suggest a line of enquiry linked to the focus of the interpretation. To justify your chosen line of enquiry you need to use your own knowledge by referring to specific people, events or situations. You also need to base your suggested line of enquiry on one or more second-order concepts (although there is no need to use terms like change, causation, significance).

Let's look at the following question:

If you were asked to do further research on one aspect of Interpretation F (on page 77), what would you choose to investigate? Explain how this would help us to understand and analyse the purpose of Norman castles.   (5 marks)

The table below gives some examples of second-order concepts. Your job is to suggest a possible line of enquiry based on each one.

Second-order concept	Possible enquiry
Typicality (Was this the same everywhere?)	
Diversity (Was it the same for everyone?)	
Chronology (Was it the same throughout the period?)	
Continuity and change (What changed? What stayed the same?)	
Causation (Why did this happen?)	
Significance (What was the impact? How is it remembered?)	

Now use the table to write some sample answers to the question. Remember to use your knowledge and to base your answer on a second-order concept, for example, 'It would be good to explore how Norman castles changed over the period because it would tell us ...'.

TIP

Remember that Question 6b tests your ability to suggest appropriate lines of enquiry. Your answer does not need to refer to the interpretation used in Question 6, but you can use it for ideas.

3.13 Domesday Book

In **December 1085**, William ordered a survey to record **every piece of land and property** in England

- This was a difficult time for William. The King of the Danes and the Count of Flanders had joined forces to invade England.
- After a long conversation with his advisers, he ordered a survey of England, listing every piece of land and every item of property in the country, and who owned it.
- Domesday Book is not a single book. 'Little Domesday' covers Essex, Norfolk and Suffolk. 'Great Domesday' covers the rest of the kingdom, except the areas the king did not control directly, for example, in the north.
- William did not call it Domesday Book. In the eleventh and twelfth centuries it was the Book of Winchester, the Book of the Treasury or the King's Book.
- The name 'Domesday' was given later – it means the Day of Judgement. What was in the book was final.
- The book contains around 2 million words, and is important because it tells us a huge amount about the changes caused by the Norman Conquest.

Commissioners visited **every manor**, asking the **same list of questions** in each

- The 34 English shires were divided into seven **circuits** (regions), with four commissioners in each circuit.
- The commissioners worked quickly. The information for the whole country – over 13,400 manors – was collected in just six months.

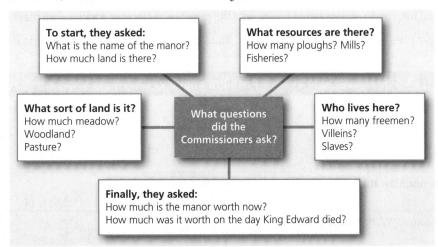

Land ownership had **changed**, so **inquests** were held to decide who owned what

- There had been a lot of change in land ownership in the twenty years since the Conquest. Some people had written proof that they owned land, but William had given some land verbally, so the owners had no proof.
- In the spring of 1086, special sessions of the shire court were held. These were called 'inquests' and jurors from each hundred (group of manors) listened to evidence from witnesses.
- The inquests made final, binding decisions about who owned what – which must have caused a lot of worry for landowners.

Key point

William commissioned Domesday Book in 1085 to tell him what land and property there was, who owned it, and what it was worth. It confirmed William's rule and Norman ownership of England.

 Test yourself

1 How many circuits were there? How many commissioners in each?
2 The commissioners collected information for which two dates?
3 Why do some historians disagree that Domesday Book was designed to help collect taxes?

TIP

There are a lot of facts and figures in this topic. For your revision, make sure you know what Domesday Book was and why William might have commissioned it, and concentrate on remembering details that support your points.

Some **historians** think **Domesday Book** was about **money**, others think it was about **power**

- For many years, historians believed that William ordered Domesday Book as a sort of tax database, so he could squeeze more money out of England.

- This view was based on William's need for money to defend against possible invasion. He also gave instructions that commissioners should note where 'more could be taken than is now being taken'.

- However, recent historians have pointed out that the book is not laid out in a way that would help tax collection.

- They suggest that the book was designed to show that the Normans had the legal right to the land, and that William was the undisputed ruler of England and the legal heir to King Edward.

Challenge question

Why do you think William chose to collect information about England in 1066 and 1086?

 ## Develop the detail

The sentences below were written to support points made in an exam answer to the following question:

An encyclopedia entry about the Domesday Book says that the book was used 'to settle land disputes and collect taxes'. How far do you agree?

However, the statements are vague and general. Add further details so that the statements support the answer more effectively. One example has been done for you.

Original sentence	Developed sentence
In 1085, there was a survey of England	In 1085, King William ordered a survey of all the land and property in England, who owned it, and what it was worth
The Domesday Book is actually two books: Great Domesday and Little Domesday	
William divided England's shires into circuits and appointed commissioners to collect information in each circuit.	
The commissioners asked a lot of questions about each manor in England	
They collected information for two different dates	
Many historians say the Domesday Book was to help collect taxes, but it might not have been	
The Domesday Book showed that the Normans owned the land	

3.14 The impact of the Norman Conquest on the English people, 1066–87

The **English elite lost their land to William's men,** who were rewarded with it

- Once William had secured the English throne, he rewarded the men who had fought for him or funded his invasion by giving them the land of the English earls and thegns who had died at Hastings.
- At first, other English nobles were allowed to keep – or buy back – their land, but he changed his mind after repeated rebellions in the first four years of his reign.
- The effect on the English nobility was shattering. By 1086, only four of William's 180 **tenants-in-chief** (major landowners who received land from the king) were English.
- Many English nobles migrated to other European countries, such as Scotland, Ireland and Scandinavia. Those who stayed often had to rent land that they had once owned.

> **Key point**
>
> Although most people still worked on the land for a lord, there were fundamental changes in ordinary people's lives after the Conquest. English nobles lost their land, Norman landlords ruled more harshly and charged higher rents, and many people became poorer as a result.

The **change in land ownership** brought **other changes** to the way the **country was governed**

- Although some Norman lords were given vast estates, the way William gave out land changed – Saxon earls had amassed huge territories which gave them a lot of power.
- William made sure that his nobles could not build up a power base to challenge him, by spreading their land out. William's cousin, Alan Rufus, owned land in twelve different shires, for example.
- Saxon thegns had divided up their property when they died, but the Norman system passed everything to the eldest son.
- Norman lords built castles in the middle of their estates and often treated the people who lived on their lands harshly and charged high rents.

The **Norman Conquest** had a **huge impact** on **ordinary people** in England as well as **landowners**

- In areas which rebelled against Norman rule, the consequences were severe. The Harrying of the North, for example, meant that the population of Yorkshire in 1086 was 25 per cent of the 1066 population.
- Most people continued to work on the land, and the cycle of the farming year stayed mostly unchanged.
- However, the number of free peasants fell radically, and many people struggled to pay the high rents their Norman lords demanded. Norman landowners increased the income from their land by 30 per cent.
- The new lords also introduced curbs on the peasants' freedoms:
  - forcing them to build the unpopular castles as part of their duties on the manor
  - stopping them fishing in the rivers
  - banning the collecting of firewood in the forests
  - charging high fees for using the mills to grind corn.
- The one group who may have benefited were the slaves – slavery had died out in Normandy, and after 1066, the number of slaves in England fell.

Quick quizzes and answers at **www.hoddereducation.co.uk/myrevisionnotesdownloads**

The **Normans** took control of **market towns**, making it **more expensive for traders to** earn a living

- The changes brought by the Normans did not just affect the countryside. Life in the towns changed too. Trade with Normandy meant that some Saxon towns grew, and a few new towns were created.

- On the whole, though, the impact was negative. Towns in rebellious areas were attacked, and houses and workshops were destroyed to make room for castles.

- While some towns grew, others such as York, Norwich and Oxford, saw their populations fall. Other smaller towns were hit even harder.

- English townspeople depended on the town markets to make their living, but the Normans saw the potential for profit and took control of the markets, charging traders high rents and tolls.

- William also exploited the efficient Saxon system for collecting tax (the geld). He increased the geld dramatically and this higher tax burden lasted for at least twenty years after the Conquest.

Test yourself

1 What percentage of land was owned by English landowners in 1086?
2 How did William prevent his nobles becoming a threat to him?
3 List three changes to towns under the Normans.

Support or challenge?

Below are a sample exam-style 20-mark question and a table showing various examples that could be used in an answer. For each one, decide whether it supports or challenges the overall statement, then challenge yourself to add three more examples.

In 2017, the historian R. Kennett stated, 'The Normans changed England for the better.' How far do you agree with this view? **(20 marks)**

Examples	Supports statement	Challenges statement
The number of free peasants fell sharply under the Normans	The number of free Peasants fell under the Normans	
William used the Anglo-Saxon system for collecting taxes		✓
Trade with Normandy meant that some English towns grew	✓	
Before and after the Conquest, most people worked on the land		✓
The number of slaves in England fell after 1066	✓	
The Normans increased rents and tolls at the markets		✓
The number of slaves in England were declined	✓	

TIP

The idea of the 'Norman Yoke' is key in your exam specification. You will need to show the examiner that you understand the concept, and consider to what extent it was true. To do this, you will need to be able to refer back to Anglo-Saxon England as well as describe Norman rule.

Challenge question

Why do you think the idea of the 'Norman Yoke' became so popular?

3.15 Laws, language and the Church

The **Normans** introduced **new laws,** and **adapted** some Anglo-Saxon laws

- We know about English law in the Norman period from a book called the *Textus Roffensis* (or Book of Rochester) which was written by a monk in the 1120s.
- The *Textus Roffensis* lists nearly 40 laws dating from 600 to 1100, and allows us to compare Saxon and Norman laws. The Normans kept some Saxon laws, and introduced new ones.
- The Saxons used 'trial by ordeal', which involved the accused holding a red-hot iron or putting their hand in boiling water. If the wound healed, it was a sign from God that they were innocent.
- The Normans kept trial by ordeal, and added 'trial by combat', which was a sword fight between the accused and their accuser. It was believed that God would intervene to decide the winner.
- The Normans also introduced two new laws, which were unpopular with the English:
  - If a Norman was murdered, the local community had to pay an enormous fine called the **Murdrum** until the murderer was found.
  - King William enjoyed hunting and created royal forests to hunt in. **Forest Law** introduced harsh punishments for hunting in these forests – killing a rabbit would get two of your fingers chopped off.

Norman French was spoken only by the ruling class but eventually it influenced the English language

- Before the Conquest, most manuscripts were written in English. The use of written English came to a sudden stop in 1066. Latin became the written language of government and the Church.
- The spoken language changed too. Instead of everyone speaking English, the ruling class spoke Norman French, making the difference between the conquerors and conquered even clearer.
- However, eventually the two languages began to blend together. French words were added to English. Around a quarter of the words in modern English came from Norman French.
- The influence of French made English richer and more flexible, and eventually led to it being one of the world's most widely spoken languages, although at the time for the English it was a symbol of their inferior status.

<aside>
Key point

William took a 'pick and mix' approach to ruling England. He continued to use Anglo-Saxon systems and laws that worked for him, and changed or added to those that did not. Norman French became the language of government, and the Church was thoroughly reformed.
</aside>

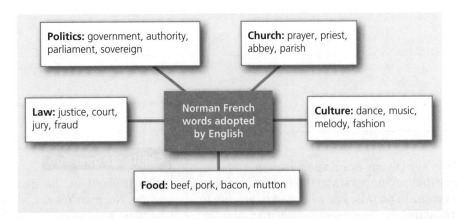

Politics: government, authority, parliament, sovereign

Church: prayer, priest, abbey, parish

Law: justice, court, jury, fraud

Norman French words adopted by English

Culture: dance, music, melody, fashion

Food: beef, pork, bacon, mutton

William's religious reforms included rebuilding cathedrals, monasteries and churches

- William was a devout Christian. In 1070, papal legates crowned William a second time, giving the Pope's blessing to his rule. William and the legates then discussed the reform of the English Church.
- Stigand was removed as Archbishop of Canterbury and replaced by Lanfranc, a Norman. Thomas of Bayeux became Archbishop of York. By 1080, only one of England's sixteen bishops was English.
- Normandy was famous for its beautiful churches, and King William began to rebuild England's cathedrals, replacing them with larger and grander buildings in the Norman style.
- The Norman Conquest also led to a revival of monasticism, with new monasteries built, old ones restored, and monks from Norman monasteries being brought to England.
- Nearly all the Saxon parish churches were destroyed and replaced with new ones. Very few of the Anglo-Saxon saints survived, as the Normans dedicated churches to their own saints.

 Test yourself

1 What was the Murdrum fine?
2 What was the main written language after the Conquest?
3 List three changes to the Church under the Normans.

 Spot the second-order concept

This extract from an exam answer to the question on page 83 contains several examples of second-order concepts. Highlight where they occur and note the second-order concept in the margin.

The Norman Conquest had an enormous impact on England. In some ways, the social structure stayed the same – power came from land, and everyone had a lord – but in other ways there were big changes. Norman lords replaced English ones and rents and taxes went up, forcing people into poverty. Although the Normans kept many Saxon laws, such as trial by ordeal, they introduced their own as well. Books such as the 'Textus Roffensis' tell us that trial by ordeal was extended to trial by combat, a sword fight between the accused and accuser. Forest Law reserved huge swathes of the forest for the king to hunt in and severely punished anyone hunting there – even collecting firewood was banned. This was hugely unpopular because before the Conquest, many people had depended on the forests as a source of food. Another new law was the Murdrum fine. If a Norman was killed, the local community had to pay an exorbitant fine until the murderer was caught. The fact that this law was necessary shows how unpopular the Normans were – and how vulnerable they must have felt, surrounded by hostile subjects.

TIP

To make sure you are using second-order concepts in your answers, try to use phrases like:
- This was particularly important because …
- This had a big impact, because …
- The drawback of this was …
- This is significant because …
- We know this because …
- On the other hand …
- Another reason for this is …

Challenge question

What do you think were the most significant changes made by the Normans? Do you think people at the time would have agreed with you, or would they have seen things differently?

4.1 Elizabeth and her Court, the Privy Council and the rebellion of the Earl of Essex

Key point

Elizabeth successfully governed with the help of William Cecil for 40 years, but at the end of her reign she faced a rebellion from her favourite, the Earl of Essex.

TIP

All the words in **purple** are defined in the glossary of key terms that you can find here: www.hoddereducation.co.uk/myrevisionnotesdownloads. Make sure that you can spell them, know what they mean and aim to use them in your written work.

The **Royal Court** was the **centre** of political life

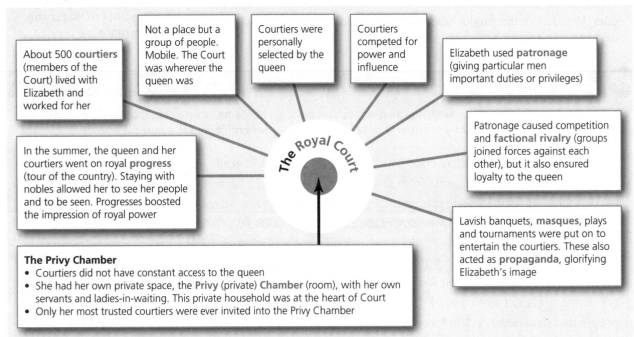

About 500 **courtiers** (members of the Court) lived with Elizabeth and worked for her

Not a place but a group of people. Mobile. The Court was wherever the queen was

Courtiers were personally selected by the queen

Courtiers competed for power and influence

Elizabeth used **patronage** (giving particular men important duties or privileges)

In the summer, the queen and her courtiers went on royal **progress** (tour of the country). Staying with nobles allowed her to see her people and to be seen. Progresses boosted the impression of royal power

Patronage caused competition and **factional rivalry** (groups joined forces against each other), but it also ensured loyalty to the queen

Lavish banquets, **masques**, plays and tournaments were put on to entertain the courtiers. These also acted as **propaganda**, glorifying Elizabeth's image

The Royal Court

The Privy Chamber
- Courtiers did not have constant access to the queen
- She had her own private space, the **Privy** (private) **Chamber** (room), with her own servants and ladies-in-waiting. This private household was at the heart of Court
- Only her most trusted courtiers were ever invited into the Privy Chamber

The **Privy Council** was Elizabeth's **small close group** of key ministers

- The **Privy Council** was a group of ministers selected by Elizabeth to help her govern the country. It met at Court almost daily.
- Elizabeth's council had nineteen members – far smaller than her predecessor Mary's.
- Her first council was a clever compromise of nobles. Later it became an effective group of full-time politicians drawn from the gentry.
- Cecil and Walsingham were her most important ministers.

William Cecil (Lord Burghley), Secretary of State 1558–72 and 1590–98; Lord Treasurer 1572–90	Sir Francis Walsingham, Secretary of State 1572–90
• Elizabeth's main minister for 40 years. She relied heavily on him • Correspondence passed through him • Moderate Protestant but more willing to **suppress** Catholics than the queen • Avoided foreign religious disputes which could lead to costly wars • Never a 'yes' man. Prepared to challenge Elizabeth. Loyal but knew how to manage the queen	• Responsible for foreign affairs • Strong Puritan. Believed Catholics were a threat and should be **repressed** • Cold and distant. Did not flatter the queen • Elizabeth's 'spy master'. Ran a network of informers uncovering plots against Elizabeth • Elizabeth once lost patience with him and threw her slipper at him • Hardworking, well educated. Died following a fit probably caused by exhaustion

The 1590s was a challenging decade for Elizabeth

- Elizabeth's closest advisers died (Walsingham in 1590 and Cecil in 1598). This opened up opportunities for new courtiers to compete to gain influence.
- England experienced a series of bad harvests, famine, plague and rising poverty.
- England's expensive war with Spain dragged on.
- Elizabeth had no heir so there was uncertainty around succession.
- Elizabeth was less popular. Her previously tight control of the Royal Court broke down.

Test yourself

1 What was the Royal Court?
2 What was patronage?
3 What's the difference between the Privy Chamber and the Privy Council?

Essex dared to defy the queen and was executed for treason in 1601

1 Essex was one of Elizabeth's favourite courtiers but he defied Elizabeth in 1589 by joining Drake's failed attack on Lisbon and again in 1590 when he married without her permission.

2 When William Cecil died, the queen made Robert, his son, Secretary of State. This was the job Essex wanted. Essex was jealous.

3 Elizabeth sent Essex to Ireland in 1599 to defeat a Catholic rebellion led by Hugh O'Neill, the Earl of Tyrone. Instead Essex made a truce.

4 Elizabeth was cross with Essex, so banned him from Court in 1600 and took away his government jobs. He was financially ruined.

5 Essex led a short-lived rebellion in 1601. He underestimated how much support there was for Elizabeth. He was arrested and executed.

Make revision cards

In your exam you will need to use precise, relevant and detailed information in your answers. Revision cards can help to make the details stick. Write a topic heading on the front and then put up to five key words/phrases on the back. Use the words to explain your knowledge on the topic. Once you have made your cards you should test yourself, or work with a friend to test each other.

We suggest you make three cards:
- William Cecil
- Francis Walsingham
- The Earl of Essex.

On each card have the following headings:
- name, job and main dates
- background
- religion
- character
- role and his approach to his duties
- relationship with Elizabeth.

Spot the mistakes

This paragraph attempts to describe the role and importance of Elizabeth's councillor William Cecil. However, there are some mistakes in the paragraph. Find them and correct them.

> As her Secretary of State all correspondence passed through Cecil and he controlled access to the queen. He always did what she wanted and never questioned her judgement because he was so loyal. Like Elizabeth he was very cautious and wanted to avoid expensive foreign wars. Cecil was a strong Puritan who worked hard as Elizabeth's spymaster to stamp out Catholic plots. He pushed her into signing the death warrant for the execution of Mary Queen of Scots and she never saw him again. But when he died she was devastated. His son Robert Devereux took over as Secretary of State.

4.2 Elizabeth and her Parliaments, including opposition from the Puritans

Elizabethan government was **not democratic.** Parliament was **less important** than it is today

- The queen ruled mostly by royal **proclamation** (royal orders that had the force of law).
- However, if Elizabeth wanted to change the laws or raise taxes she summoned Parliament.
- The queen could open and close Parliament whenever she liked.
- MPs were not elected, they were selected by local lords.

- Parliament sat for only 35 months of Elizabeth's 45-year reign.
- Between 1580 and 1603, Elizabeth called Parliament more often than previously because she needed laws and financial support to deal with religious threats and war with Spain.

> **Key point**
>
> Elizabeth had various ways to control Parliament. She often compromised. Most of her requests were granted without difficulty. As her reign continued, some MPs, particularly Puritans, opposed her.

Elizabeth and her ministers decided what Parliament could discuss

- Privy councillors organised parliamentary business. Some served as MPs.
- The queen appointed the **speaker**, who decided on the agenda.

- Some topics such as religion, marriage, foreign affairs and the **succession** (who would inherit the throne) could not be raised by MPs.

In later years of her reign Elizabeth faced greater opposition or criticism from Puritan MPs

- Some MPs grew in confidence and started to discuss sensitive topics.
- Even privy councillors such as Cecil and Walsingham stirred up 'off limits' issues such as foreign policy or the succession, which they wanted the queen to confront.
- **Puritans** wanted freedom of speech for MPs. Two Puritans were hanged in 1583 for putting forward such views. But this issue was raised again in Parliament in 1584 and 1586.

- In November 1579, John Stubbs, a Puritan MP, wrote a pamphlet criticising Elizabeth's proposed marriage to the French Catholic, Duke of Anjou. Stubbs had his right hand cut off, as did his accomplice, William Page.
- In 1593, Puritan MP Peter Wentworth was imprisoned in the Tower of London for urging Elizabeth to name a Protestant successor. He died there four years later.

Purveyances and monopolies were criticised

Date	Complaint	Elizabeth's response
1589	MPs complained about **purveyances** (the queen's right to buy supplies at cheap prices)	Elizabeth said this did not concern MPs, but that she would look into their complaints
1597	A **monopoly** was the exclusive right to make or sell a product. Elizabeth had the right to grant or sell a monopoly to a favourite courtier. For example, she granted Walter Raleigh a monopoly of tin. MPs complained about monopolies in the 1597 Parliament.	The queen agreed to look into the issue but did not take action
1601	Elizabeth had done little about monopolies and MPs complained again, much more forcefully. There was more opposition from MPs on this issue than on any issue at any other time in Elizabeth's reign	Elizabeth realised she needed to compromise and made a 'Golden Speech' to parliament flattering MPs and reinforcing how much she loved her people. She cancelled some monopolies and promised to look into others

Support or challenge?

The most valuable question on your depth study exam will be an essay question that asks you to agree or disagree with a statement.

Below are a sample exam-style 20-mark question and a table showing pieces of evidence that could support or challenge the statement given. Use the information on this spread and your own knowledge to make a decision by ticking the appropriate column. When you have done this, add three more examples and show whether they support or challenge the statement.

'Parliament was unimportant in Elizabeth's reign. MPs simply did whatever the queen and her ministers wanted.' How far do you agree with this view? **(20 marks)**

Evidence	Supports	Challenges
During 1584 and 1586, Puritan MPs demanded there should be more reform of the Church. Elizabeth banned the debate		
If the queen did not like a law passed by Parliament she could simply refuse to sign it and it would not become law		
Between 1580 and 1603, Elizabeth had to call Parliament more often because she needed laws and financial support to deal with religious threats and war with Spain		
In 1586, MPs demanded the execution of Mary Queen of Scots. Elizabeth gave a vague answer but agreed to the execution three months later		
Most of the time Elizabeth ruled by royal proclamation. But if she wanted new laws, new punishments or new taxes these had to be approved by Parliament		
The queen's Privy Council decided what Parliament should debate		
Puritan MP Peter Wentworth demanded that Elizabeth name a Protestant successor. Elizabeth put him in the Tower of London		
The queen decided when Parliament would meet. She could dissolve it when she wished		
The queen set strict limits on what Parliament could discuss. Foreign policy, succession, her marriage and religion were forbidden topics		
Even privy councillors such as Cecil and Walsingham stirred up 'off limits' issues such as foreign policy or the succession, which they wanted the queen to confront		

 ## Test yourself

1 Which issues were MPs forbidden from discussing?
2 Name someone who criticised Elizabeth and outline what happened to them.
3 List three Puritan demands that were raised in Parliament.
4 What are monopolies?

TIP

There is no right or wrong answer to a 20-mark question, but make sure you start with a clear statement of your overall judgement and support this with specific knowledge.

4.3 Elizabeth and her people; local government and propaganda

Elizabeth used **trusted local officials** to help her **control her subjects**

- Two of the most important roles were **Lord Lieutenant** and **Justice of the Peace (JP)**. It was considered a great honour to be chosen to serve queen and country in this way.

Lord Lieutenant: one per county	JPs: around 40 per county
• Had overall responsibility for each county for ensuring people obeyed Elizabeth's laws • Elizabeth usually chose the most powerful **noble** in each area for this role • Told the Privy Council of any local problems • Provided the queen with part-time soldiers when needed	• Came into direct contact with the people and did most to keep the county running smoothly • Usually selected from educated, gentry families • Unpaid. But people wanted to do this job because being a JP gave a man considerable influence in his local area • We know about their vast range of duties from a 600-page book written by William Lambard, a JP in Kent. These included enforcing Poor Laws, collecting taxes, setting wages and arranging road repairs • Every **quarter** (three months) they held **sessions** where they judged criminal cases • Some JPs were lazy. Others favoured powerful families. Others turned a blind eye to Catholic activities • Elizabeth could dismiss JPs who failed in their duties, but did not do this if it might make her unpopular in an area

- Towns were different. Their affairs were run by councils elected by wealthy citizens.

Key point

Elizabeth used local officials to oversee law and order around the country. She ensured loyalty through a mixture of propaganda and censorship.

Elizabeth used **propaganda** to present a strong image to keep her subjects **loyal**

Progresses: every summer Elizabeth and her Court stayed with nobles who competed to impress the queen. This meant Elizabeth was regularly seen by her most powerful subjects

Plays were performed at Court showing the importance of monarchy and hierarchy

Pageants: the Privy Council made Ascension Day (17 November) the day to celebrate Elizabeth becoming queen. Local communities lit bonfires and performed bell ringing

Publications: books were published on topics such as Elizabeth's 'Golden Speech'

Portraits of the queen showed her looking young and powerful. Elizabeth expected courtiers to wear miniature portraits of her. Courtiers commissioned portraits to flatter the queen

Pennies: most people never saw a painting of Elizabeth. Their image of her came from coins

Prayers: attending church each week was compulsory. Services included the 'Prayer for the Queen's Memory', which reinforced Elizabeth's position as God's divinely appointed ruler

Preaching: preachers had to have a government licence. The queen selected Church leaders who would spread a message of loyalty through sermons, prayers and songs

Challenge question

What do you think was a more powerful tool: propaganda or censorship?

Quick quizzes and answers at **www.hoddereducation.co.uk/myrevisionnotesdownloads**

Censorship was also used to ensure loyalty and discourage criticism

- Elizabeth saw plans for plays in advance so could cut anything that she did not approve of.
- There were only 60 printing presses in England so the Privy Council could easily prevent publications they disapproved of.
- The image used in portraits of the queen was carefully controlled. For example, in 1596:
  - a new template was produced for artists to copy which showed her younger than she was and to hide the fact she had decayed teeth and wore a wig
  - the Privy Council ordered unacceptable portraits of the queen to be burned.

TIP

The two mistakes to avoid with Question 6a are:
- writing too much
- not focusing on the interpretation but waffling on about other things you know.

Eliminate irrelevance

The depth study exam focuses on interpretations – how the past is presented by writers and artists. The first question on your exam will be like this:

In Interpretation A, the writer Tracy Borman presents Elizabeth as someone obsessed with her public image. Identify and explain one way in which she does this. (3 marks)

INTERPRETATION A *From an article by Tracy Borman. It appeared in 2015 on History Extra, a website for adults, under the title '7 things you (probably) didn't know about Elizabeth'.*

Elizabeth used dirty tactics to outshine her rivals. Elizabeth exalted in [enjoyed] being the queen bee at court. But although for the early part of her reign she was the most desirable bride in Europe, as her physical charms began to fade she employed dirty tactics to make sure that she kept all the male attention to herself. Thus, while Elizabeth appeared at court bedecked [dressed] in lavish gowns of rich materials and vivid colours, her ladies were obliged to wear only black or white.

This answer addresses the question above and has some good points but some irrelevance.

Read the answer and a) cross out any parts that are irrelevant and b) in three colours, highlight three parts of the answer that:

- identify a feature in the interpretation
- explain how this feature supports the interpretation.

Elizabeth came to the throne in 1558. She had a troubled past but that made her tough. In the interpretation, Tracy Borman focuses on Elizabeth's obsession with clothes. She tells the story that as she got older Elizabeth boosted her own image by making her servants wear black and white so her own dresses would look more spectacular. She had 500 courtiers who were always trying to get one up on each other by getting her attention. You can tell how important clothes and jewellery were to Elizabeth's image from her portraits because she was always shown wearing spectacular dresses full of coded symbols. One example is the Armada Portrait. Painters were told what to paint and portraits that were not approved might be destroyed.

Test yourself

1. List three responsibilities held by a) Lord Lieutenants and b) Justices of the Peace.
2. List three ways the Elizabethan authorities used: a) propaganda and b) censorship.

4.4 The enforcement of Elizabeth's religious settlement after 1580

Elizabeth's **religious settlement** was intended to be a **compromise**

- Under Edward and Mary, England had changed between Protestant and Catholic ways.
- Elizabeth was a Protestant. She rejected Catholic beliefs such as **transubstantiation**. But she was not a religious **radical** like the **Puritans**. She still liked church decoration and music.
- Elizabeth passed two important laws in May 1559 to establish her Church: the **Act of Supremacy** and the **Act of Uniformity**.

> **Key point**
>
> Elizabeth's reign saw one of the deepest and longest-lasting shifts in British history – the move from Catholicism to Protestantism. The vast majority of English Catholics conformed, but Catholic opposition posed a great danger to Elizabeth from the 1580s.

Act of Supremacy	Act of Uniformity
• Re-established that the Church of England was independent – not ruled by the Pope in Rome • Made Elizabeth Supreme Governor of this independent Church of England	• Attendance at Anglican services made compulsory. You could be fined for not attending • Bible and services should be in English • Clergy could marry • Catholic practices such as pilgrimages and saints' days banned • Altars replaced with communion tables But as a compromise to Catholics • candles and **vestments** (colourful robes) were allowed

Responses to the religious settlement varied **around the country**

Conformers	Church papists
• Many Catholics went along with the changes, became Protestants and dropped their Catholic beliefs • They were persuaded to convert after listening to sermons • They avoided the social and financial penalties of continuing to be a Catholic • Conformers were mainly in the south and east	• Most English Catholics, especially in the north-west, attended Protestant church services but kept some loyalty to the Pope • Going to church prevented them from paying fines but did not change their beliefs • On the inside they may have still held Catholic beliefs but they did nothing to challenge the queen • They hoped Catholicism would return with Mary Queen of Scots as Elizabeth's successor but did not plot against her
Plotters	**Recusants**
• Catholics who plotted against Elizabeth • Probably fewer than 200 people • Fiercely loyal to the Pope • Believed their opposition to Elizabeth was justified as it was God's will to remove her	• Several thousand wealthy English Catholics, based especially in the north and west • Refused to attend church services and continued to hear or attend Mass • Could afford to pay the fines and hoped Catholicism would return when Mary Queen of Scots replaced Elizabeth

- Most Catholics showed loyalty and attended church services. Few could afford the non-attendance fines. As long as they outwardly conformed, Elizabeth and her ministers were happy.

Test yourself

1 What were: a) the Act of Supremacy, b) the Act of Uniformity and c) the Act of Persuasions?
2 What is the difference between a Church papist and a recusant?
3 What was the effect of Elizabeth's excommunication?

> **TIP**
>
> The Depth Study is arranged thematically but you should always be looking out for connections between the sections. For example, the issue of religion affects government (pages 86–91), popular culture (pages 104–7) and overseas exploration (pages 110–15).

From 1580, **recusancy** became **more common** as Catholics fought to keep the old faith alive

- Mary Queen of Scots had been in England since 1568. Her presence was a real problem for Elizabeth. She became the focus of Catholic hopes to return the country to the 'true' faith.
- Through the 1570s, the Catholic Church began an organised effort to rebuild the Catholic faith in England.
  - Elizabeth was **excommunicated** (expelled from the Catholic Church) by the Pope in 1570, as a **heretic** (an unbeliever). This meant her subjects did not have to remain loyal to her.

- Catholic **missionaries** and priests were trained in Europe then sent to England to keep the faith alive (see next page).
- From 1580, these measures began to have an effect and more Catholics (particularly the rich ones who could afford the fine) started to disobey the rules and refused to attend church.
- A few went further and became plotters. There were never that many but Elizabeth's government felt very threatened by them.

The **authorities responded** with strict laws to **punish recusants**

- The 1581 **Act of Persuasions** raised recusancy fines by 10,000 per cent! This meant that only the wealthiest could afford to pay.
- The 1585 Act against Priests. Priests were seen as the heart of Catholic resistance. Those who offered shelter or aid to priests could face the death penalty.
- Margaret Clitherow became the first female Catholic **martyr** (someone who dies for their beliefs). She died under torture when she was accused of sheltering priests in York in 1586.
- The 1587 **Recusancy Act**. Two-thirds of the land owned by a recusant could be taken. Even the wealthiest Catholics, such as Thomas Tresham, who

spent time in prison and was on a list of disloyal subjects accused of sheltering priests in 1581, were now forced into debt.
- In 1588, amid fears of an English Catholic uprising to support the Spanish **Armada**, eleven Catholics were executed.
- The 1593 **Act Restraining Recusants**. Catholics had to stay within five miles of their homes and not hold large gatherings. This meant that the authorities could keep a closer watch on potentially disloyal subjects and Catholics became isolated from one another.

Getting from A to B

With a complicated topic like this it is important to keep a strong hold of the chronology. The flow chart below picks out the main steps from 1580 to 1603 as Elizabeth dealt with the Catholic threat. Copy the chart and in each box explain its impact or importance. You will need to refer to the next four pages to complete some of the boxes.

1580	1581	1583	1585
Missionary priests arrived	Act of Persuasions	Campion executed	Throckmorton Plot	Act against Priests

1586	1587	1588	1593	1603
Babington Plot	Recusancy Act	Mary Queen of Scots executed	Defeat of the Spanish Armada	Act Restraining Recusants	Elizabeth died

4.5 Catholic links abroad and the Elizabethan spy network

Seminary priests and Jesuits were sent to England to keep the Catholic faith alive

- When Elizabeth became queen, most Catholic priests left England and became **exiles** (people forced to live abroad) working in Catholic countries in Europe.
- Elizabeth was relieved that there were no longer priests in England to encourage others to break her laws when the Pope excommunicated her in 1570.
- By the 1580s, this situation had changed as two types of priests were sent to England: **seminary priests** and **Jesuits**.

> **Key point**
>
> Elizabeth feared that Catholics in England would get help from Catholics abroad. That is exactly what happened, although Walsingham dealt with the threat ruthlessly.

Seminary priests	Jesuits
• Trained by William Allen (an English priest in exile) at seminaries (priest schools) in northern France and in Italy • Main role was to encourage faithful Catholics by saying Mass and hearing confession • Told not to try to convert anyone	• Specially trained to win people back to Catholicism • They were dedicated to serving the Pope • Robert Persons (sometimes called Parsons) and Edmund Campion were the first to arrive • They came in disguise and used 'safe houses' to avoid arrest

Priests were sheltered by wealthy Catholics but hunted by Walsingham's spies

- By 1580, over 100 priests had arrived from Europe.
- Their mission was dangerous. Two seminary priests were executed as traitors in 1577.
- Wealthy Catholics made secret hiding places in their houses, called **priest holes**.
- The most famous designer of priest holes was Nicholas Owen. It is claimed that he saved hundreds of priests from arrest.
- These priests succeeded in influencing many wealthy people to stay Catholic.
- Walsingham built up a network of spies and informers to learn about the plans, plots and the movement of Catholic priests.
- Local JPs were ordered to search for priests in the houses of the gentry.

After Campion was executed in 1581, attitudes hardened and a propaganda war followed

- Edmund Campion, the first Jesuit priest to arrive in 1580, was found hiding in a priest hole.
- Campion insisted he had never encouraged rebellion against Elizabeth. He claimed he was a loyal Englishman, but that Elizabeth was just wrong about religion.
- He was tortured on the rack, then hung, drawn and quartered as a traitor.
- As a result, Catholic opposition to Elizabeth increased. More priests came to England.
- Catholics published propaganda showing images of torture to expose the cruelty of Elizabeth's regime. Elizabeth's government countered this with pamphlets to justify torture.
- After 1585, priests on trial were asked the '**Bloody Question**' about who they would be loyal to in the event of an invasion of England.
- The execution of priests peaked in 1588 when England was under threat from Spanish invasion.

The **threat faded** after 1588 and **Elizabeth triumphed**

Wrong place: they concentrated on the south-east but recusancy was strongest in the north and west

Wrong people: they concentrated on the gentry yet the majority of people in England were from the lower orders. They had no one to encourage them to stay Catholic

Reasons why the Catholic threat faded

Too few: Walsingham's spy network was more extensive than the Catholic network

Too divided: Seminary and Jesuit priests argued over tactics. The Pope appointed an archpriest and the two groups argued about him too

 Test yourself

1 What was a priest hole?
2 Who was Edmund Campion and what happened to him?
3 Give three reasons why the priests failed to keep the Catholic faith alive.

Suggest a line of enquiry

The second interpretations question on your exam asks you to plan an enquiry. For example:

If you were asked to do more research on one aspect of Interpretation B, what would you choose to investigate? Explain how this would help us to analyse and understand the persecution of Catholics in Elizabethan England.   **(5 marks)**

INTERPRETATION B *Monument to Nicholas Owen at St Mary's Church, Harvington, 1825. The building at the back represents the Tower of London, where Nicholas Owen died under torture in 1606.*

For high marks you need to justify your chosen line of enquiry by using your own knowledge of specific people, events or situations. You also need to base your suggested line of enquiry on one or more second-order concepts:

- **typicality** (Was this the same everywhere?)
- **diversity** (Was it the same for everyone?)
- **continuity and change** (What changed? What stayed the same?)
- **causation** (Why did this happen?)
- **significance** (What was the impact? How is it remembered?).

Below are some possible lines of enquiry on the persecution of Catholics in Elizabethan England on Interpretation B.

- If they are too narrow and don't involve a second-order concept then cross them out.
- If they do involve a second-order concept then draw a line to link them to one of the concepts in bold above.
- Choose one line of enquiry and write two or more sentences to explain how this would help you understand the persecution of Catholics.

Who was Nicholas Owen?	What is the person on the bottom left doing?
Why were Catholic priests in hiding?	When was Owen busiest?
Was he the only priest-hole maker?	What's the sculpture made of?
Why did they make this monument in 1825?	Why was Owen tortured?

4.6 Mary Queen of Scots, plots against Elizabeth, the Armada and war with Spain

The presence of **Mary Queen of Scots** in England created an **ongoing threat** for Elizabeth

- Mary was Elizabeth's Catholic cousin.
- When Protestants **deposed** (removed) Mary from the Scottish throne, she came to England in 1568 hoping for Elizabeth's help.
- Elizabeth kept Mary in comfortable captivity, but regularly moved her so no one could easily plan her escape.

- As feared, Mary soon became the focus of Catholic plots. She was a real threat to **national security**, made worse by:
  - In 1570, the Pope excommunicated Elizabeth and denounced her as a heretic; attacking England could now be justified.
  - In 1580, the Pope sent specially trained priests to help spread the Catholic faith.

> **Key point**
>
> Lying behind much of the religious tension of the 1580s was the problem of Mary Queen of Scots and the Catholic plots to make her queen. Eventually this led to war with Spain.

The **Throckmorton Plot of 1583** aimed to replace Elizabeth with Mary

- In 1583, the Pope, Philip II of Spain and a French Catholic army devised a plan with Francis Throckmorton, to place Mary on the throne.
- Walsingham's spies uncovered the plot, Throckmorton was arrested, but Mary was spared because they could not prove her involvement.

- A **Bond of Association** followed whereby anyone who plotted or who would gain from a plot to kill Elizabeth could be executed.

Walsingham finally trapped Mary with the **Babington Plot** in 1586

- In 1586, Anthony Babington communicated with Mary, using coded messages, about a plot to kill Elizabeth (the '**Babington Plot**').
- They were both unaware that their correspondence was being intercepted by one of Walsingham's spies. This provided evidence of Mary's guilt.

- Mary was put on trial, found guilty of treason and executed at Fotheringay Castle on 8 February 1587.
- Elizabeth had signed Mary's death warrant but had asked for it not to be sealed. She was furious that the execution had gone ahead anyway.

Anglo-Spanish hostility built up through Elizabeth's reign, leading to the **Armada invasion plan**

1559	Elizabeth rejected an offer of marriage from King Philip II of Spain. Philip was a Catholic who viewed the queen as a heretic and wanted to restore Catholicism in England
1570s	Elizabeth supported privateers who attacked Spanish treasure ships in the New World
1583	Philip supported the Throckmorton Plot to depose Elizabeth
1584	The Dutch rebel leader, William of Orange, was assassinated by a Catholic subject of Philip II. Elizabeth feared this could happen to her
1585	Elizabeth sent an army to help Dutch rebels fight against Spanish rule
1587	Philip prepared a fleet of ships – the Armada – to invade England. When Mary Queen of Scots was executed, Philip was even more determined to succeed in his crusade against England

> ✎ **Test yourself**
>
> 1 State the name, date and outcome of two plots against Elizabeth.
> 2 Give three reasons the Armada failed.
> 3 In which year did plotters make their last famously failed attempt to restore Catholicism?

The **Armada failed** through a combination of bad planning, bad **luck** and skilful English **tactics**

TIP

There are sample answers to all the practice questions at www. hoddereducation.co.uk/ myrevisionnotesdownloads

- **Planning**: the Armada was supposed to pick up troops in the Netherlands and take them to invade England. But communication between Armada and troops was impossible, so this never happened.

- **Luck**: strong winds drove the Armada northwards so the English could attack.

- **Tactics**: English vessels changed direction more easily. Fireships drove the Spanish ships into open sea. At the Battle of Gravelines, English guns were reloaded more quickly.

 Develop the detail

Each of the following statements is vague and general. Add further details to show that you understand the general point being made. One example has been done for you. This will help with most questions as it is important throughout your exam to use 'detailed, accurate and relevant knowledge'.

General statement	Supporting detail
Mary Queen of Scots was a problem for Elizabeth	*As an alternative queen, already living in England, with a clear claim to the throne, she was a focus for Catholic plotters*
Elizabeth was called a heretic	
The Armada was badly planned	
The Babington Plot trapped Mary	
Elizabeth was indecisive	

 Support or challenge?

Below are a sample exam-style 20-mark question and a table showing various pieces of evidence. For each one, decide whether it supports or challenges the overall statement, then add three more pieces of evidence.

In his 2012 book, *The Watchers*, the historian Stephen Alford argued that the threat from Catholics created 'dangerous and uncertain times' in Elizabethan England. How far do you agree with this view? (20 marks)

Evidence	Supports	Challenges
By 1603, there were very few Catholics in England		
Elizabeth was seen as a heretic by Catholic Europe		
Mary was a ready-made Catholic queen in England		
Mary was kept in comfortable captivity as a prisoner		
Most people were happy to go along with Elizabeth's religious changes		
The Armada was aiming to invade England with 30,000 Spanish troops		
The leader of the Dutch Protestants was killed by a Catholic assassin		
The Pope and Spain supported Throckmorton's plot to make Mary queen		
There were about 200 people involved in Catholic plots. They all failed		
Walsingham had spies all over the country to inform on Catholic plots		

4.7 The contrasting lives of rich, middling and poor Elizabethans

During the sixteenth century, the gap between rich and poor widened further

- Elizabethan society was hierarchical. At the top were those who owned land (the **landed gentry**) – the privileged few. At the bottom were those who worked on the land – the vast majority.
- Living standards depended on where you were in this hierarchy.

- The rich became richer during Elizabeth's reign, and the number of poor people grew. The gap between rich and poor widened.
- People could move up this hierarchy, for example a skilled craftsman or trader could make money and buy some land.

> **Key point**
>
> Some people in Elizabethan England lived very comfortable lives. For others, life was a real struggle.

To show off wealth, the gentry built big houses

- The gentry owned land – this is what made them rich. They only made up two per cent of the population, but owned over 50 per cent of the land in England.
- The gentry also had political power. As JPs, they enforced the queen's rules locally and as MPs they helped her to govern.
- To display their wealth and power, individuals built magnificent country houses like Montacute House in Somerset or Hardwick Hall in Derbyshire.
- These houses were based on **Renaissance** ideas of symmetry and proportion.

- They had huge glazed windows, tall decorated chimneys, ornate fireplaces and decorative oak panelling.
- A fashionable feature was a long gallery running the length of the house, used for exercising, dancing and socialising. The walls displayed works of art.
- The rich ate well. Plentiful food was supplied from the farms, gardens and orchards around the house. The gentry could also afford to import fine wines and luxury foods from Europe.

The 'middling sort' led comfortable lives, but were less wealthy and powerful than the gentry

In the towns the 'middling sort' were	In the country the 'middling sort' were
Tradesmen and craftsmen who owned their own businesses	**Yeomen** or husbandmen who farmed some land of their own
Poorer than the merchants who ruled the town, but much more wealthy than the labourers	Nowhere near as wealthy as the gentry, but more comfortable than the labouring poor

- A yeoman's house had between five and ten rooms separated into upstairs and downstairs. Sometimes service buildings like a bake-house, dairy or brew-house were attached.
- The parlour was a sleeping room with feather mattresses and linen sheets. Children and servants slept upstairs.
- Chimneys, ceilings and glass windows were new home comforts.

- The middling sort ate well but there was less ceremony than in gentry homes:
  - they had some meat (beef, mutton and pork) reared on their own land.
  - bread was an important part of their diet
  - they drank beer and mead rather than wine.

> **TIP**
>
> There are Elizabethan houses all over the country. You might have the opportunity to visit one. It could prove very useful for answering questions about the daily lives of rich Elizabethans.

The **labouring poor** made up half the population

- They struggled to make a living because most did not have regular work on the farms. At harvest time it was busy, but at other times it was hard to afford rent, food and fuel.

- Houses were small, dark and smoky. They usually had two rooms with a bare earth floor. There were no upper rooms, glass or chimneys. Smoke escaped through the thatch.

- Their diet was limited. Bread was the main food and was made from **rye**, a cereal cheaper than wheat. **Pottage**, a thick soup, was the usual meal.

- Wet weather led to poor harvests in 1594, 1595 and 1596. Many labouring people starved to death during this difficult decade.

 Sorting into a table

Look at the nine pieces of information to the right of the table. Put the correct number in the correct box in the table.

	Gentry	Middling sort	Labourers
Houses			
Food			
Work			

1 Ate meat. Drank beer and mead. Could not afford luxuries like grapes

2 Choice of meats, fish and sweets. Imported French and Italian wines

3 Didn't own land. Men and women did manual work. Women did household chores

4 Hard to know due to little evidence remaining. Small and poorly built houses

5 Magnificent Renaissance-inspired buildings with 50 rooms

6 Mainly ate bread and pottage, a thick soup made from vegetables in the garden

7 Managed their estate and acted as MPs and JPs. Servants did the housework

8 Oak-framed houses with five to ten rooms and chimneys to channel away the smoke

9 Men were tradesmen, craftsmen or merchants. Women helped the men. Some had servants

 Test yourself

1 What did the gentry own that the poor did not?
2 What did the 'middling sort' drink?
3 What was the main food eaten by the labouring poor?
4 Describe three features of a labourers' cottage.

4.8 Family life: husbands and wives, parents and children, wider kinship

Young people got **married** when they could **afford it** or when the girl got **pregnant**

- Couples saved up money before getting married. Men usually married in their late twenties and women in their mid-twenties. Gentry couples were richer so could marry younger.

- There was no reliable contraception but **illegitimate births** (babies born to unmarried mothers) were uncommon because the Church forbade sex outside of marriage.

- However, the decision to marry was often triggered by becoming pregnant. Up to 30 per cent of brides were pregnant at their wedding.

- In wealthy families, a young person would need their parents' approval of their choice of partner because property and status mattered. Young people in middling or labouring families were freer to choose their own partners.

- Same-sex marriage was unknown.

> **Key point**
>
> In many ways, Elizabethan families were similar to families today although family life varied depending on whether you were rich or poor.

There were **clear roles** for **husband and wife**

- Wives were expected to obey their husbands. Husbands were advised to respect their wives. A woman's property belonged to her husband.

- Elizabethans disapproved of violent husbands and scolding, domineering wives.

- In poor and middling households, wives helped their husbands in their work.

- Divorce was difficult and required an Act of Parliament. But couples could separate informally. It was more common for marriages to end with death.

- When a partner died, their spouse often remarried. Many children in England were brought up by step-parents.

Families were small. **Children** had to grow up quickly

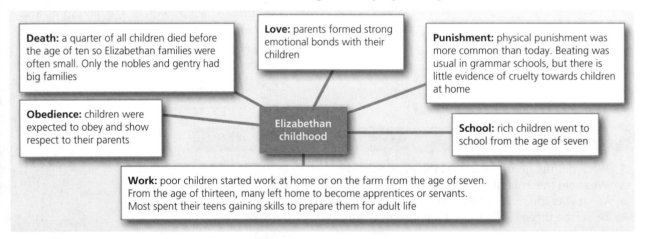

Death: a quarter of all children died before the age of ten so Elizabethan families were often small. Only the nobles and gentry had big families

Love: parents formed strong emotional bonds with their children

Punishment: physical punishment was more common than today. Beating was usual in grammar schools, but there is little evidence of cruelty towards children at home

Obedience: children were expected to obey and show respect to their parents

Elizabethan childhood

School: rich children went to school from the age of seven

Work: poor children started work at home or on the farm from the age of seven. From the age of thirteen, many left home to become apprentices or servants. Most spent their teens gaining skills to prepare them for adult life

The **immediate family** was more **important** than the extended family (kinship)

- The structure of Elizabethan households was similar to today.

- Households rarely included members outside the **nuclear family** (a couple and their dependent children). Sometimes an elderly parent or orphaned child was taken in.

- Young people left home to work, so most extended families were scattered. Relatives did not live in the same village, although people usually had relatives in nearby villages and towns.

- In difficult times people relied on neighbours for support.

- Unlike today, few Elizabethan people had relatives living abroad.

Comparing interpretations

Question 7 of your exam will ask you to compare two interpretations. For example:

Interpretations C and D both comment on home life in Elizabethan times. How far do they differ **and** what might explain any differences? **(12 marks)**

- 'How far do they differ' means compare what each interpretation tells us about home life and consider the similarities and differences.
- 'What might explain any differences' means compare the provenance (who wrote it, when and why).

Fill out this table to help you compare these interpretations. Then write two paragraphs to explain how far they differ and why.

Content	Interpretation C	Interpretation D
Detail of the house		
Detail of the family		
Familiar or strange?		

Provenance	Interpretation C	Interpretation D
Authorship		
Date		
Purpose		

INTERPRETATION C *From* Family Life in Shakespeare's Time, *an online resource for American schools by Joseph Papp and Elizabeth Kirkland, 2003.*

If you woke up one morning and suddenly found yourself in a sixteenth-century family, you might be surprised at how familiar everything seemed. Although you would be getting off a lumpy straw mattress and planting your feet on a floor covered with rushes instead of rugs, when you went downstairs you would find a very modern-looking nuclear family—mother, father, and a few sisters and brothers—sitting on stools around the breakfast table drinking their morning beer (*that* might be different!) and eating their bread and butter before getting on with the day's work.

INTERPRETATION D *From a BBC television series,* The Time Traveller's Guide to Elizabethan England, *2013, written and presented by the historian Ian Mortimer.*

Imagine you have come to stay with one of your ancestors in the 1560s. It's not unusual to find seven or even eight people living in a house like this ... The thing that will strike you most is that it is very dark. You'll find it's very basic. Just one room with an earth floor. What will really hit you is the thick smoke filling the whole room. Candles, you think, are the obvious answer. [But] candles are expensive and poor families simply can't afford lots of light. This family's only possessions are a few pots, some spoons and ladles, a basket and a bench.

TIP

Remember to read the interpretation caption as carefully as the text. It may include helpful details about the purpose and audience.

 ## Test yourself

1. Why were illegitimate births uncommon?
2. When did children go to school?
3. Did couples get divorced?

4.9 Poverty: its causes, Elizabethan explanations and responses

> **Key point**
>
> Poverty became a serious problem at the end of Elizabeth's reign. Local action led to the Elizabethan Poor Law of 1601. For the first time, looking after the poor became the responsibility of the state.

In the 1590s, long- and short-term causes combined to increase poverty to crisis point

- There had always been poor people in England but from the 1580s the number increased massively. Ordinary labouring people found themselves facing real hardship.

Long-term problems during Elizabeth's reign	**Rising population.** Between 1520 and 1600, England's population almost doubled from 2.4 million to 4.1 million	**Rising prices.** Population increase meant that despite some improvements in farming there was not enough food to meet demand, so prices soared	**Low wages.** Rising prices meant yeoman farmers had increased incomes. But with such competition for work the wages of the labouring poor stayed low and did not keep pace with the rising price of bread
Short-term pressures in the 1590s	**Harvest failure.** Bad weather in 1586, 1595, 1596 and 1597 led to bad harvests and food shortages. Food prices rocketed	**Downturn in cloth demand.** From the early 1580s, demand for English woollen cloth reduced, which increased unemployment and vagrancy	**Plague.** More frequent outbreaks of the plague made the situation worse

- Short-term pressures made the long-term problems worse. The 1590s was a crisis time.
- Large areas of England suffered from famine. Deaths due to starvation rose across the country, particularly in Cumbria, Yorkshire, Northumberland, Staffordshire and Devon.
- Those who could travel went looking for work or food where they could find it. The number of **vagrant poor** (homeless labourers who moved from place to place looking for work) increased significantly.
- Those who could not travel (women with children or elderly people) stayed where they were and tried to get by. The problems of these **settled poor** increased in times of famine.

Central government was slow and unwilling to grasp how big the problem was

- The government was more worried about the threat posed by vagrant poor than helping the settled poor.
- It feared that the vagrant poor were dangerous – that they might steal or beg to get money. They were classed as **vagabonds**.
- There was already a law from 1572 that vagabonds could be burned through the ear with a hot iron and sent away, or could be hanged for repeated offences.
- New laws were added including in 1589, one of which made it illegal to shelter vagrants.
- The settled poor were seen as a local problem. Therefore, they were to be looked after by local people.

The **towns** could not ignore the local problem and took **practical steps**

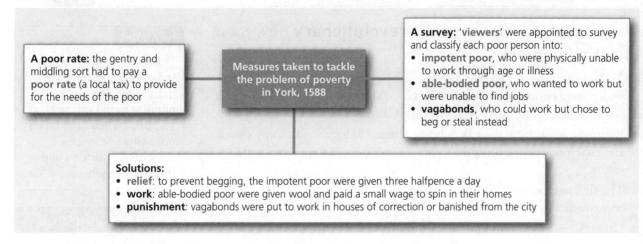

A poor rate: the gentry and middling sort had to pay a **poor rate** (a local tax) to provide for the needs of the poor

Measures taken to tackle the problem of poverty in York, 1588

A survey: 'viewers' were appointed to survey and classify each poor person into:
- **impotent poor**, who were physically unable to work through age or illness
- **able-bodied poor**, who wanted to work but were unable to find jobs
- **vagabonds**, who could work but chose to beg or steal instead

Solutions:
- **relief**: to prevent begging, the impotent poor were given three halfpence a day
- **work**: able-bodied poor were given wool and paid a small wage to spin in their homes
- **punishment**: vagabonds were put to work in houses of correction or banished from the city

The **Elizabethan Poor Law, 1601,** was a landmark law which **tackled all aspects of poverty**

- Through the 1590s, the problem got so great that the government had to act. A series of laws were updated and brought together as the Poor Law Act in 1601.
- These were closely based on the solutions that towns had come up with in the 1580s:
  - JPs appointed overseers of the poor to collect the poor rate. This money was used to support the poor.
  - Begging was forbidden.
  - Vagrants were whipped and sent back to the parish where they were born.
  - The impotent poor were looked after in almshouses.

- Work was provided for the able-bodied poor.
- Anyone refusing to work was forced to do hard labour.
- The law did not solve the problem of poverty but it provided a safely net and ensured that large numbers of people would no longer die if harvests failed.
- It also set the principles that:
  - taking care of the poor was the responsibility of the state
  - it should be paid for through local taxation.

 Support or challenge?

The historian Keith Wrightson has described late Elizabethan England as a 'period of crisis' for many people. How far do you agree with this view? **(20 marks)**

From your study of the **last six pages** and your wider knowledge, compile two lists of evidence that can be used to support or challenge Keith Wrightson. Use your lists to decide how far you agree with the statement.

Support – it was a period of crisis	Challenge – it was not a period of crisis
Famine hit large parts of England in the 1590s	The rich were building magnificent new houses around the country

---

 Test yourself

1 Who were the 'settled poor'?
2 List three long-term causes of poverty.
3 List three short-term causes of poverty.
4 List the key features of the 1601 Elizabethan Poor Law.

TIP

When you're explaining both sides of an argument, use phrases like: 'On the one hand ...', 'On the other hand ...', 'However' and 'Further evidence is ...'.

4.10 Theatres and their opponents

The London theatres were a **revolutionary** new form of **entertainment**

- At the beginning of Elizabeth's reign, many people enjoyed 'miracle plays' which were performed on carts and showed scenes from the Bible. These were banned because they were seen as a Catholic tradition.
- Roaming actors faced the risk of being arrested as vagabonds. Only settled and established acting companies with a noble **patron** (supporter) were secure.
- The first purpose-built playhouse, called 'The Theatre' opened in Shoreditch, just outside London's walls, in 1576.
- Others soon followed in Bankside – just over the river from the City of London.
- In 1599, 'The Theatre' was dismantled beam by beam and rebuilt on Bankside as 'The Globe'. This is where some of Shakespeare's most famous plays were performed.

Elizabethan dramatists contributed most to the cultural 'golden age' in Elizabethan England

- In Elizabethan times, there were significant developments in art, literature and music but developments in theatre overshadow the other achievements.
- The most celebrated dramatist was William Shakespeare, who created many plays that were popular in their time and are still performed and praised today.
- Theatre was 'popular culture'. An outing to the theatre was affordable for all. It was enjoyed by all sections of society. Theatres were lively, bustling places.
- Shakespeare's comedies, tragedies and histories were full of strong characters and emotion.
- The themes of Elizabethan plays had something for everyone: kingship, magic, superstition, love, cruelty, violence, exploration, the Renaissance.

> **Key point**
>
> The first permanent theatres were built in London. They were popular with both rich and poor. They also faced opposition from the London authorities and Puritan preachers.

> **Test yourself**
>
> 1 When was the first London theatre built?
> 2 Whereabouts in the city were London theatres built?
> 3 List three popular themes for Elizabethan plays.
> 4 List three reasons people opposed the theatre.

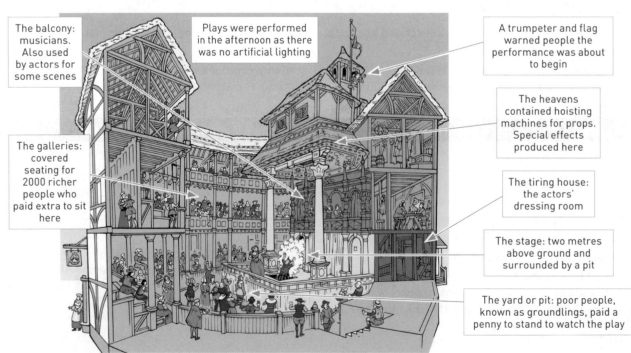

The balcony: musicians. Also used by actors for some scenes

Plays were performed in the afternoon as there was no artificial lighting

A trumpeter and flag warned people the performance was about to begin

The heavens contained hoisting machines for props. Special effects produced here

The galleries: covered seating for 2000 richer people who paid extra to sit here

The tiring house: the actors' dressing room

The stage: two metres above ground and surrounded by a pit

The yard or pit: poor people, known as groundlings, paid a penny to stand to watch the play

There was **opposition** to the theatre from the **London authorities** and **Puritan preachers**

London authorities	Puritan preachers
• Feared that the theatres attracted rogues, thieves and prostitutes, who would commit crime and spread plague • Feared that disorder in the suburbs of Bankside and Shoreditch, just outside the city boundaries, might spread into the city • Claimed that servants and apprentices were being enticed away from their work • Wrote many times to the Privy Council asking for the closure of theatres, but with little success	• Puritanism was strong in London • Theatre was seen as pagan (a non-Christian set of beliefs) • Theatres also reminded Puritans of Catholic miracle plays • Thought that theatregoing and plays encouraged sinful behaviour, particularly sex outside of marriage

 Analyse the interpretation

The writer of Interpretation E clearly thinks that Elizabethan theatre was very successful. Highlight all the words and phrases that show us this.

> **INTERPRETATION E** *From the website www.elizabethan-era.org.uk by Linda Alchin, which describes and celebrates all aspects of Elizabethan England.*
>
> Elizabethan theatre was a booming business. People loved the theatre. The Elizabethan plays and theatres were as popular as the movies and cinemas of the early 20th century. Vast amounts of money could be made. The inn-keepers increased their profits by allowing plays to be shown on temporary stages erected in the yards of their inns (inn-yards). Soon purpose-built playhouses and great open theatres were being constructed.

 Suggest a line of enquiry

If you were asked to do more research on one aspect of Interpretation E, what would you choose to investigate? Explain how this would help us to analyse and understand Elizabethan theatre. **(5 marks)**

Here is a sample answer.

> I would investigate who opposed the theatre, what motivated them and how successful they were. I would want to know why the Puritans and the London authorities feared that theatres caused crime, spread disease, encouraged dissent and immoral and ungodly behaviour and what arguments they used. This would help us to understand the diverse beliefs and attitudes in Elizabethan England, both of people who loved theatre and people who hated it.

Choose some other aspect of Elizabethan theatre and write your own answer using this same writing frame:

I would investigate …	
I would want to know …	
This would help us …	

4.11 The Puritan attack on popular pastimes

There were four types of Elizabethan **merrymaking**

Parish feasts (or 'parish ales')	The alehouse
• Festivals to celebrate the saint of the local parish church • There would be a procession, plays, Morris dancing, bull-baiting, cock-fighting and much eating and drinking	• The centre of village life for the middling sort and labouring poor • The numbers of alehouses in towns also increased after 1580 • Beer, sing-songs, good company, gambling and prostitution were all available at the alehouse
Sports Violent and cruel sports were popular: • Football was the most popular sport, but was very different from today. Players fought for possession of the ball which they kicked across the countryside. There were no pitches, few rules and many injuries! • Bare-knuckle boxing, wrestling and cudgel fighting with sticks • Bear-, bull- and badger-baiting involved tying an animal up to be attacked by dogs. People bet on the outcome • 'Throwing at cocks' (where a cockerel was tied up and sticks or stones were thrown to kill the bird) was also common	**Calendar customs** Linked to the religious and farming calendar: • Christmas – twelve days of feasting, singing and dancing with 'mumming plays' • Shrove Tuesday – a day of feasting before Lent • Whitsun – a popular time for 'parish ales' and 'rush-bearing' when rushes were spread on the floor of the parish church • May Day – when Maypoles were erected on village greens for May games • Midsummer's Eve – when bonfires were lit and a lot of ale was drunk • Harvest Home – at the end of the farming year in August. A time of feasting, drinking and dancing

> **Key point**
>
> Towards the end of Elizabeth's reign there was a decline in 'merrymaking' because the Puritans saw such activities as 'ungodly' pursuits.

Merrymaking declined at the end of Elizabeth's reign due to Puritan influence

- From the start of Elizabeth's reign these pastimes were in decline.
- Some areas continued their traditional festivities, but by the end of Elizabeth's reign many places had fewer parish feasts, May games, plays and Morris dancing.
- The main reason was the rise of Puritanism.
- Puritans thought these activities were wrong. Puritan ministers condemned them in their preaching and in pamphlets.
- Puritan ministers worked together with local gentry to ban these events.
- The greatest decline in popular festivals happened where Puritans were in charge of local government – for example where the JP or constable was also a Puritan.

The Puritans curbed merrymaking because they wanted people to live godly lives

- A popular interpretation is that Puritans curbed these pastimes simply because they were killjoys who wanted to stop people having fun. But it was more complicated than that.
- They wanted people to live godly lives because that meant they would go to heaven. It was for people's own good.

 Test yourself

1 What was a parish ale?
2 When did popular pastimes decline?
3 How did the Puritans curb merrymaking?
4 Why did the Puritans curb merrymaking?

Protecting the Sabbath: Puritans thought the Lord's Day should be set aside for rest and prayer, not dancing and drinking	**Stopping Catholic practices:** some popular customs were linked to superstitious Catholic beliefs and traditions	**Stopping pagan practices:** some festivities could be traced back to pagan times and Puritans felt this was inappropriate in Christian communities

Why the Puritans curbed popular pastimes

Keeping control: some festivals were unruly and disorderly behaviour took place	**Preventing unwanted pregnancies:** sex outside marriage was seen as a great sin. May games were a traditional time for love-making

 ## Looking at the question

6a. In Interpretation F, the illustrator shows the popularity of a May Day celebration in Elizabethan times. Identify and explain one way in which the illustrator does this. **(3 marks)**

For this Question 6a there is lots you could focus on. Remember you don't only need to name a feature – you have to say how your chosen feature contributes to the message of the interpretation. This table describes key features of the interpretation.

Find the feature in the interpretation then complete the second column to explain how it contributes to the overall message that May Day celebrations were popular.

INTERPRETATION F *An engraving of a May Day celebration in Elizabethan England, made around 1860.*

Feature	What this shows
Maypole: carefully decorated with blossom and ribbons	People have put a lot of effort in. Shows it's important to them
Environment: idyllic springtime scene. Birds in the sky. Lush grass	
People: all ages. Men and women. Rich and poor. Gentry and minister watch approvingly. Finely dressed	
Activity: dancing. Games in background. People dressed as horses – mock jousting	
Composition: people sitting or standing neatly	Orderly and balanced. Shows it's not a rowdy or drunken occasion

6b. If you were asked to do further research on one aspect of Interpretation F, what would you choose to investigate? Explain how this would help us to analyse and understand popular culture in Elizabethan England. **(5 marks)**

For Question 6b, remember to show some of your own knowledge and use a second-order concept. Choose one aspect of the interpretation and write your answer using this writing frame:

- I would investigate ...
- I would want to know ...
- This would help me ...

4.12 The persecution of witches

Belief in magic was common and was seen as useful in daily life

- Supernatural beliefs helped people to cope with the challenges of daily life.
- People might use magic to try to find out the sex of an unborn child, cure an illness or recover stolen goods.
- People known as 'cunning folk' or 'wise women' were thought to have special magical powers that they had inherited.
- People often relied on their specialist knowledge of herbs and spells to cure illnesses.

> **Key point**
>
> Belief in magic and the supernatural was widespread. Witchcraft, however, involved a harmful type of magic. Prosecutions for this crime increased in late Elizabethan England.

Elizabethans became increasingly fearful of witchcraft

- Elizabethans also believed that supernatural powers could be dangerous. A witch's curse could make someone ill or damage their property.
- The Elizabethans passed a law in 1563 that made **witchcraft** a criminal offence:
  - an accused person could be brought to court and if found guilty of using witchcraft to kill someone could be hanged
  - witches who harmed people or damaged property could be imprisoned.
- Anyone could accuse another of 'bewitching' them. So anything that went wrong in your life – from a sick cow to the death of your child – could be blamed on witchcraft.
- Witches were said to use small animals known as '**familiars**' to commit their evil acts.
- In the 1560s, there had been fewer than 40 witch trials but in the 1570s this increased significantly. Accusations peaked in the 1580s.
- A witch-hunt was sweeping continental Europe. The English witch craze was not so extreme.

Various explanations have been given for increased witchcraft accusations in late Elizabethan times

Social explanation: village tensions	Gender explanation: an attack on women	Religious explanation: the rise of Puritanism
- In late Elizabethan England poverty was a big problem - People were less willing to help poorer neighbours, which led to tensions in village life This explanation is backed up by the facts that: - Accusations did often follow a dispute between neighbours - A typical case started with an elderly woman asking a neighbour for help which was refused. The elderly woman cursed the neighbour. If the neighbour then had a problem or an illness the neighbour accused the old woman of witchcraft	- Some historians see witchcraft accusations as part of the repression of women in Elizabethan times, which stemmed from **misogyny** (negative attitudes towards women) in Elizabethan England This explanation is backed up by the facts that: - The vast majority of people accused of witchcraft were women, while the magistrates and jurors were always men - Many of the accused were independent, single women who were thought to have special powers However, many of the accusers were also women, which challenges this explanation	- Under Elizabeth, England became decisively Protestant. Puritanism grew stronger - Puritans believed that the Devil (Satan) was actively trying to harm good people and draw them away from the truth and into sin - Puritans were determined to root out these people, just as they were determined to end Catholic or pagan practices This explanation is backed up by the facts that: - Most witchcraft accusations were in Essex, where Puritanism was strong - Where Puritan ministers were trying to establish 'godly communities', witchcraft accusations were particularly high

Comparing interpretations

Interpretations G and H both focus on witchcraft in the sixteenth century. How far do they differ and what might explain the difference? **(12 marks)**

INTERPRETATION G *From a BBC television series*, The Time Traveller's Guide to Elizabethan England, *2013, written and presented by the historian Ian Mortimer.*

This brings us to one last point about witchcraft; it is heavily biased against women. The 1563 Act itself is not sexist but despite this 90 per cent of those accused of witchcraft in England are women. You may suspect this is a consequence of women being so thoroughly disempowered by society; for many women their only chance to get back at those who have wronged them is by way of spells and curses. Alternatively you may suspect that accusations of witchcraft are entirely made up and just another form of female oppression.

INTERPRETATION H *From John D. Clare*, Investigating History 1500–1750 Foundation Edition, *a simplified textbook for Key Stage 3 pupils, 2004.*

Why did people believe in witchcraft? People did not know about germs or science so they blamed disasters and bad luck on witches. Accusing a person of being a witch was a good way to get back at someone you had fallen out with. Pretending to be a witch was a good way for an old woman to stop younger people bullying her.

Use a table as on page 101 to compare the interpretations. Use this writing structure.
- Paragraph 1: compare the content – how similar or different are they?
- Paragraph 2: compare the provenance. Make sure you connect this to paragraph 1. How does the provenance explain the differences?

> **TIP**
>
> You have about fifteen minutes for this question – including time to read the interpretations carefully. Don't spend too long writing about the detail in the interpretations. The question is equally interested in **why** they differ.

 ## Support or challenge?

'Elizabethan England was Merry England.' How far do you agree with this statement? **(20 marks)**

From your study of the **last six pages** and your wider knowledge, compile evidence that can be used to support or challenge this statement. Use your lists to decide how far you agree with the statement.

Support – Elizabethan England was merry	Challenge – Elizabethan England was not merry

 ## Test yourself

1 What was the difference between a wise woman and a witch?
2 What was a familiar?
3 How did the law change in 1563?
4 Which county saw the highest number of witchcraft cases?

4.13 Imperial ambition; the motives and achievements of Elizabethan adventurers

John Dee had a vision of a 'British Empire' to rival Spain's, and provided practical help for explorers

- John Dee was an adviser to the Queen on science and astrology.
- In 1577, he presented a plan to shift the **balance of power** from Spain to England, which appealed to Elizabeth.
- Spain had built up a huge empire in Central and South America. Dee proposed that English adventurers should search for new routes to the rich markets of China and the East Indies.
- He advised the Queen to establish **colonies** (land taken and ruled by a foreign power) in North America and claim her right to rule there.
- He called his vision 'British Empire'.
- Dee also produced a map and books to help with navigation.

> **Key point**
>
> The queen encouraged overseas exploration. She wanted an empire to rival Spain. Elizabethan adventurers expanded English interests across the globe.

Francis Drake became a national hero when he sailed around the world

- Drake and his crew were the first Englishmen to sail around the world.
- On his way, Drake claimed territory and captured Spanish treasure.

November 1577	Left Plymouth with five ships and 170 men. Began plundering small Spanish and Portuguese ships off the coast of west Africa
Spring and summer 1578	Entered the Strait of Magellan. Claimed several islands for the queen, then sailed into the Pacific. No English sailor had been there before
Winter 1578–79	Raided native settlements along the coast of Chile and Peru. Attacked Spanish treasure ships
June 1579	Landed in California. He claimed the territory for Elizabeth, calling it 'New Albion'
Summer 1579	Headed west across the Pacific towards the Cape of Good Hope. In the Moluccas (Spice Islands) he traded linen cloth for cloves, ginger and pimento
September 1580	Returned to England with vast amounts of pillaged treasure for investors, the queen and himself
April 1581	Was knighted by the queen on board his flagship, the *Golden Hind*

The achievements of four other Elizabethan adventurers are covered on the next four pages.

> **TIP**
>
> To make sure you are using second-order concepts in your answers, use phrases like:
> - this is important because …
> - this had a big impact, because …
> - we need to know this because …
> - another reason for this is …

Develop the detail

Each of the following statements is vague and general. Add further details to show that you understand the general point being made.

General statement	Supporting detail
England and Spain were rivals	
Francis Drake became famous	
John Dee was clever	
Elizabethan England's horizons were broadening	

Practice question

In Interpretation I, the illustrator shows Sir Francis Drake as a hero. Identify and explain one way in which the illustrator does this. **(3 marks)**

If you were asked to do further research on one aspect of Interpretation I, what would you choose to investigate? Explain how this would help us to analyse and understand attitudes towards Elizabethan adventurers. **(5 marks)**

INTERPRETATION I *An illustration of Drake's arrival in Plymouth in September 1580 from the children's magazine* Look and Learn, *May 1978.*

Test yourself

1   What was John Dee's plan to change the balance of power with Spain?
2   List three significant events in Francis Drake's circumnavigation of the globe.

4.14 Roanoke: England's attempt at an American colony

Gilbert claimed territory in Newfoundland, but failed to establish a colony

- Humphrey Gilbert, as a Protestant Englishman, was driven by his hatred of the Spanish.
- Gilbert searched for a sea route around the top of North America to provide England with a trade route to China.
- His first attempt in 1579 was a disaster and only the ship captained by his younger half-brother, Walter Raleigh, made it across the Atlantic.
- A second voyage in June 1583 was more successful.
- He claimed land in Newfoundland for the queen by digging a piece of turf and erecting a post with the arms of England engraved in lead.
- He did not establish a **colony**. The land was barren, the climate cold and food scarce.
- One of his ships was wrecked, killing 80 men, and the others returned home. Gilbert himself drowned on the return voyage.

Raleigh made plans for a colony at Roanoke in Virginia

- Walter Raleigh thought America could be the gateway to the riches of Asia. As a loyal courtier he hoped to find silver and gold for Queen Elizabeth (and wealth and fame for himself).
- An initial survey in April 1584 convinced Raleigh that Roanoke would be a good place to found England's first colony.
- It had a natural harbour and the local people, the Algonquian, were friendly.
- The territory was named Virginia in honour of the 'Virgin Queen'.
- Richard Hackluyt wrote a pamphlet outlining the benefits of colonising America:
  - goods that could be bought and sold
  - potential for **missionary** work
  - opportunities to attack Spanish treasure ships.
- The queen did not want to part with her favourite, Raleigh, so Richard Grenville and Ralph Lane led the expedition of 600 soldiers, sailors and colonists.
- They also took a scientist, Thomas Harriot, and an artist, John White, to study and record the people, landscapes and wildlife.

> **Key point**
>
> Despite ambitious plans, no lasting English colonies were established in America during Elizabeth's reign. However, the mistakes made by the first colonists paved the way for later, more successful attempts.

Test yourself

1 What did Humphrey Gilbert achieve on his voyage in 1583?
2 What did Hackluyt's pamphlet say were the three benefits of colonisation?
3 Who led the 1585 voyage to Roanoke?
4 List three reasons why the colony in Roanoke failed.

> **Challenge question**
>
> Do you think the attempts to found a colony in Elizabeth's reign were a total failure?

The colony **failed**. The colonists fell out with the **Algonquian** and had to leave **after one year**

1	600 colonists set out from Plymouth in April 1585
2	The journey to Roanoke was treacherous. Grenville got split from the group
3	They arrived in July 1585, but the fleet got stuck on sandbanks in a storm. They lost many of their supplies, including their seeds
4	Grenville returned to England for more supplies. Lane stayed on as governor with 107 colonists and built a fort
5	The colonists knew they would have to rely on the Algonquian people if they were to survive the first winter
6	Wingina, the Algonquian chief, initially supplied corn, but later became wary of the colonists
7	Lane learned Wingina was planning to attack the colony so he attacked first. Wingina was killed
8	The Algonquians became hostile and Drake came to rescue the colonists in June 1586

Much was **learned** from early **failures**

- Harriot and White turned their careful records into a book, *A Brief and True Report of the New Found Land of Virginia*. This helped the next colonisation attempt to succeed (at Jamestown in 1607).

- Raleigh's next expedition was to the city of Manoa in Guiana, South America. This also failed but his record of it, *Discovery of the Large, Rich and Beautiful Empire of Guiana*, encouraged later attempts at empire building.

> **TIP**
>
> Some reasons why interpretations differ:
> - Writers use different sources. (Later writers often have more sources available.)
> - Writers use their imagination to fill gaps in the sources.
> - Writers are influenced by their own background or beliefs.
> - Writers write for different audiences.
> - Writers write for different purposes (for example, to entertain or to inform).
> - Some writers are more careful in their research and writing than others.

 Practice question

> Interpretations J and K both comment on Walter Raleigh. How far do they differ and what might explain any differences?
>
> (12 marks)
>
> **INTERPRETATION J** *From* Little Arthur's History of England, *a history book for children written by Maria, Lady Callcott in 1835. It was a best seller and was still in print 150 years later.*
>
> In many things, the next admiral I will tell you about was a greater man than any of the rest. His name was Sir Walter Raleigh. He was both a sailor and a soldier. The first time the queen took notice of him was one day that she was walking in London and came to a splashy place just as Sir Walter was going by. Sir Walter took off a nice new cloak and spread it on the dirt so that the queen might walk over without wetting her shoes. She was very pleased, and desired him to go to see her at her palace; and as she found that he was very clever and very brave, she made him one of her chief admirals.
>
> **INTERPRETATION K** *By Agnes Latham, an academic, for the* Encyclopedia Britannica.
>
> In 1580 [Raleigh] fought against Irish rebels in Munster, and his outspoken criticism of English policy in Ireland brought him to the attention of Queen Elizabeth. By 1582 he had become the monarch's favourite, and he began to acquire lucrative [valuable] monopolies, properties, and influential positions ... Although Raleigh was the queen's favourite, he was not popular. His pride and extravagant spending were notorious, and he was attacked for unorthodox thought [ideas].

4.15 Trade with the east, including first contacts with India

There was **demand** in England for **luxury goods from India**. Portugal dominated this trade

- Wealthy Elizabethans wanted luxury goods from India and China:
  - ○ silk, cotton, jewels and perfumes were fashionable for clothing and furnishings
  - ○ spices such as cinnamon, nutmeg, cloves, ginger and pepper were used for preserving and flavouring food; they fetched high prices in England.
- In past centuries, such goods came overland via the Mediterranean. Portuguese traders started to use the sea route around southern Africa.
- Spain invaded Portugal in 1580, leading to fears that the spice trade would be disrupted.
- As a result, London merchants formed the Turkey Company in 1581. They were granted a monopoly – the sole right to trade in the eastern Mediterranean.

Ralph Fitch established England's first direct links with **the Mughal Empire**

1 The Turkey Company sent Ralph Fitch to research trade opportunities in India, South-East Asia and China.

2 He carried letters of introduction from the queen to the **Mughal** and Chinese emperors – the leaders of the greatest civilisations in the world.

3 He set off from Falmouth with four other men in March 1583. Only Fitch returned.

4 They reached Basra in May. John Eldred stayed behind to trade.

5 In Hormuz (a Portuguese trading station) they were arrested as spies and taken to Goa, a Portuguese colony in India.

6 In Goa they were released, but James Story joined the Jesuit College there.

7 They carried on to Fatepur Sikri, the Court of the Mughal emperor at Agra. William Leedes was so impressed he stayed to work as a jeweller. John Newbury returned to England over land. He was not heard of again.

8 Fitch carried on alone. At the Portuguese fort of Malacca he not allowed to continue into the South China Sea, so he headed home.

9 He arrived back in England in April 1591, eight years after he had left.

> ### Key point
>
> Elizabethan adventurers built trade links with India. They laid the foundations for the British Empire when they set up the East India Company.

>
>
> ### Test yourself
>
> 1 Why was there a demand for luxury goods in England?
> 2 Which country dominated the European trade in luxury goods?
> 3 What role did Fitch play in setting up the East India Company?
> 4 Where and when did Lancaster establish England's first trading post in the East?

Map showing the outward and homeward journeys, with locations: Lisbon, OTTOMAN EMPIRE, Aleppo, Mosul, Baghdad, Tripoli, Basra, Hormuz, MUGHAL EMPIRE, CHINA, Agra, Hooghly, Pegu, Goa, Cochin, Colombo, Malacca. Scale: 0 1000 2000 3000 Kilometres. Key: Outward journey, Homeward journey.

> ### TIP
>
> It is vital to practise planning essays before the exam so that it becomes instinctive. Try and do this as much as possible.

Fitch's account of his travels showed the opportunities available to England in the east

- Fitch learned a lot about the wealth and trade of India, China and the Spice Islands.
- He saw the gems, spices, cloth, dyes and drugs that were easily available in India.
- He wrote about the people, customs and goods he had seen.

- Merchants in England were very interested in the trade opportunities he described, and also worried about losing out to competitors (particularly the Dutch) in exploiting them.

The East India Company was established in 1600. It changed England's trade forever

- In April 1601, John Lancaster was given command of the East India Company's first fleet.
- His expedition established England's first trading post in the east, in Java, in 1602.
- English ships began to bring home spices just as Portuguese and Dutch merchants were doing.

- Lancaster's voyage of 1601–3 was an important moment in British history. Dr Dee's dream of a 'British Empire' had begun to be realised.
- 200 years later, the East India Company was the biggest trading company in the world.

 Essay plan

The most valuable question in your depth study exam (Question 8 or 9) will be an essay question based on a quotation from an interpretation. You will have to make a judgement. It will deal with some of the big issues from the specification such as the significance of Elizabethan England's connections with the wider world.

In 2012, newspaper columnist A.N. Wilson wrote 'British explorers went out to every corner of the known world to form the foundation of power and prosperity for future generations.' How far do you agree with this view? **(20 marks)**

The secret of writing a good essay is good planning. Here is a plan.

Plan	Purpose/points to include	Comment
Introduction	State how far you agree or disagree	This sets your essay off on a positive track and gives you an argument to hold on to throughout your answer
		The question asks 'how far you agree …', so words and phrases such as 'mostly', 'partly' and 'totally' will be useful
Paragraph 1	Reasons to agree Explain how the statement can be supported	Use the words of the statement *'every corner of the known world', 'power and prosperity for future generations'*. This helps to ensure you focus on the actual statement
		Support everything you say with detailed and precise knowledge
Paragraph 2	Reasons to disagree Explain at least one other angle on the statement	Look at the wording. Does it hold true entirely or just for part of the time or just in some instances? Does it overstate the situation?
		Once again, make sure you support everything you say with detailed and precise knowledge
Conclusion	Restate your judgement as to how far (to what extent) you agree or disagree and give one killer argument as to why	This should be easy to write if you have kept your focus through the rest of the essay
		Use your final minutes to check your work. Correct it if necessary

1. In note form, write down two reasons to agree and two reasons to disagree, using the last six pages.
2. Decide on your argument – based on your notes in step 1. How far do you agree or disagree?
3. In the exam, step 3 would be to write your full essay. For this task just practise writing your conclusion.

The Period Study

This part of the GCSE develops your understanding of the history of a distinct period of time in world history. In this book the period is The Making of America, 1789–1900. It is worth twenty per cent of your total GCSE. You must be able to:

Explain the unfolding narrative (the big story) of America from the first President in 1789 to 1900 when the USA was set to become a global superpower.

You do not need to know every single part of the story but knowing the big picture from the start to the end is crucial.

Identify, describe and explain events, situations and developments relating to **three key groups**:
- Native Americans
- African Americans
- White Americans

Each of these groups had a very different experience of America from 1789 to 1900. Make a timeline for each and know how they are different.

Explain five smaller stories that sit within the big story of America 1789–1900. The five stories are:
- **America's expansion 1789–1838.** Why America expanded; the impact of slavery; and relations with Native Americans.
- **The West 1839–1860.** Why white Americans began migrating West and what they found there.
- **Civil War and Reconstruction 1861–77.** The reasons for the war and attempts to rebuild afterwards.
- **Settlement and conflict on the Plains 1861–77.** The impact of white Americans on the Plains and the conflicts that arose from this.
- **American cultures 1877–1900.** How the end of the century changed the lives of the three key groups.

Just like the 'unfolding narrative' point above, you do not need to know every single part of each of these stories, but knowing the key events will help. For each story, try to make a flow chart of the key parts of the story and how they link together.

What do I need to do in the Period Study exam?

TIP

Remember 40 marks for this exam and 52.5 minutes!

- The Period Study exam is taken together with the World Depth unit. The paper in total is 1 hour 45 minutes and worth 80 marks.
- There are **40 marks** available for the Period Study half of the paper and you have **52.5 minutes** to complete it.
- There is a total of **five questions, of which you must answer four**. On the next page is a guide to how to do this.

The Making of America, 1789–1900
Answer Questions 1 (a–c), 2 and 3.

1. (a) Name **one** example … [1]
   (b) Name **one** way in which … during the period … [1]
   (c) Give **one** … in the period … . [1]

2. Write a clear and organised summary that analyses … Support your summary with examples. [9]

3. Why did … in the period … have limited impact? Support your answer with examples. [10]

Answer **either** Question 4 **or** Question 5.

4. '[statement].' How far do you agree with this statement? Give reasons for your answer. [18]

5. How far do you agree that …? Give reasons for your answer. [18]

Key skill: answering the 'write a clear and organised summary' question

For Question 2 you will be asked to 'write a clear and organised summary'. This is something that historians often do in their writing. You should be used to writing summaries from your Key Stage 3 history course. Here are some examples:

- Write a clear and organised summary that analyses the impact of the Indian Removal Act of 1830. Support your summary with examples. (9 marks)

- Write a clear and organised summary that analyses the culture of the Plains Indians. Support your summary with examples. (9 marks)

- Write a clear and organised summary that analyses the changes in the lives of African Americans during the Civil War. (9 marks)

- Write a clear and organised summary that analyses the difficulties faced by settlers on the Plains.

You can actually write your answer to any of these in a number of different ways but there are three important things to think about:

TIP

With this question type avoid just telling the story. Use the second-order concepts to structure an answer into paragraphs!

Structure	Support	Analysis
The question says an 'organised summary', therefore you need to think about the structure of your answer. This will depend on the question. For some questions, you would need to structure your answer around a chain of events. For others, you will focus on different aspects of a situation. You could write one long paragraph or several short paragraphs	It's important that your summary is supported by precise and accurate knowledge. Specific examples will make your summary stronger and will gain marks in the exam	The question is not just asking you to tell a story or describe a situation. It also requires you to analyse. You do this by using one or more second-order concepts that relate to the particular question, for example, cause, consequence, change, continuity, significance, diversity. Don't feel that you have to name the second-order concept that you are using

5.1 The growth of the USA, 1789–1838

The USA was a new, **democratic republic** – but only white, property-owning men had voting rights

- The United States of America was only a few years old in 1789. It had fought for independence from Great Britain between 1776 and 1783.
- The USA was a **republic** (a country without a king or queen) and followed a set of rules set down in a document called the Constitution.

- The USA was a **democracy** (a system where people vote for the leaders). However, only white, male, property-owning (usually land-owning) Americans could vote.

> **Key point**
>
> The growth of the USA between 1789 and 1838 was extremely rapid. This growth created tensions which lasted throughout the nineteenth century.

The USA was a **federal country,** meaning that each of the **thirteen original states** also had its own powers

- The USA was made up of **states** (smaller political units which are part of the country of the United States). Each state had its own government led by a state governor.
- The state government could make its own laws but they could not go against the rules set down in the Constitution.
- The Constitution could be **amended** (changed) if Congress and enough states agreed.

- Each state in the USA sent **representatives** (politicians) to **Congress** (a bit like Parliament in the UK) where they would help to make laws for the whole country.
- Each state helped to elect a **President** (the head of state) every four years. The President could suggest laws, but Congress had to agree to them.
- **Territories** (areas with too few people to have their own state government) were controlled directly by Congress and run by a territorial governor.

The USA **grew rapidly** in the **northwest 1789–1838,** partly thanks to the **expansion of slavery**

- In 1790, the United States of America had only thirteen states. The rest of the land which now makes up the United States was lived in by **American Indians,** or claimed by European powers.

- The original thirteen states were: Connecticut, Delaware, Georgia, Maryland, Massachusetts, New Hampshire, New Jersey, New York, North Carolina, Pennsylvania, South Carolina and Virginia.
- Between 1790 and 1838, the number of states in the USA doubled to 26 as the USA expanded. See the outline map here.

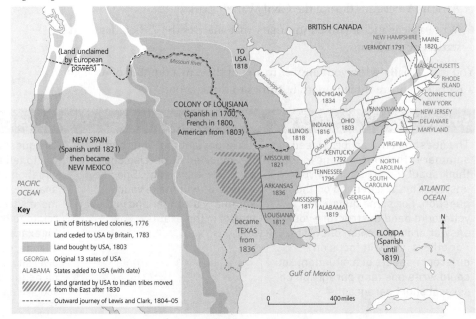

Key

- - - - - - Limit of British-ruled colonies, 1776

Land ceded to USA by Britain, 1783

Land bought by USA, 1803

GEORGIA   Original 13 states of USA

ALABAMA   States added to USA (with date)

////////   Land granted by USA to Indian tribes moved from the East after 1830

- - - - -   Outward journey of Lewis and Clark, 1804–05

There were **many different reasons** why the USA expanded so rapidly

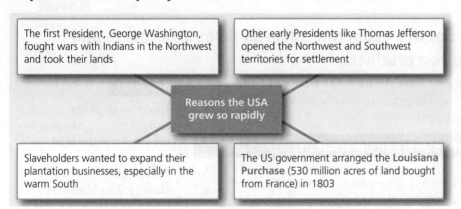

The first President, George Washington, fought wars with Indians in the Northwest and took their lands

Other early Presidents like Thomas Jefferson opened the Northwest and Southwest territories for settlement

Reasons the USA grew so rapidly

Slaveholders wanted to expand their plantation businesses, especially in the warm South

The US government arranged the **Louisiana Purchase** (530 million acres of land bought from France) in 1803

The country's **growth caused divisions and conflict** between **different groups** living in the USA

Divisions between ...	Division/conflict caused
White Americans and American Indians	Many of the lands taken over by the US government were already occupied by American Indian tribes. Thousands of Indians were forced to move further west to escape the growing USA
White Northerners and white Southerners	Northern business owners thought that slavery was unfair competition for their factories. They also saw slavery as old fashioned
White Southerners and white Northerners	Many people in the South thought Northern business owners were greedy and morally corrupt. They saw a powerful North as a threat to their way of life
Abolitionists and other white Americans	A small number of white and free-black Americans called **abolitionists** (people who were against slavery) thought that the growth of slavery was immoral. They set about trying to stop it altogether

 ## Turning statements into reasons

Below are a sample exam-style 10-mark question and a series of statements. In a 10-mark question you need to structure your answer clearly. For a question that asks why something happened, it is a good idea to structure your answer around different reasons. You can use a separate paragraph for each reason. Read the question and turn each of the statements into a relevant reason which could be used to help structure your answer.

Why did the USA grow so rapidly between 1789 and 1838? Explain your answer. **(10 marks)**

Statement	Reason
The USA was surrounded by potential enemies after 1789	The USA expanded to protect itself from attack by countries like Britain and France
Not everybody in the USA owned their own land. People without land could not vote	
The French government was short of money in 1803	
People in Kentucky and Western states had already settled lands outside the borders of the USA	
Lands in the south of America were good places to grow cash crops like cotton or tobacco	

5.2 The growth of the Deep South, cotton plantations and slavery, 1793–1838

Cotton was key to the South's economic success through exports and the North's through cotton products

The Deep South was opened for settlement around 1790. Between 1790 and 1838, thousands of slave **plantations** (large farms, usually growing a single crop like cotton) were set up in the new territories.

	Impact of cotton and slavery on the economy
In the South …	• By 1820, cotton made up 42 per cent of all US exports. By 1819, New Orleans was the fourth largest city in the USA • Southern traders shipped cotton to overseas markets in Europe • Between 1815 and 1819, around 100,000 slaves were sold in the South
In the North …	• Northern factory owners bought Southern cotton and turned it into cloth. This was sold across America • Northern business people invested in the sale of slaves like someone today might invest in Apple or Microsoft

> **Key point**
>
> The growth of cotton and cotton slavery made the whole of the USA much richer, so very few Americans tried to end slavery. The Missouri Compromise of 1820 was created as an attempt to keep the power of slaveholders in check.

Many different factors contributed to the expansion of slavery

In 1789, many Americans had believed that slavery would die out naturally because it was outdated and old fashioned. This meant that few white Americans did much to end slavery. Despite the prediction, however, by 1820, slavery was growing faster than ever. Why?

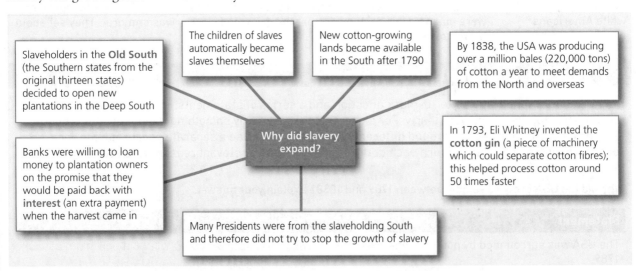

Expansion caused tension as the North grew agitated at the growing power of Southern slaveholders

- By 1838, there were over 2 million slaves living in Southern states. Slaves could not vote and white Americans had all the power.

- Many people in the North became worried that slaveholders in the South were becoming too powerful.

- A handful of abolitionists believed that slavery was **morally wrong** (against the Christian religion) and spoke out against it.

- People were worried that if a new slave state, or new free state was added to the USA, it would upset the balance of power.

- In the end, the government created the **Missouri Compromise** of 1820 to solve the issue.

The **Missouri Compromise of 1820** tried to **stop the battle** between **slave and non-slave states**

- The Missouri Compromise drew a virtual line across the middle of the country. Any states created in the West which fell below this line could be slave states, any above had to be free states.
- The Missouri Compromise said that all territories in the West would be **free** (not allow slavery) until they joined as states.
- The Missouri Compromise set down a pattern of adding states to the USA in pairs: one slave and one free, to keep the balance of power in government.

 What sort of cause?

Below is a sample exam-style 10-mark question which asks for a range of reasons. Understanding the difference between types of causes can help give structure to an 'explain why' or 'why' question. You could answer the question by covering all the political factors, then the social ones, and so on. The chart offers a range of factors which are relevant to the answer to the question. Use the information on this spread, and your own knowledge, to decide what type of cause each factor is.

Why did slavery in the Deep South grow so rapidly between 1789 and 1838? Explain your answer.   **(10 marks)**

Factor	Political	Social	Economic	Technological
Eli Whitney invented the cotton gin in 1793				
There was a growing demand for cotton in North America and Europe				
By the 1830s, railroads were being built across America				
Banks were willing to lend money to slaveholders and plantation owners				
Many people did not believe slavery was morally wrong				
Presidents like James Madison and Andrew Jackson were slaveholders				
Many Southerners believed that slavery was part of the natural order				
Existing slaveholders saw the chance to make huge profits in the Deep South				

 Test yourself

1   How many slaves lived in the South by 1838?
2   What piece of machinery did Eli Whitney invent?
3   How much cotton was the USA exporting by 1838?
4   Explain how the Missouri Compromise tried to solve divisions over slavery in the USA.

5.3 Securing growth: the removal of Eastern tribes, 1830–38

REVISED

The 'Five Civilised Tribes' tried to live alongside white Americans

- In the south-east of America, several key tribes tried to adapt and live alongside white Americans. These tribes became known as the **Five Civilised Tribes** (the Cherokee, Chickasaw, Choctaw, Creek and Seminole).
- The Cherokee tried to use the same political structures as the USA. They set up a capital city, used money for the economy and even created a written language.
- By the 1820s, the Cherokee had their own churches, schools and even a newspaper. The other four tribes took a similar approach.

> ### Key point
> The demand for cotton land in the Southern states led to the forced removal of tens of thousands of Indians from the East.

White settlers and cotton planters demanded the removal of Indians from the East to free up land

- White settlers had begun coming into the lands of the Five Civilised Tribes as early as the 1790s. Many of these settlers wanted to farm the land or create plantations for slaves.
- In 1830, the slaveholder Andrew Jackson (President 1830–38) became President.
- Jackson persuaded Congress to pass the **Indian Removal Act of 1830** (a law which promised tribes money if they agreed to relocate).
- Jackson set aside a permanent **Indian Territory** (a piece of land specially put aside for the Indian nations) west of the Mississippi river in modern-day Oklahoma.
- Jackson believed that Indian nations needed to be treated like children. He said that moving West was in their best interests.

Many Indian tribes were unhappy with the Indian Removal Act (1830)

- Not all tribes had the same experience of removal. The table below shows how some tribes reacted to the Act.

Choctaw and Chickasaw	• Quickly signed treaties and began moving West
	• Between 1831 and 1833, the Choctaw gave up around 11 million acres of land and around 15,000 moved to Indian Territory
	• Despite their cooperation, thousands died due to harsh winters, lack of government funds and disease
Cherokee	• Took their case to the Supreme Court to complain at the actions of the state of Georgia in trying to remove them
	• In 1832, the Supreme Court ruled that the Cherokee should stay
Creek	• Refused to sign a treaty at all

Quick quizzes and answers at **www.hoddereducation.co.uk/myrevisionnotesdownloads**

Between 1830 and 1838, the US Government used a range of tactics to remove Eastern tribes, causing much suffering

The Seminole
- In 1830, a small group of Seminole signed a treaty with the US government and moved to Indian Territory
- Not all Seminole agreed to go. The government declared war against them (1835–42)
- The USA lost the war but had Osceola, the Seminole chief, killed during peace talks
- After the loss of Osceola, the remaining Seminole were forced to move West

The Creek
- The Creek were unwilling to move and so signed a treaty giving up some land in 1832
- Some white settlers and planters moved on to land which had not been sold in the treaty
- By 1835, the Creek began attacking the settlers and stealing their livestock
- Between 1836 and 1837, the army forcibly removed over 15,000 Creek to Indian Territory

The Cherokee
- Most of the Cherokee refused to move after the Supreme Court judgment of 1832
- By 1838, only 2000 Cherokee had moved West and the army was sent to remove the 16,000 Cherokee who had stayed in Georgia
- The Cherokee were forced into concentration camps until the winter
- The Cherokee were force-marched to Indian Territory on 'The Trail of Tears', where 4000 Indians died

 Spot the second-order concept

Second-order concepts are the things that historians use to make sense of the past. They include: cause, consequence, change, continuity, significance and diversity. In the exam you will gain marks by using second-order concepts in your answers, but don't feel that you have to name the second-order concepts that you are using.

This extract from an exam answer contains several examples of second-order concepts. Highlight where they occur and note the second-order concept in the margin.

Write a clear and organised summary that analyses the impact of the Indian Removal Act of 1830. Support your summary with examples.

(9 marks)

Between 1830 and 1838, the US government removed almost all the American Indians who lived in the Southern states. The Creek, Seminole, Chickasaw, Choctaw and Cherokee were all moved into Indian Territory by Andrew Jackson. However, not all Indian tribes in the South had the same experience of removal. Most of the Seminole refused to sign any sort of treaty with the US government. Instead, they fought a long, bitter and costly war against the United States. It was only after the Seminole chief, Osceola, was killed by the army in 1842 that the Seminole had to start moving to Indian Territory. By contrast, many of the Choctaw Indians moved peacefully after signing a treaty with the Government in 1831. However, many Choctaw died on the journey West and thousands more were killed by disease and poor weather. In some ways, this was a similar experience to the Creek, who lost over 5000 people when they were forced to move to Indian Territory.

 Test yourself

1 Name three of the Five Civilised Tribes.
2 Which tribe challenged the Indian Removal Act in the Supreme Court?
3 Which President was responsible for the Indian Removal Act?
4 What was the 'Trail of Tears'?

Challenge question

Why might the growth of slavery have played a role in the Indian Removal Act of 1830?

5.4 The lives and culture of the Plains Indians, including the Lakota Sioux

The **Plains** were **vast and dangerous**. White Americans saw them as **uninhabitable** before the 1840s

- The **Plains** (an area of open grassland) lie between the Mississippi River in the East and the Rocky Mountains in the West.
- There are few resources such as wood or water on the Plains, and

temperatures vary from well below freezing in the winter to over 40 °C in the summer.

- Most white Americans saw the Plains as a great desert before the 1840s and not worth settling.

> **Key point**
>
> Plains Indians adapted their way of life to suit their life on the Plains. There were big differences between the Plains tribes.

The **Lakota tribe adapted** their culture to **suit life** in the **hostile environment**

- The **Sioux** (a powerful Indian nation) were divided into several large groups: the Lakota, the Dakota and the Nakota.
- Until the mid-eighteenth century, the Lakota Sioux lived in the area around Minnesota, just north of the Plains.
- The Lakota moved on to the Plains from the late eighteenth century for several reasons:
  - They were experienced with horses: this allowed the Sioux to follow the buffalo on to the Plains and have a source of food.

- By the 1830s, the Lakota Sioux had obtained guns from white American traders.
- The Sioux homelands began to fill up with other Indian tribes escaping white expansion in the East.

- By the 1830s, the Lakota had moved permanently on to the Plains and their culture changed to match this new life.

There were **similarities and differences** in the cultures of **different tribes**

	Lakota Sioux	Cheyenne	Nez Perce
Leadership and organisation	• Organised into tribes and each tribe into bands. Usually led by a powerful warrior • **Nomadic lifestyle** (constantly moving around) following the buffalo	• Organised into tribes and bands. Usually led by a powerful warrior or trader • Partially nomadic but it depended on the tribe. Some settled near trading posts	• Organised into villages. Each village elected a **headman** (leader), chosen on his ability to organise and negotiate trade • Not really nomadic. Had fixed villages
Food	• Mainly ate buffalo and buffalo products, like tongue	• Mainly ate buffalo but also traded supplies with white traders	• Hunted buffalo on the Plains in the summer but ate fish and camas roots in the winter
Shelter	• Lived in **tipis** (tents) made from buffalo hides	• Lived in buffalo tipis	• Lived in huts in the winter and tipis in the summer
Warfare	• Fought on horseback using bows and guns • Young men learned to fight from childhood • Warrior **societies** (groups) were very powerful in Sioux politics	• Fought on horseback using bows and guns • Young men learned to fight from childhood • Warrior societies, like the Dog Soldiers, were a powerful force	• Fought on horses but only during summer buffalo hunts. Sold horses to other Plains tribes • Warrior societies were less influential than headmen

	Lakota Sioux	Cheyenne	Nez Perce
Beliefs	• Believed in the Great Spirit, Wakan Tanka • Believed that the Black Hills of Dakota were the **sacred** (holy) centre of Sioux power • Believed that no one could own land and that farming was disrespectful to the earth	• Believed in the All Being • Thought that the Noaha-vose hill was the sacred centre of Cheyenne lands • Believed that the Cheyenne were a 'called out people'	• Believed in the importance of staying near the Bitterroot Mountains, which they saw as their sacred home • Believed that land could not be bought or sold by people
Relationship with white Americans	• Generally hostile to white Americans. Fought to keep control of lands and made **treaties** (agreements) to protect their interests	• Saw trade with white Americans as key to their survival on the Plains. Brought trade items to sell to other Indian tribes • Married into white trading families	• Friendly with white Americans. Helped to rescue the Lewis and Clarke expedition to the West in 1804–05

 ## Complete the paragraph

Below is an incomplete paragraph from an answer to the question:

Write a clear and organised summary that analyses the cultures of the Plains Indians, 1839–60. Support your summary with examples. (9 marks)

The paragraph begins with a relevant comment but is lacking detail and examples. Read the paragraph and complete it, adding in the missing information.

> In some ways the cultures of Plains Indians were quite similar in terms of the way they were organised, what they ate and how they fought wars. In terms of organisation the Sioux …
>
> This was similar to …
>
> The diet of the Sioux and Cheyenne was also similar …
>
> There were also similarities in the way that the Sioux and the Cheyenne fought wars …

 ## Make revision cards

In your exam you will need to use precise, relevant and detailed information in your answers. Revision cards can help to make the details stick. Write a topic heading on the front and then put up to five key words/phrases on the back. Use the words to summarise your knowledge on the topic. Once you have made your cards you should test yourself, or work with a friend to test each other.

Create a set of revision cards for each tribe:

- Sioux
- Cheyenne
- Nez Perce

Topics:

- leadership and organisation
- food
- shelter

- warfare
- beliefs
- relationship with white Americans.

 ## Test yourself

1 Name two of the three main divisions of the Sioux Indians.
2 What was the main source of food for the Cheyenne?
3 What was the name of the sacred centre of Sioux culture?
4 Explain why the Sioux moved on to the Plains.

Challenge question

In what ways was Lakota culture well suited to life on the Plains?

5.5 Journeys to Oregon and California and the settlement of Utah

People began **travelling West** in large numbers **from the 1840s**. **Most went across the Plains** to the Far West

- Very few people had tried to travel to the West before 1838. There were few routes mapped to the West and the journey was as much as 3000 miles.
- Hundreds of thousands of white settlers travelled to the West between 1839 and 1860.
- Most of these overlanders (travellers who went over the land to the West rather than by sea) went in wagons and travelled to territories in the **Far West** (California, Oregon and Washington).

> **Key point**
>
> Journeys to Oregon and California were extremely long and difficult, and needed careful preparation. The Mormons tried to escape persecution and create an entirely new type of settlement in the West.

Some reasons **pulled people out to the West**, other reasons **pushed them to leave** their home states

People travelled westwards for a whole range of reasons:

- The banking system in the USA had collapsed in 1837 – many people had no money and were unemployed.
- Land in the East was beginning to fill up. Competition between Eastern farmers was high.
- Explorers had begun to map safe routes to make the journey to the Far West.
- In 1848, the land of California was taken from Mexico in a war and so became US land.
- Some believed they had a mission to convert Indians living in the West to Christianity.
- Territories like Oregon and California ran advertising campaigns to encourage people to travel West.

Journeys to California or Oregon **were long** and people who went faced many **different types of danger**

The timeline below shows a typical journey to Oregon in the 1840s.

Stage	Detail on the stage of the journey	Issues and dangers
1	Before they went they had to decide which route they wanted to take and which **company** (group) of travellers they wanted to join	Buying the right equipment, supplies and travel guides was important for **emigrants** (travellers moving to the West)
2	Families loaded their possessions into a covered wagon and joined a wagon train heading on either the Oregon or California Trails (common routes to the West)	The wagon needed to carry enough supplies for the whole journey. Many families took guns but more people injured themselves with these than were ever killed by Indian attacks
3	The first part of the journey was easy going, but the wagons meant that families only travelled around twenty miles a day	Wagons got stuck and injuries like broken bones or crushed limbs were common Many people died of cholera or typhoid
4	Wagons were taken through one of the few **passes** (crossing places) over the Rocky Mountains	Groups who arrived at the Rockies too late in the autumn had to spend winter on the Plains or risk crossing the mountains. Either way, many died
5	The final leg into Oregon and California was a little easier. Local Indian tribes often helped to ferry travellers down the rivers	Diseases continued to be a major issue. Late summer or autumn floods could also claim many lives

The **Mormon settlement of Utah** was very different from others, due to the **organisation** of the **Mormon Church**

- One group of people who tried to settle in the West were the **Mormons** (a religious group set up in the early nineteenth century).

- Mormons wanted to practise their religion and **polygamy** (marrying many wives) freely.

- Their leader, Brigham Young, chose Utah Territory as the place to build a new settlement at a place called the Great Salt Lake.

- Salt Lake City (the capital of Utah) was established in the late 1840s and by 1852 had a population of over 10,000.

- The city was planned carefully from the beginning and had **irrigation ditches** (these helped to water the land) to allow farming to begin straight away.

- The Mormon Church decided how much land each family got. Nobody was allowed to own water.

- The Mormon temple was built at the centre of the city. The city itself was modelled on the streets of Paris.

- In 1850, Brigham Young became the first Governor of Utah.

Prioritisation

Below are a sample exam-style 10-mark question and a list of reasons which could be used in the answer. Prioritising reasons is one way to structure an 'explain why' question. Using your own knowledge and the information on these pages, decide the order of priority you would give each of these factors by writing a number from 1 (most important) to 6 (least important) next to them. Once you have done this, add some specific detail or examples which you could use to back up the factor in your answer.

Why did many migrants find the journeys to Oregon and California so difficult in the 1840s? Explain your answer. **(10 marks)**

Reasons	Importance (1–6)	Detail and examples
Deadly diseases were easy to catch on the trails		
Indians could attack wagon trains		
It was difficult to travel as a group for so long		
The journey was extremely long		
The Rocky Mountains were dangerous to cross		
The weather was not always good		

Write a summary

Writing a summary is an important skill for any historian and helps you to remember key information. The process of turning notes into sentences is especially helpful for the 9-mark questions which ask you to write a clear and organised summary. Another thing which can really help you to remember details is trying to write summaries from memory.

Without looking back at your notes, summarise a typical journey to Oregon using between 80 and 100 words. Once you have done this, use your notes to check you have not missed anything out.

Test yourself

1 Name two diseases which killed people on the trails to Oregon and California.
2 What were migrants to Oregon and California known as?
3 Who led the Mormons to Utah?
4 Why were the Mormons so keen to settle in the West?

Challenge question

In what ways could the Mormon settlement of Utah be considered unique?

5.6 The California and Pike's Peak gold rushes

The discovery of **gold** in **California, 1848**, led to a **rush of settlers**

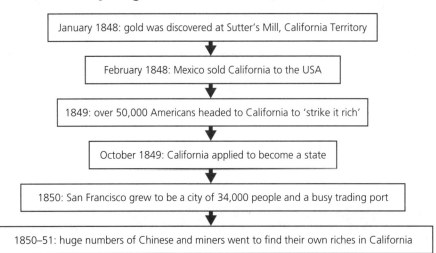

January 1848: gold was discovered at Sutter's Mill, California Territory

↓

February 1848: Mexico sold California to the USA

↓

1849: over 50,000 Americans headed to California to 'strike it rich'

↓

October 1849: California applied to become a state

↓

1850: San Francisco grew to be a city of 34,000 people and a busy trading port

↓

1850–51: huge numbers of Chinese and miners went to find their own riches in California

> **Key point**
>
> The Californian and Pike's Peak gold rushes sped up the settlement of the American West. However, the gold rushes had an enormously damaging impact on the relationship between the US government and Indian tribes.

Mining settlements were established in California. They were **often rough and violent** places

- **Mining settlements** (quickly built towns for miners) were heavily male dominated and were often full of gambling dens and saloons.
- Many miners forced native peoples from the land so that they could set up mining camps.
- Mining settlements could be violent places: robberies and murders were much more common than in other types of settlement.
- Women did come to mining settlements: some as prostitutes, but many more made a good living by selling food or doing laundry for the miners.

Some people made a **lot of money** from the gold rush, but **few** of them were **individual gold miners**

- Small-business owners could make a lot of money by selling shovels or gold-washing pans.
- A whole industry grew up selling maps and supplies to get to California.
- After 1852, huge **crushing mills** (machines to get gold out of rock) were needed to extract the gold from the rock. These crushing mills were paid for by rich businessmen from the East.

The **Californian gold rush** had an **enormous impact on the West**, the **Plains**, and the **people** who lived there

Impact on	Nature of impact
Californian Indians	Californian 'Digger' Indians were pushed off land to make way for miners. A law was brought in which allowed Indians to be sold into slave labour
Immigrants in the West	In 1850, California passed a law which said that all non-US miners had to pay a $20 tax. This forced thousands of Mexicans and Chinese to leave
Plains Indians	The miners who travelled West cut right through Plains Indians' hunting grounds. The government was forced to sign the **Fort Laramie Treaty** in 1851 which promised not to disrupt Plains hunting or to settle on the Plains
California	San Francisco grew to have 56,000 people by 1860 and was the fifteenth largest city in the country. Mining led to environmental destruction, clogging rivers with silt and putting harmful chemicals into the water supply
America as a whole	California became a **free state** (without slavery) very suddenly in 1850. This threw the delicate balance of slave and free states into crisis. It also led to demands to connect the country up fully with a **railroad** (railway)

The **Pike's Peak gold rush (1858–59)** began the settlement of the Great Plains. War seemed inevitable

- In 1858, a new gold strike was made at Pike's Peak in Kansas Territory (modern-day Colorado). This land was occupied by the **Cheyenne Indians** (a powerful Plains tribe).

- Huge numbers of people came to Pike's Peak – over 100,000 by 1859.

- New mining towns like Denver needed food. This led to thousands more people settling in the eastern half of Kansas Territory and establishing farms.

- The settlement of Kansas proved that the Plains were not just a desert land and soon more settlers came flooding on to the new lands.

- The settlement of Kansas and Colorado broke treaties the USA had signed with Indian tribes in the 1850s. Tribes like the Cheyenne and Kiowa began to fight back against white settlers on the Plains.

- By 1860, war between the USA and the Plains tribes seemed inevitable.

 Getting from A to B

It is very important to see the 'unfolding narrative' in period studies. When studying events like the Californian gold rush, it is easy to get caught up in the detail and miss bigger stories like how it contributed the breakdown of relations between the USA and Plains Indians over time. The discovery of gold in California began a story of conflict. The question is: how do we get from A to B?

You are not going to remember all of this story so you must select the most important parts. Four of the boxes below are empty. Your challenge is to decide what are the four most important steps that led from A to B. Complete the empty boxes to tell the story of how the gold rush contributed the breakdown of relations between the USA and Plains Indians.

A Discovery of gold in California in 1848					**B** Relationships between the USA and Plains tribes broke down by 1860

 Test yourself

1 Where was gold first discovered in California in 1848?
2 Name two states or territories added to the USA between 1839 and 1860.
3 Why do you think more people came to Colorado than California to search for gold?
4 How did the Californian government try to stop foreign miners from coming to the USA?

5.7 The causes of the Civil War

In **1861**, the **Northern and Southern states** of the USA went to **war** with each other

- The **American Civil War** was fought between 1861 and 1865.
- Over 750,000 people died during the Civil War.
- The Civil War was fought between the Northern and Southern states of the USA, as shown in the map below.
- The Northern states were known as the **Union** and the Southern states as the **Confederacy**.

> **Key point**
>
> The issues which led to Civil War had been there for many decades before the outbreak of the conflict. However, the election of Abraham Lincoln caused a serious division which helped to bring on the start of the war.

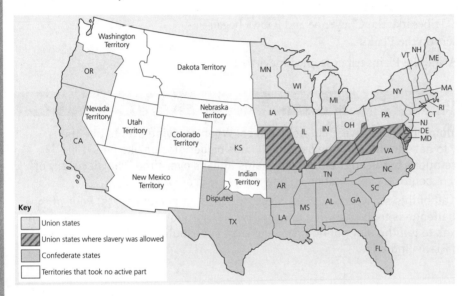

Key

- ☐ Union states
- ▨ Union states where slavery was allowed
- ▨ Confederate states
- ☐ Territories that took no active part

The **Civil War** was a result of **political, economic and social divisions** which had built up over **many years**

The following are the main causes of the Civil War:

- People in the South saw the cities and industry of the North as too modern and ungodly.
- By 1850, the population in the Northern states was growing rapidly, giving the North more political power.
- The **1850 Compromise** (a law which said that free states had to return escaped slaves to their holders) handed more power back to slaveholders in the South. In return, California was allowed to become a free state.
- Between 1850 and 1854, there were many arguments over whether slavery should be allowed to expand as the USA grew.
- The **Kansas–Nebraska Act** of 1854 said that states could decide for themselves if they wanted to be slave or free states – this overrode the Missouri Compromise.

- In 1857, the **Supreme Court** (the highest court in the USA) said that slaves had absolutely no rights and that the US government could not ban slavery in territories. This made the slaveholders more powerful again.
- Frederick Douglass (an important abolitionist) was successful in gaining a lot of support from the public for ending slavery.
- The **Republican Party** (a new political party) was set up in 1854 as an anti-slavery party. It wanted to stop the spread of slavery.
- Slaveholders in the South were afraid that the Republican Party would try to end slavery in the South altogether.
- In 1860, Abraham Lincoln was elected as President of the USA. He was a Republican.
- John Brown (an abolitionist) tried to start a slave uprising in 1859. He was stopped and hanged, but he became a hero in the North.

The **presidential election** of **Lincoln** was one of the **triggers** which ultimately led to war

Many have argued that civil war was inevitable once Lincoln was elected. The timeline below shows the steps from Lincoln's election to the outbreak of war.

1 Lincoln was elected in November 1860 with lots of Northern support but almost none in the South.

2 In November 1860, South Carolina voted to **secede from** (leave) the USA in protest at Lincoln's election.

3 By February 1861, six other states had seceded: Mississippi, Florida, Alabama, Georgia, Louisiana and Texas. They formed a new political group called the Confederacy.

4 The Confederacy elected its own President, Jefferson Davis.

5 When Lincoln became President fully on 4 March 1861, he said that the Confederacy was illegal.

6 On 12 April, Davis ordered his gunboats to open fire on **Fort Sumter** (a Union fort) in South Carolina.

7 On 15 April, Lincoln declared war and said he would defend the Union of the United States.

8 Between April and June 1861, four more states joined the Confederacy: Virginia, Arkansas, North Carolina and Tennessee.

 ### Identifying causes

Below is a sample exam-style 10-mark question, which asks for a range of causes. Understanding the difference between different types of causes can be a good way to structure an answer. The chart that follows gives a range of causes that are relevant to answer the question. Using the information on this spread and your own knowledge, decide if each cause is a political (P), social (S) or religious (R) cause of war. Once you have done this, try to add some detail which you could use in your answer.

Why did the American Civil War break out in 1861? Explain your answer. (10 marks)

Cause	P, S or R?	Useful detail for the answer
People in the North were worried that slaveholders were becoming more powerful		
The Kansas–Nebraska Act allowed states to choose if they wanted to be slave or free states		
People in the South were terrified that ending slavery would destroy their way of life		
Many slaves were willing to rebel against their holders		
People in the South were angry at the election of President Lincoln		
People in the North and South were suspicious of each other's way of life		
The Supreme Court supported the rights of slaveholders over the rights of slaves		
Christian abolitionists in the North were getting much more support for ending slavery		

 ### Test yourself

1 Which political party was established in 1854?
2 Who tried to encourage slaves to rebel in 1859?
3 Which Act allowed states to decide if they wanted to be free or slave states?
4 What happened after the election of Abraham Lincoln which led to the Civil War?

Challenge question

If Lincoln had not been elected, would war have come anyway? Take some time to consider both sides of this question, it will help you to consider your response to the 18-mark exam question.

5.8 The experiences of black Americans during the Civil War, 1861–65

REVISED

Key point

The Civil War had a positive impact on the lives of black Americans; however, the changes were quite minor until the passing of the Emancipation Proclamation. Despite the important role played by black soldiers, there was still a lot of racism in America after 1865.

In **1861, black Americans** had some **extremely limited rights** in the **North, and none** at all in **the South**

Factor	In the North	In the South
Jobs	Black workers could get jobs; however, they often did not get equal pay. Black workers could not be in charge of white workers A few black Americans got professional jobs (for example, lawyers, doctors)	Most black Americans were slaves. They could not get jobs or earn money A few free-black Americans could get work, but this was rare
Housing	Most black Americans lived in poorer areas of cities with high rents. A handful of professional black Americans had better living conditions	Plantation housing was small and cramped. Diseases spread easily and medical care was non-existent
Education	Most schools were **segregated** (separate for black and white students) but black students had access to basic education. There were a few universities for black students but they struggled to get jobs afterwards	In most Southern states it was illegal for black Americans to learn to read or write

One of the **most significant changes** for black Americans in the **South** was **the ending of slavery**

Period	Positive changes	Limits
1861–62	• By 1862, South Carolina was freed and ex-slaves began setting up regiments • Land in the **Sea Islands** (islands off the coast of South Carolina) was given to freed slaves from the South • Missionaries came to teach the ex-slaves how to read and write. This was known as the Sea Islands Experiment	• The Union refused to commit to ending slavery throughout the whole of the USA • Some escaped slaves were used to do very hard labour (for example, digging ditches) for the Union army • There was a lot of opposition to having black regiments
1863–65	• On 1 January 1863, Lincoln issued the **Emancipation Proclamation** which made all slaves in the Confederate states free • Volunteers continued to teach freed slaves how to read and write – over 200,000 by 1865 • Ex-slaves took on jobs such as field hands, mechanics and barbers, and started earning money • Many slaves in the Deep South were given 40 acres of land by General Sherman (a Union general) • Hundreds of thousands of ex-slaves joined the Union army and helped to defeat the Confederacy • Many black women supported the armed forces by working as cooks or nurses	• Some slaves continued to work on cotton plantations even after they had been freed • Black soldiers were often given some of the worst jobs: late-night guard duties, cleaning and ditch digging • The Emancipation Proclamation would not be a full Constitutional Amendment until the war was over

Black Americans in the **North** suffered the usual racism, but with signs of **improvement**

- In 1861, many black Northerners tried to join the Union army but they were told that this was not allowed.
- Lincoln claimed that slavery was nothing to do with the Civil War and even considered a solution to send black Americans 'back to Africa'.
- **Race riots** (violence against minority groups) broke out in many Northern cities where white Americans were being forced to join the army. They blamed black Americans for this.
- After 1863, black soldiers were allowed to join the army. However, they were not allowed to be officers and did not get the same pay as white soldiers.
- Many black workers did not volunteer to join the army because they could get work more easily when white soldiers were away fighting. This led to a huge race riot in New York in 1863.
- By 1864, black soldiers fought for and won the right for equal pay in the army. However, black soldiers could still not serve as officers.

Test yourself

1 When was the Emancipation Proclamation issued?
2 Which city saw huge race riots in July 1863?
3 In what year did black soldiers get equal pay in the army?
4 What was the Sea Islands Experiment?

Make revision cards

Use the headings below to help you summarise the information from this spread and make revision cards about the changes in the lives of black Americans during the Civil War.

Key words/phrases:

- major issues before 1861
- positive changes 1861–62
- limitations of change 1861–62
- positive changes 1863–65
- limitations of change 1863–65.

Spot the second-order concept

This extract from an exam answer contains several examples of the concepts of continuity and change. Highlight where they occur and note them in the margin.

Write a clear and organised summary that analyses the changes in the lives of African Americans during the Civil War, 1861–65. Support your summary with examples. (9 marks)

> The end of 1862 was a major turning point for African Americans in the South. When South Carolina was defeated by the Union, lands were given out to ex-slaves in the Sea Islands. Over 10,000 freed slaves got their own land. Some of these slaves went on to set up the South Carolina Volunteers, a black regiment which fought for the Union – this was a significant change as African Americans were now actively fighting for the Union.
>
> 1863 was another key change point for African Americans. In 1863, Lincoln passed the Emancipation Proclamation. This promised all slaves in the South that they would be free when the Union defeated the Confederacy. As each Confederate state was defeated, ex-slaves were given paid work for the first time. Over 200,000 freedmen were taught to read and write, and tens of thousands were given their own land. For the first time, Southern African Americans were able to earn wages and own their own property.

5.9 Reconstruction after the Civil War and its impact on black Americans, 1863–77

President Lincoln took a number of key steps to rebuild the USA even before the end of the war

- Lincoln persuaded Congress to help make the Emancipation Proclamation (the law which had freed slaves in the South) the **13th Amendment** to the Constitution in January 1865.

- He began trying to persuade the Union states to support the 13th Amendment and help it to become permanent.

- He set up the **Freedman's Bureau** (a charity to help ex-slaves), which gave out land confiscated from plantation owners to ex-slaves.

- He began to raise important questions about whether black Americans would be citizens.

- He wanted to make sure the South could not block African Americans from becoming citizens.

> **Key point**
>
> There were three major phases of Reconstruction: Presidential Reconstruction, Radical Reconstruction and a general loss of direction. Radical Reconstruction brought the most significant and lasting changes for black Americans, thanks to the 14th and 15th Amendments.

Presidential Reconstruction (1865–66) by President Johnson did little for black Americans

- Lincoln was shot dead in April 1865 and replaced by Andrew Johnson (the Republican Vice President).

- Johnson believed his most important job was to bring the whole country back together again (see diagram).

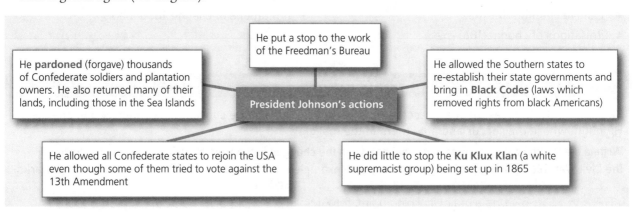

He put a stop to the work of the Freedman's Bureau

He **pardoned** (forgave) thousands of Confederate soldiers and plantation owners. He also returned many of their lands, including those in the Sea Islands

President Johnson's actions

He allowed the Southern states to re-establish their state governments and bring in **Black Codes** (laws which removed rights from black Americans)

He allowed all Confederate states to rejoin the USA even though some of them tried to vote against the 13th Amendment

He did little to stop the **Ku Klux Klan** (a white supremacist group) being set up in 1865

Between 1866 and 1870, radical Republicans took control of Reconstruction and made enormous changes in the South

Many Republican politicians were extremely angry at Johnson. In February 1866, they began forcing through their own changes. This period became known as the period of **Radical Reconstruction**.

- February 1866: the Freedman's Bureau was re-established.

- March 1866: Congress brought in a **Civil Rights Bill** (a law to protect the rights of all black Americans).

- April 1866: Congress proposed the **14th Amendment** to the Constitution which said that anyone born in the USA should be a US citizen whatever the colour of their skin.

- March–July 1867: ex-Confederate governments were shut down and taken over by the North; people who fought the Union in the Civil War were banned from voting; and the military were sent to the South to protect the rights of black Americans.

- July 1868: the 14th Amendment became law.

- March 1870: the **15th Amendment** gave all black Americans the right to vote.

- November 1870: more than 2000 black Americans were voted into political office.

Not everybody was happy with Reconstruction, especially in the South

- Reconstruction was not always popular. Many in the South said it was a way for corrupt Northerners to take control of land and money in the South.

- Many white business owners grew very rich out of Reconstruction. They won expensive contracts to build railways or factories and took a lot of profits for themselves.

- Northerners who moved to the South to make money out of Reconstruction became known as **carpetbaggers**.

- By the mid-1870s, many people in the North and the South began to think that Reconstruction had been a mistake.

After 1870 many of the radical changes in favour of black Americans were reversed

- In 1872, the Freedman's Bureau was shut down.

- Many black Americans worked on plantations as **sharecroppers** (farmers who did not own their land).

- In 1873, the Supreme Court said that voting rights at state level were the choice of the state.

- In 1875, the Supreme Court said that it was not the role of the US government to stop black Americans being bullied out of voting booths.

- In 1877, the US government withdrew the soldiers it had stationed in the South after the war.

 Support or challenge?

Below are a sample exam-style 18-mark question and a table showing various points. For each one, decide whether it supports or challenges the overall statement, then add three more examples.

'The Civil War and Reconstruction were a time of great progress for African Americans in the South.'
How far do you agree with this statement? Give reasons for your answer. (18 marks)

Point	Supports	Challenges
The Freedman's Bureau was set up to help ex-slaves earn a living, receive an education and become self-supporting		
President Johnson allowed ex-Confederate states to introduce 'Black Codes' between 1865 and 1866		
The Ku Klux Klan were established in 1865 and little was done to stop them growing		
The 14th and 15th Amendments were passed by 1870, giving all black Americans some civil and voting rights		
Black soldiers were allowed to join the US army and form black regiments from 1863 onwards		
President Johnson returned much of the land given to ex-slaves by the Union Army and Freedman's Bureau		

5.10 Railroads, ranches and cow towns

The **new Transcontinental Railroad united** the **Eastern and Western states** of America

- The American government had been exploring the idea of building a **Transcontinental Railroad** (one which crossed the whole country) since the 1850s.
- In 1862, Abraham Lincoln approved a **Pacific Railroad Act**. It promised to provide money to companies willing to build a railroad connecting the East and West of the country.
- Railroad companies were given land and money to construct the railroad lines.
- The **Union Pacific** company built from the East towards the West. The **Central Pacific** company built from the West towards the East.
- The line was completed in 1869, by which time both companies owned more land than the whole state of Texas.

> **Key point**
>
> Railroads, cow towns and cattle ranches helped many people to realise that the Plains were an untapped opportunity to make money or to settle and start new lives. This caused a lot of tension between white Americans and Indians.

Railroads had **positive and negative impacts** on groups in the USA

Impact on railroad companies and investors	Impact on Indians	Impact on workers	Impact on the USA
Railroads made these companies and people associated with them very wealthy	The railroads cut through Indian lands and disrupted the buffalo hunting grounds. They also encouraged more settlers and cattle ranchers to settle on Indian lands on the Plains	Thousands of workers were needed to build the lines. Over 12,000 workers were **Chinese immigrants** (people coming to the USA from China). They received little pay and worked in dangerous conditions. Accident rates among all workers were high, especially when blasting through the Sierra Nevada Mountains	New towns were created on railroad lines. Many of these were violent, drunken and unruly. However, towns soon grew and law and order improved. The first railroad inspired the building of other lines across the West. By the 1880s, the journey across the USA could be made in days instead of months

The **cattle industry grew** thanks to **railroads** and **grass** on the Plains, although there were **conflicts**

- The American Southwest was full of **Texas Longhorns** (hardy cattle). As early as the 1850s, some ranchers in Texas had kept and sold these cattle for money.
- After the Civil War, many Texan soldiers returned home to find that their cattle stocks had grown hugely while they had been away at war.
- Some people realised they could make money by driving the cattle to railroad stops and then selling the beef to cities or **Indian agents** (people who managed Indian reservations).
- In 1866, Charles Goodnight and Oliver Loving made $24,000 by selling 2000 cattle. They hired eighteen cowboys to help them make the journey.
- Taking cattle over the Plains to be sold became known as the **long drive**. Soon many people were trying to make their money from it.
- The long drives caused conflict with Indian tribes whose **hunting grounds** (buffalo hunting lands) were disrupted by the cattlemen.

 Test yourself

1 Name the two companies who built the first Transcontinental Railroad.
2 What sort of cattle were taken on the long drives?
3 Name a cow town set up in the 1860s/1870s.
4 Why did the cattle industry cause tension and conflict on the Plains?

Some pioneering Americans tried to **make even more money** by setting up **cow towns** and **cattle ranches**

Cow towns	• Located on railroad lines. They became places where cattle were bought and sold. One of the first was Abilene (in Kansas) • Cowboys could rest and spent their wages at cow towns • Early cow towns were violent and drunken places but by the 1870s many of them had developed their own laws and hired **sheriffs** (police)
Cattle ranches	• Located on the Plains. They were set up so that cattle did not have to be driven all the way from Texas • One of the first cattle ranchers was John Illiff, who bought his cattle from Charles Goodnight and emigrants on the Oregon Trail • Cattle ranches needed a lot of grass and water. Overgrazing was a big problem

 You're the examiner

Below is an extract from an answer to the question:

What was the impact of railroads and the cattle industry on the Plains in the 1860s? Explain your answer.

(10 marks)

Use the simplified mark scheme to decide which mark you would award. You need to annotate the extract and then explain why you have awarded the mark.

> Railroads and the cattle industry had an enormous impact on the Plains. The Transcontinental Railroad was built between 1862 and 1869 and connected states in the East to the new ones in the West. The impact of the railroad was huge, because it was thousands of miles long. The workers had to cut through the Sierra Nevada Mountains so that it could get to California. This had a big impact on the environment. The railroad also affected the Plains because it disrupted the lives of Native Americans living there. Many Plains tribes hunted buffalo, but the buffalo herds were disrupted by the trains running across the country. As well as this, the railroads allowed more and more settlers to travel and settle on the Plains. This meant that more people were farming the land, but also disrupting Indian ways of life.

Mark scheme for 10-mark questions:

- **Level 5 (9–10 marks):** demonstrates strong knowledge of key features and characteristics of the period in ways that show secure understanding of them. Uses these to show sophisticated understanding of one or more second-order concepts in a fully sustained and very well-supported explanation.

- **Level 4 (7–8 marks):** demonstrates sound knowledge of key features and characteristics of the period in ways that show secure understanding of them. Uses these to show strong understanding of one or more second-order concepts in a sustained and well-supported explanation.

- **Level 3 (5–6 marks):** demonstrates sound knowledge of key features and characteristics of the period in ways that show some understanding of them. Uses these to show sound understanding of one or more second-order concepts in a generally coherent and organised explanation.

TIP

A good 10-mark answer should clearly address the question at the start and end of each paragraph. A good way to do this is to reuse some of the key words from the question. This helps to show you have fully understood the focus of the question.

5.11 Living and farming on the Plains

There were **many push and pull factors** which led to **people moving** to the **Plains**

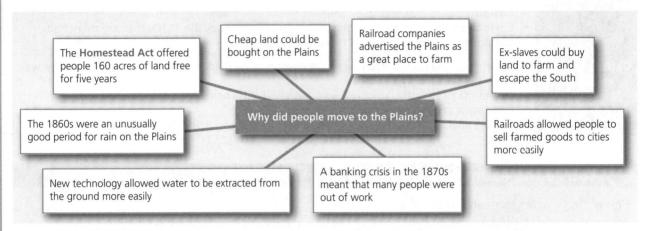

The **Homestead Act** offered people 160 acres of land free for five years

Cheap land could be bought on the Plains

Railroad companies advertised the Plains as a great place to farm

Ex-slaves could buy land to farm and escape the South

The 1860s were an unusually good period for rain on the Plains

Why did people move to the Plains?

Railroads allowed people to sell farmed goods to cities more easily

New technology allowed water to be extracted from the ground more easily

A banking crisis in the 1870s meant that many people were out of work

Homesteaders setting up new lives on the Plains faced a lot of difficulties

- The Plains were a long way from big towns. Getting supplies was extremely difficult – most people had to improvise.
- There were few trees on the Plains so building houses was difficult.
- Many houses were small and the lack of wood to burn meant that they were cold in winter.
- A lack of clean water meant that diseases like **cholera** (a waterborne disease) and **typhoid** (a serious bacterial disease) were common and killed many, especially children.
- Families often lived miles from the nearest town. People became lonely and felt isolated.

> **Key point**
>
> The Plains were a hostile environment and farmers had to be very adaptable and inventive to survive. Many homesteaders did not manage to last a full five years on the Plains.

The Plains were a hostile and difficult environment to farm in

- The Plains were very open. This meant that harsh winds could destroy crops.
- In the summer, the extreme heat could cause fires on the prairie grasses and crops struggled to grow as there was so little water.
- Ploughing the land to grow crops was extremely hard as the land had never been farmed before.
- Buffalo and wild cattle could trample across farmland and ruin a year's crops.

Homesteaders came up with many clever solutions to survive on the Plains

- **Homesteads** (houses built on the Plains) were built of **sod** (earth) instead of wood. The sod houses could be built quickly and easily at a low cost.
- As more people moved to the Plains, farmers grouped together to build churches and schools. Small stores opened and communities began to be created.
- **Wind pumps** were used to harness the prairie wind. They could be drilled into the ground and draw up clean water from deep down.
- Farmers learned dry-farming techniques and brought over new types of wheat, such as Turkey Red, which needed less water.
- **Barbed-wire fencing** was a cheap and easy way to enclose a large area of land.
- Homesteaders often worked together to **plough** land (make it ready for planting crops) – it was better to have one effective farm than three or four failing ones.
- Women helped with ploughing, something they would not have done very much in the East or back in Europe.
- Settlers shared crops if one family was unable to plant in time for the spring.
- Children were often given the task of collecting **buffalo chips** (dung) which could be burned for cooking and heating.

Match the examples

Making connections between historical facts is very useful when you are trying to remember a lot of detail. Each of the solutions settlers came up with to survive on the Plains is clearly connected to an issue they were trying to solve. If you link the two in your head, it will make them both easier to remember. Use the information on this spread and your own knowledge to complete the table, connecting the difficulty with the solution. The last two rows are blank for you to add your own examples.

Difficulties faced by settlers on the Plains	How they dealt with the difficulties
There was very little water on the Plains so growing crops was difficult	
	Barbed-wire fencing allowed farmers to close off their fields and keep them safe
There was very little wood on the Plains for making fires or building houses	
	People worked together to plough fields. It was quicker for a number of people to plough one person's field than for each person to try and plough their own alone

Complete the paragraph

Below is an incomplete paragraph from an answer to the question:

Write a clear and organised summary that analyses the difficulties faced by settlers on the Plains and how they tried to overcome these. Support your summary with examples. (9 marks)

The paragraph begins with a relevant comment but is lacking detail and examples. Read the paragraph and complete it, adding in the missing information.

Homesteaders faced many difficulties when they tried to settle on the Plains. One such difficulty was …

One solution to this problem was …

This solved the problem by …

Another major problem was …

This was a big issue because …

The best solution to this problem was …

This was effective because …

Test yourself

1 Give two reasons why people moved to the Plains.
2 What variety of wheat was brought by homesteaders to the Plains?
3 What did homesteaders use buffalo chips for?
4 Which three problems do you think were the most severe faced by homesteading families?

TIP

A good 9-mark answer should be supported by a range of specific examples. Make sure you have plenty of clear examples to give for each of the topic areas on the specification.

5.12 The Indian Wars

Growing tensions between white settlers and Indians led to the reservation policy

- By the 1860s, the Plains were being viewed as potentially usable land for white settlement.
- The Transcontinental Railroad disrupted Indian hunting grounds and led to growing tensions.
- The settlement of Colorado and the Plains after the Pike's Peak gold rush led to conflict over land and resources, especially grass and water.
- The government began a policy of moving Indians on to **reservations** (set-aside areas of land) so they would not interfere with white settlement.
- Many Indian tribes, especially the Sioux, refused to keep reservation agreements.

> **Key point**
>
> White Americans and Plains Indians came into conflict during the 1860s and 1870s due to competition over land and resources. Although the Sioux were successful at the start, by 1877 they had lost the vast majority of their lands.

Little Crow's War was fought as a protest against government policy towards the Sioux

Causes	Events	Aftermath
• Little Crow (Chief of the Santee Sioux) had signed a reservation agreement in 1861 in return for supplies from the US government • When the Santee were starving in 1862, the reservation agent refused to open up the emergency stores	• In the summer of 1862, Little Crow led his warriors and attacked white farms and settlements in Minnesota. They killed around 500 settlers • The Minnesota **militia** (soldiers) fought back and Little Crow was surrounded and killed	• On 26 December 1862, 38 Santee were publicly hanged, while hundreds more were sent to prison. Some white settlers were angry that so many Sioux had been spared • The remaining Santee Sioux were forced to move to a reservation in Dakota

Red Cloud's victory against the US government forced them to give the Sioux more land

Causes	Events	Aftermath
• In 1851, the Sioux had signed a treaty with the US government who promised to respect Sioux lands • In 1862, gold was discovered on the Sioux reservation and miners began pouring in along the **Bozeman trail** (a mining trail) • Red Cloud of the Lakota Sioux led attacks against some of these miners • The US government began setting up army forts on Sioux land	• Between 1866 and 1868, Red Cloud and his warriors fought the US army • Eventually the government was forced to admit defeat	• The government signed another treaty at **Fort Laramie** (a key US fort) in 1868. The treaty gave the Sioux even more land and promised that no settlers would enter the lands without permission • The defeat was humiliating for the government and many argued that tougher policies were needed

The **Great Sioux War**, the **last major conflict**, had a **lasting impact** on the Sioux

Causes	Events	Aftermath
• Gold was discovered in the Black Hills of Dakota (on Sioux lands) in 1874 • The government tried to buy the Black Hills from the Sioux but the hills were sacred to them and they did not want to sell • The US government ordered all Sioux Indians to come back from their hunting grounds by January 1876 • By spring, a band led by Sitting Bull (a powerful chief) had not returned so the army was sent to bring them back	• On 25 June 1876, General Custer found Sitting Bull's camp on the Bighorn • Custer and his 210 cavalrymen attacked the 6000-strong camp • It took just a few minutes for Custer's soldiers to be defeated	• Although Sitting Bull won, the US army kept chasing him and the other Sioux • All Sioux bands were rounded up by the army, even if they had nothing to do with the fighting. Rations were stopped on the reservations • Eventually the Sioux were forced to sell their land and were moved to smaller reservations

 Make revision cards

Use the headings below to help you summarise the information from this spread and make revision cards about Little Crow's War, Red Cloud's War and the Great Sioux War.

Headings:

- causes and events of Little Crow's War
- results of Little Crow's War
- causes and events of Red Cloud's War
- results of Red Cloud's War

- causes of the Great Sioux War
- the Battle of the Little Bighorn
- results of the Great Sioux War.

 Complete the paragraph

Below is an incomplete paragraph from an answer to the question:

Why did Red Cloud and the United States come into conflict in the 1860s? Explain your answer. (10 marks)

The paragraph begins with a relevant comment but is lacking detail and examples. Read the paragraph and complete it, adding in the missing information.

There are many reasons why Red Cloud and the United States came into conflict. One reason is that Red Cloud's lands were being flooded by miners. Miners were arriving in Sioux territory because …

Red Cloud was especially angry that miners were coming on to Sioux lands because …

Because of this Red Cloud and his warriors …

This led to war because …

 Test yourself

1   In what year did Little Crow's War begin?
2   Who led the Lakota Sioux to victory against the US government in 1868?
3   Where was General Custer defeated?
4   What were the results of the Great Sioux War, 1875–77?

Challenge question

Can you find any similarities between the causes of the three main Sioux wars? Why do you think the wars did not happen in the 1840s?

5.13 The changing lives of Plains Indians, 1877–1900

After 1877, US government policies became much harsher. Many tribes were forced to move to reservations

- After the **Great Sioux War**, many Plains tribes were forced on to US government reservations. Tribes were deliberately split up to prevent them fighting back.
- The government did not put a lot of money into reservations. Supplies, medical aid and food rations were often far too low.
- The growth of the railroad network brought many hunters to the Plains to shoot and kill buffalo. As many as 3 million buffalo were killed by 1883. The government did little to stop the slaughter.
- The arrival of homesteaders, ranchers and big businesses on the Plains pushed many tribes to starvation. Again, the government did almost nothing to stop this.

> **Key point**
>
> After 1877, the vast majority of Indian tribes were forced to move to reservations where they were made to adopt white ways of life. The Ghost Dance movement was the last attempt by the Plains Indians to resist in the nineteenth century.

It was official reservation policy to force Plains Indians to give up their own cultures

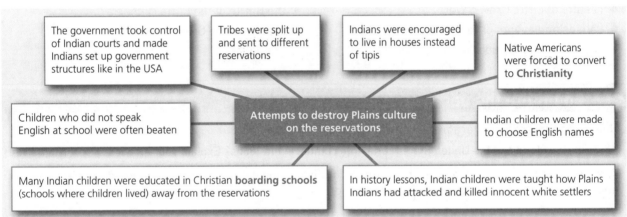

- The government took control of Indian courts and made Indians set up government structures like in the USA
- Tribes were split up and sent to different reservations
- Indians were encouraged to live in houses instead of tipis
- Native Americans were forced to convert to **Christianity**
- Children who did not speak English at school were often beaten
- **Attempts to destroy Plains culture on the reservations**
- Indian children were made to choose English names
- Many Indian children were educated in Christian **boarding schools** (schools where children lived) away from the reservations
- In history lessons, Indian children were taught how Plains Indians had attacked and killed innocent white settlers

Groups such as 'Friends of the Indian', were set up to help but often helped to destroy Indian cultures

A group called the **Friends of the Indian** was set up in 1883 to protect the rights of Native Americans. It tried to solve some of the problems below:

Problem	What the Friends did
Many government agents who ran reservations were corrupt	They reported corrupt agents and monitored how the money on reservations was spent
Indian children had no formal education	They set up schools to help Indian children learn English, so that they could access jobs in white America
Indians were not full citizens of the USA so they had no rights and could not vote	They persuaded the government to pass the Dawes Act in 1887. It gave each Indian family 160 acres and citizenship if they gave up their claim to their tribal lands

- The Friends' solutions were well meaning but they also meant that tribes lost huge amounts of their land.
- By 1900, nearly two-thirds of the land held by Native Americans in 1877 had been taken by white settlers.

The **Ghost Dance movement** was the **last major** attempt at **resistance** by Plains tribes in the nineteenth century

- During the 1890s, a new religious movement called the **Ghost Dance** movement sprang up on the reservations. It was led by a holy man named Wovoka.

- The Ghost Dancers believed that if they danced and prayed, the white settlers would be swept off the land and the buffalo would return.

- In 1890, the government sent in the army to stop the Ghost Dance movement. Many of the Ghost Dancers ran away to Dakota.

- The Ghost Dancers were eventually tracked down at a place called Wounded Knee. The army opened fire and killed over 250 men, women and children.

- On 15 January 1891, over 4000 Ghost Dancers surrendered. This was the last Indian attempt at resistance in the nineteenth century.

Getting from A to B

You have been given the start and the end of a story. Complete the blank boxes to show the key steps the US government took that contributed to the destruction of Sioux Indian culture.

| **A** The Sioux were defeated during the Great Sioux War of 1877 | → | → | → | → | **B** Most Sioux Indians stopped trying to resist the US government by 1900 |

Mind map

Below are a sample exam-style 18-mark question and the basic structure of a mind map connected to the question. A good mind map should help you to organise ideas and evidence. Complete the mind map by adding examples of the impact of each of the headings. Use information from this spread and your own knowledge. This will help you to structure an answer to the question below.

'The destruction of the buffalo was the main reason why Indian culture had been largely destroyed by 1900.'
How far do you agree with this statement? Give reasons for your answer. **(18 marks)**

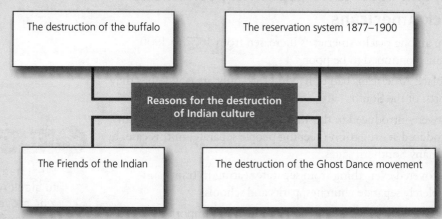

The destruction of the buffalo

The reservation system 1877–1900

Reasons for the destruction of Indian culture

The Friends of the Indian

The destruction of the Ghost Dance movement

Test yourself

1 Roughly how many buffalo were killed by white hunters?

2 Give three ways that Indian schools tried to force Native American children to adopt white culture.

3 Which group tried to protect the rights of Native Americans?

4 Why do you think the Dawes Act is sometimes seen as very negative for Plains Indians?

TIP

A good conclusion should answer the question in a few sentences. Thinking about your conclusion before you write can help you structure your answer. Try writing a conclusion to the practice question before you answer it fully.

5.14 The changing lives of black Americans, 1877–1900

REVISED

Black Americans continued to live in poverty after the end of Reconstruction

Life in the South	Opportunities in the West
• The cotton industry collapsed after the Civil War • Black Americans were generally prevented from getting better paid jobs • The majority of black Americans in the South worked as sharecroppers on land owned by former slaveholders	• The Homestead Act was open to black Americans • In 1877, Benjamin Singleton tried to encourage ex-slaves to move to Kansas and claim land under the Homestead Act • By 1879, over 6000 black Americans had moved to Kansas. By 1880, this had doubled. They became known as the **exodusters**
Challenges in the North	**Education**
• Between 1877 and 1900, many black Americans left the South for Northern cities • Due to racism, black workers were much less likely to get a job than white workers, even if they were more qualified	• In 1882, Booker T. Washington set up a school to train black children to be farmers, craftsmen and house servants. Some people criticised this approach • In 1900, Washington established the Negro Business League to support black businesses • By 1900, there were 23,866 black teachers, 417 black doctors and 300 black lawyers in the USA

In the South, Jim Crow laws kept living conditions poor for black Americans

- Land ownership among black Americans increased from 1877 to 1900. However, housing continued to be poor.

- In cities, most black Americans had to live in black-only areas whether they were in the North or the South.

- Jim Crow laws were introduced in the 1890s in many Southern states. Jim Crow laws introduced **segregation** (keeping people separate, in this case, by skin colour) in many Southern states.

- Jim Crow laws covered everything from separate seating in trains and theatres to completely separate churches, parks and schools.

- Despite the Jim Crow laws, black churches became more important in the lives of ordinary black Americans. They helped to build a sense of community and identity.

- There was a growth in published output from black scholars. Over 100 books and 206 journal articles were published by black authors between 1865 and 1893.

 Test yourself

1. What name was given to black Americans who moved to Kansas between 1877 and 1879?
2. What name is given to the laws which introduced segregation in the South?
3. How many black lawyers were there in the USA by 1900?
4. How did Southern governments try to stop black people from voting?

Challenge question

To improve your notes, find out a bit more about the work of black civil rights campaigners such as Booker T. Washington, Ida Wells or William DuBois. Pick one of these campaigners and record ten interesting facts about them and their work.

Political violence against black Americans increased due to the Ku Klux Klan and other factors

The Redeemers	The Ku Klux Klan
• Many Southern state governments were run by ex-slaveholders • These governments called themselves **Redeemer governments**. They tried to undo the changes made after the Civil War • Redeemer governments brought in literacy tests to stop black Americans from voting, introduced segregation laws and ignored violence against black Americans • In 1905, in Louisiana just 1342 black Americans were registered to vote	• The KKK was a violent group who believed that black Americans were inferior to whites • The KKK was banned in the 1870s, but had re-formed secretly by the 1890s • The KKK had a lot of influence among people in power, including state politicians and the Southern police forces
Constitutional changes	**Lynching**
• Black Americans continued to campaign for better treatment because the 13th, 14th and 15th Amendments still existed and promised them equality • Whatever the South did, it could not make black Americans slaves again, or remove their right to vote altogether	• One way in which black Americans were kept in fear was through **lynching** (hanging someone without a proper trial) • In 1892 alone, 161 black Americans were lynched by white mobs, mainly in the South

 ## Support or challenge?

Below are a sample exam-style 18-mark question and a table showing a number of points which might be made to address it. For each one, decide whether it supports or challenges the overall statement, then add some supporting detail from the spread. When you have finished this, add three more points.

'There was little progress for black Americans between 1877 and 1900.' How far do you agree with this statement? Give reasons for your answer. **(18 marks)**

Point	Supports statement	Challenges statement
Black Americans continued to have little political power		
Black Americans did not see much improvement in their living conditions		
Black Americans continued to live in poverty		

5.15 The growth of big business, cities and mass migration, 1877–1900

Key point

The USA changed dramatically between 1877 and 1900 as corporations took control of American industries, and many more people became wageworkers instead of landowners. However, these changes did provide some people with opportunities.

Big business created some opportunities but brought many challenges too

Industry	Impact on people
Cotton and tobacco • The number of cotton mills in the South doubled between 1880 and 1900 • The American Tobacco Company controlled 90 per cent of cigarette production	• More cotton factories meant more demand for cotton. Cotton was usually picked by poorly paid black Americans or sharecroppers • New factories created jobs but these were low paid and low skilled and usually for white workers • Because the American Tobacco Company controlled nearly all production there was no reason to improve wages for workers
Farms and ranches • Huge **bonanza farms** (farms over 10,000 acres) and ranches began to appear in the 1880s • By 1900, most farms and ranches in the West were owned by a handful of people	• People who could not afford their own land could get employment on a farm or ranch and save to buy their own • Bonanza farms controlled the best land, water and railroads, stopping smaller farmers from competing • Bonanza ranches sometimes used violence to intimidate small-scale ranchers • Black and minority farmers could not usually compete with the bonanza farmers
Minerals • The growth of railroads led to a demand for coal, iron, steel and other **minerals** (for example, oil) • Coal production in the South increased ten-fold between 1875 and 1890	• Big **corporations** (companies) used their power and political influence to pay workers as little as possible • When steel workers went on strike in 1892, the local militia were sent in and six strikers were killed • Black and Mexican workers were employed by companies when white workers went on strike • **Trade unions** (organisations set up to protect workers' rights) had a little power and usually used this power to stop black or Mexican workers from getting employment • Big companies could 'blacklist' troublesome employees, stopping them from getting other work

Cities grew massively, creating new opportunities – but they often contained poor areas

- In 1870, there were fourteen cities with more than 100,000 people in the USA. By 1900, there were 38.

- Cities controlled local water supplies and used these to increase their own power.

- Cities attracted people, especially in the American West, where access to water was a key part of surviving.

- Many cities were overcrowded. It was not uncommon for 32 families to share a six- or eight-storey **tenement** (apartment building).

- Overcrowding led to disease. In Chicago, 60 per cent of babies died before the age of one.

- However, cities also drew people in with promises of work, entertainment, education and freedom.

- Women and black Americans gained some benefits from city life. Western cities were a driving force behind women getting the vote in the USA in the 1920s.

Challenge question

What connections can you identify between overcrowding in cities, the growth of industries and increased immigration?

Immigration continued to grow. Immigrants often met racism and hostility when they arrived

Reasons for coming to America
- the American economy was booming by the 1880s
- travel to America was faster and cheaper thanks to steam ships
- Jews and other minority groups were being persecuted in places like Russia
- America offered freedom of religion and thought

Mass migration to the USA

Arriving in America
- 600,000 immigrants came from Italy alone in the 1890s
- Ellis Island (in New York) opened in 1892 to process immigrants
- Immigrants had to pass a basic language test and a medical examination

Living in America
- most immigrants went to cities to find work
- anti-immigrant violence was common
- laws prevented Chinese workers from moving freely in California
- immigrants ended up in the poorest areas of cities

Structured notes

Making brief notes on a topic is a very good way to help you remember key dates and details. Use the four headings below to take some bullet-pointed notes on the growth of big business, cities and migration. You should aim to have three bullet points under each heading. Try to do these notes from memory as this will help the information stick in your brain better. Once you have done this, use your own notes and this spread to check your work.

What sorts of industries became rich and important between 1877 and 1900?	Why did many people move into cities?
• • •	• • •
Why did many immigrants come to America?	What happened when immigrants arrived in America?
• • •	• • •

What sort of impact?

Below is a sample exam-style 10-mark question which asks for examples of the impact of the growth of business and industry. Using concepts like similarity and difference can help give structure to an 'impact' question. The chart below uses the similarity and difference between white workers and black/immigrant workers as the basic structure. Use the information on this spread and your own knowledge to fill in the chart with specific examples of the positive and negative impacts of big businesses and industry on different groups in the USA.

What was the impact of the growth of big business and industry on the American people, 1877–1900? Explain your answer. **(10 marks)**

Group	Positive impact	Negative impact
White workers		
Black/immigrant workers		

Test yourself

1. Which company controlled most American tobacco production?
2. How many Italian immigrants came to the USA in the 1890s?
3. Name one way the USA tried to deal with the number of immigrants arriving after 1890.
4. Why did workers find it more difficult to get better wages and conditions in the 1880s and 1890s?

The World Depth Study

This part of the GCSE focuses on a traumatic and short period in world history when different cultures or ideologies were in conflict. It is worth twenty per cent of your total GCSE. You must be able to:

Understand the interplay of **politics, religion, economy, society and culture**. This means how each of these factors affected the others.

> The interplay bit is important here. To help you with this, write these words randomly across a big peice of paper and then draw links between them if they affect each other. Along the line explain why they are linked.

Identify and describe the **main features of the different societies** at the time.

> This point is linked with the one above about interplay. To truly know the features of each society at this time, you must know what the politics, economy, society and culture were like. Try to think how these features changed during this period.

Analyse **both sources and interpretations** related to this period.

> This is important as both sources and interpretations will feature in the exam. These could be written extracts or pictures. You will need to think carefully about what we can learn from different sources and interpretations.

What do I need to do in the World Depth Study exam?

- The World Depth Study exam is taken together with the Period unit. The paper in total is 1 hour 45 minutes and worth 80 marks.
- There are **40 marks** available for the World Depth Study half of the paper and you have **52.5 minutes** to complete it.
- There is a total of **four questions, of which you must answer three**. On the next page is some guidance on how to do this.

> **TIP**
>
> Remember: 40 marks for this exam and 52.5 minutes!

For Question 6 you need to analyse a single source to explain what it **tells us** about a particular subject.
- Refer to **specific details** in the source and make inferences from them
- Use your **own knowledge** to explain the source
- Consider the limitations and benefits of the source in the context of the question
- 9 minutes in total

Answer Questions 6 and 7.

6. What can extract Source A tell us about ...?
    Use the source and your own knowledge to support your answer. [7]

7. How useful are Interpretation B and Sources C and D for a historian studying ...? In your answer, refer to the interpretation and the two sources as well as your own knowledge. [15]

Answer **either** Question 8 **or** Question 9.

8. '[statement]'. How far do you agree with this view? [18]

9. '[statement]'. How far do you agree with this view? [18]

For Question 7 you will be given a collection of sources and interpretations and asked how useful they are for a historian studying a particular focus.
- Take each source or interpretation **in turn**. Pick out **specific details** in each to answer the question
- Use your own knowledge of the focus in the question
- Think about the provenance of the source or interpretation: who produced it? For whom? When? Why?
- Make an overall judgement about how useful the collection is for the focus in the question.
- 20 minutes in total

You must only answer Question 8 or 9. In your answer, you should make your own judgement, explaining how far you agree or disagree with the view in the question.
- Start by making a clear statement of your overall judgement then support this with some detailed paragraphs.
- Give reasons for agreeing and disagreeing (you could write a paragraph on each) but don't feel these have to be balanced.
- Finish with your strongest reason for agreeing or disagreeing, or with a conclusion summarising the main reasons for your judgement.
- 24 minutes in total.

The difference between a source and an interpretation

A source is a written document, picture, artefact or site that was created by people at the time. Sources such as government documents, diaries, photographs, propaganda posters and sound recordings can provide a wealth of evidence about Living under Nazi Rule, 1933–1945.

An interpretation is any version of events in the past that has been created at some later time. Interpretations such as books and articles written by historians, documentaries, websites, exhibitions, monuments, novels and films provide range of different perspectives on Living under Nazi Rule, 1933–1945.

Chapter 6 Living under Nazi Rule, 1933–1945

6.1 The Nazi Party, ideas and leaders in 1933

REVISED

The **Nazi Party** had its **origins** in the **1920s** but was not **strong** until the **1930s**

Key point

The Nazis were a highly organised and appealing party in 1933.

- The Nazi Party was founded in 1919 by Anton Drexler. It was a small **right-wing** party (fiercely nationalistic) with its main support in southern Germany.

- Adolf Hitler, a young Austrian with a natural talent for public speaking, became the chairman of the party in 1921.

- On 8 November 1923, Hitler led an unsuccessful takeover of power in Munich. The so-called **Munich Putsch** (or Beer Hall Putsch) ended up with sixteen Nazis dead, Hitler jailed and the party banned for two years.

- At his trial, Hitler gained national fame for his political ideas and in prison wrote *Mein Kampf*, which detailed these ideas and gained him more fame.

- Relaunching the party in 1925, the Nazis decided to take power through democracy. They remained a relatively small unpopular party until the Great Depression of the early 1930s.

- Faced with high unemployment and depression, the German people turned to more extreme parties such as the Nazis.

The **Nazi Party** was **run** by a handful of **driven, extremely right-wing men**

- By 1933, the Nazis had won the majority of seats in the Reichstag and had a personal membership of over 850,000. They had emerged from their weak beginning in the 1920s to become a hugely powerful force.

- The most prominent people in the party were as follows:

Adolf Hitler	An ex-soldier with charisma who could whip a crowd into a frenzy. He was portrayed as god-like and his right-wing views about race formed the backbone of the party
Joseph Goebbels	A highly educated and very anti-Semitic man who realised the power of modern media. He was tasked with spreading Nazi propaganda using newspapers, film and radio
Ernst Röhm	Fear was a key tactic of the Nazis and in order to create fear they needed force. In 1933, this came through the SA, a personal army of brown-shirted stormtroopers, led by Röhm, which was 400,000 strong
Heinrich Himmler	Fanatical about Nazi ideas, he created an elite force of soldiers, the SS, who wore black shirts and would work alongside the SA. He had strict entry requirements and its force numbered 50,000 in 1933
Herman Göring	An ex-fighter pilot who was second in power to Hitler. He would go on to create the Gestapo (the secret police) and command the *Luftwaffe* (air force)

The **Nazi Party policies** were created to **appeal to the masses** and **make Germany great again**

- Germany in 1932–33 was not in a good state:
  - The Wall Street Crash had led to a global Great Depression and it affected Germany badly. Unemployment soared and poverty was widespread.
  - The ruling government before the Nazis, the Weimar government, appeared weak and unable to provide any solutions to this worsening situation.
  - In this situation, the Nazi ideas to make Germany strong seemed very appealing and they made the most of this.

Abolish the Treaty of Versailles: in 1920, after the First World War, the Weimar government had signed a treaty with the Allies which meant that the German army was severely reduced, its territories were reduced and vast debts were owed. The Nazis promised to abolish these restrictions

Bread and jobs: the unemployed were promised food and work. During the Depression this would have been very appealing. The Nazis would nationalise industry and educate the people ready for work to revitalise the economy

Lebensraum: many German-speaking people had been forced into other countries by the Treaty of Versailles. The Nazis wished to reunite these people and conquer new land in the east so that the Germans could have space to thrive

The main Nazi Ideas

Aryans are supreme: the Nazis believed that there were distinct races of people. Natural Germans (Aryans) were seen as racially superior to others. They saw Jews as non-Aryans and racially inferior and as a result believed Jews should not have the same rights or be viewed as citizens

Destroy Communism: Russia had a Communist revolution in 1917 and the Nazis wanted to avoid this at all costs. They saw Communism as a Jewish plan to take over the world

Strong central government: the Nazis believed that a strong central government was key to Germany overcoming its problems. At the head of this government would be Hitler, whose power as *Führer* would be ultimate

 ## Structure the detail

As you can probably tell from these two pages, the Nazi Party was very strong in 1933. Two of the key things you must do in an exam is support your answer with specific evidence and explain your point. In the table below are four big reasons why the Nazis were strong in 1933. Your job is to develop these reasons. First, find specific evidence you can use to prove that this reason is true. Secondly, you should explain why this made them strong. Using the word 'because' is crucial. Some boxes have been done for you.

Reason	Evidence to prove this	Explain why this made the Nazis strong
The Nazis were well led		This made the Nazis strong because …
The Nazis were organised		
The Nazis had popular ideas		
The Nazis had force	The SA was 400,000 strong in 1933. The SS was 50,000 strong	

 ## Test yourself

1 What was the key turning point in the success of the Nazi Party?
2 Who was the man in charge of Nazi propaganda?
3 Name three of the most important Nazi ideas of the early 1930s.

TIP

Precise knowledge is the key to success in these exams. From the detail here about Nazi leadership and ideas, you need to know the names of the key individuals and at least five key terms related to the Nazi ideology.

6.2 Establishing the dictatorship, January 1933 to July 1933

Hitler became Chancellor of Germany in January 1933 but there were a lot of restrictions on his power

- The Communist Party had a large amount of support that prevented a Nazi majority in the **Reichstag** (the German Parliament).
- Germany was a democracy and the other political parties could oppose the Nazi policies.
- The people of Germany were a potential threat as they could rise up against the Nazis.
- By July 1933, all these restrictions had been removed.

> **Key point**
>
> In six months, Germany went from a democracy to a dictatorship. The most important steps were the Reichstag Fire and the Enabling Act.

Hitler used the Reichstag Fire to remove the Communists

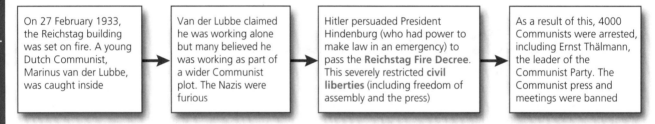

| On 27 February 1933, the Reichstag building was set on fire. A young Dutch Communist, Marinus van der Lubbe, was caught inside | → | Van der Lubbe claimed he was working alone but many believed he was working as part of a wider Communist plot. The Nazis were furious | → | Hitler persuaded President Hindenburg (who had power to make law in an emergency) to pass the **Reichstag Fire Decree**. This severely restricted **civil liberties** (including freedom of assembly and the press) | → | As a result of this, 4000 Communists were arrested, including Ernst Thälmann, the leader of the Communist Party. The Communist press and meetings were banned |

The Enabling Act gave Hitler the power to make laws without the approval of the Reichstag

- With the Communists removed, the Nazis were confident of success at the scheduled 5 March 1933 election.
- The SA and SS patrolled the German streets intimidating voters into support for the Nazis.
- The election result did not give the Nazis an outright majority. They only won 288 of the 647 seats, but forming a **coalition** (temporary alliance) with the Nationalists gave them an extra 52 seats and the majority they desired. They could now pass any law they wished.
- On 24 March 1933, the members of the Reichstag met and Hitler introduced the **Enabling Act**. Officially called *The Law to Remedy the Distress of People and Reich*, it gave Hitler the power to create any law he wished without the Reichstag.
- Surrounded by SA guards, 444 Reichstag members voted to approve the law, with only 94 Social Democrats voting against.

The Nazis began crushing the German people with fear

- With their newfound power, the Nazis now began the process of creating a state built on fear. They called this *Gleichschaltung*, meaning co-ordination or bringing into line. Below are some examples of key changes that happened in this period:

Change	Detail
Civil Service Act	On 7 April 1933, any civil servant (including teachers, judges and university lecturers) who was a political opponent or a non-Aryan (mostly Jews) was fired from their job
Anti-Semitism began	Laws to restrict Jews began, initially preventing from them working in the legal or medical professions. On 1 April 1933, a countrywide **boycott** (a campaign encouraging people not to use) of Jewish shops was held
Book burning	Encouraged by Goebbels, burning of 'un-German' (often Jewish or Communist) books began. In May 1933, many cities across Germany had large bonfires tended by Nazi student groups
Increased use of the SA	The SA began terrorising Nazi opponents including Jews, Communists, Social Democrats and trade unionists. By October, over 100,000 had been arrested. Some were placed in the newly built concentration camps such as the one at Dachau

The **Nazis removed** other political **parties and trade unions**

- By the spring, the Nazis had a vast amount of power but two external threats remained: the other political parties and the trade unions. They now acted to remove both:

Trade unions	Other political parties
• Fearing a strike organised by the trade union leaders, the Nazis arrested their main leaders • The remaining leaders worked with the Nazis as they were promised a Day of National Labour (1 May) to celebrate workers. This kept them happy • The next day, 2 May, the offices of these remaining leaders were raided and they were arrested • A new workers' organisation, the German Labour Front, was created and led by the Nazis to replace trade unions	• Although democracy had been removed by the Enabling Act, other parties still existed • The Social Democrats, the largest of these, were removed first. On 10 May, the Nazis announced the Social Democrats had used funds corruptly and on 21 June banned them altogether, arresting 3000 people • Seeing what had happened to the Social Democrats, other political parties now **dissolved** (stopped existing) rather than face the same fate • On 14 July, an act was passed to ban new parties

Getting from A to B

The chain of events that allowed the Nazis to establish a dictatorship in Germany within six months is a complex story. It has a clear start, the Reichstag Fire in February, and a clear end, with the removal of the political parties in July. The question is: how do we get from A to B?

You are not going to remember all the details of this story so you must select the most important parts. Four of the boxes below are empty. Your challenge is to decide what are the four most important steps that lead from A to B. Complete the empty boxes.

A Reichstag Fire (February 1933)				**B** Banning of political parties (July 1933)

Test yourself

1. The threat from which group was eliminated after the Reichstag Fire?
2. What power did the Enabling Act give Hitler that he did not have before?
3. Name three new laws in this period that gave Hitler and the Nazis more power.

Challenge question

Why was it so important to create fear and terror in the German public from the earliest stage of the Nazi takeover of power?

Practice question

'The Reichstag Fire was the most important step in Hitler becoming dictator of Germany.' How far do you agree with this view?   (18 marks)

6.3 Achieving total power, July 1933 to August 1934

By July 1933, Hitler was dictator but some constraints on his power remained

- The justice system and local government system needed to be brought into line.
- The SA, the Nazis' own personal army, and their leader, Ernst Röhm, were growing in power.
- Conservative politicians like von Papen were not Nazis but still remained in the government.
- President Hindenburg still technically sat above Hitler and could veto his laws.

The Nazis passed laws to control local government and courts

The People's Court	• Hitler and the Nazis were getting frustrated that the courts were not doing their bidding • As a result, they created a new type of court, the People's Court. This was a separate court outside the normal justice system to deal with **political offences**, a deliberately vague term • Only Nazi-approved judges were chosen and the number of death penalties they imposed increased year on year
Local government	• German local government had traditionally had lots of power • In January 1934, the Act for the Reconstruction of the State gave more power to central government • Germany was now a highly centralised state. It was split into 42 *Gaue*, each run by a *Gauleiter* directly elected by the Nazis

The Night of the Long Knives destroyed the threat from the SA

- By 1934, the SA were becoming increasingly violent and difficult to control.
- Röhm, their leader, began openly talking of taking over the German army, who were far better organised and equipped. When Hitler rejected this idea, Röhm called him the 'ridiculous corporal'.
- Hitler tasked the SS with making up evidence that Röhm and the SA were planning a national uprising and with constructing a list of 'politically unreliable' people.
- The **Night of the Long Knives**:
  - On 30 June 1934, the SA leadership met at a hotel outside Munich. Hitler and Goebbels, aided by the SS, arrested the most prominent leaders and sent them to prison. Many were killed.
  - Röhm was given the option to kill himself but refused, so was murdered by the SS.
  - In Berlin, Göring arranged the arrest of all of the conservative opponents including von Papen and von Schleicher.
  - In all, 85 people were murdered, including twelve prominent Reichstag deputies.

Key point

The largest threat to Hitler came from his own personal army, the SA. Hitler needed to remove this threat to have total power.

Challenge question

Can you link any of the detail from these two pages to this source to support or challenge what Goebbels is saying?

 Test yourself

1 Name the two groups who were targeted in the Night of the Long Knives.
2 Who gained most from the consequences of the Night of the Long Knives?
3 What was the name of the law that meant Hitler could become *Führer*?

TIP

Every single historical source is useful is some ways and limited in others. As a historian, you must analyse both the utility and its limitations.

The **Night of the Long Knives** had important consequences, particularly for the **SS** and the **army**

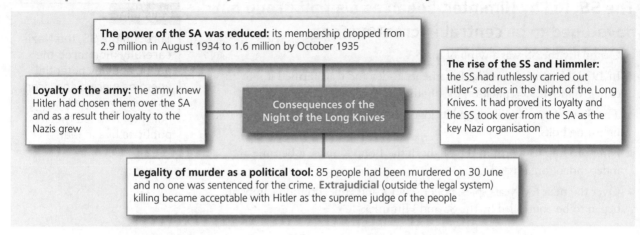

The power of the SA was reduced: its membership dropped from 2.9 million in August 1934 to 1.6 million by October 1935

Loyalty of the army: the army knew Hitler had chosen them over the SA and as a result their loyalty to the Nazis grew

Consequences of the Night of the Long Knives

The rise of the SS and Himmler: the SS had ruthlessly carried out Hitler's orders in the Night of the Long Knives. It had proved its loyalty and the SS took over from the SA as the key Nazi organisation

Legality of murder as a political tool: 85 people had been murdered on 30 June and no one was sentenced for the crime. **Extrajudicial** (outside the legal system) killing became acceptable with Hitler as the supreme judge of the people

The **death of Hindenburg** was the final hurdle **Hitler** passed to become *Führer*

- There was now only one final obstacle to complete power: President Hindenburg.
- By late July, Hindenburg's health began to deteriorate.
- Hitler and the Nazis worked quickly to pass a law to seize the moment.

- The Act Concerning the Head of State was passed. At the moment of Hindenburg's death the office and power of the President would be merged with Hitler's Chancellor into a new title, *Führer*.
- That moment came a day later, on 2 August at 9a.m.

Link the source to the correct statement

In your exam you are going to need to analyse sources and think about what they are telling us, how they are limited and why they are useful to a historian. Below is a source about the Night of the Long Knives written by Joseph Goebbels (the Minister for Propaganda).

SOURCE A *An extract from Goebbels' diary of June 1934, quoted in Toby Thacker*, Joseph Goebbels: Life and Death, *2009.*

Executions nearly finished. A few more are necessary. That is difficult, but necessary ... It is difficult, but is not however to be avoided. There must be peace for ten years. The whole afternoon with the *Führer*. I can't leave him alone. He suffers greatly, but is hard. The death sentences are received with the greatest seriousness. All in all about 60.

Below are lots of statements you could make about this source. Highlight the three that you think are most accurate.

- The source is limited as it is written by one of the Nazis
- The source is useful as Goebbels was involved in the Night of the Long Knives
- The source shows the Nazis had remorse for their actions
- The source is helpful to a historian but is only one person's opinion
- The source shows how the Nazis believed that murder was an appropriate course of action

- The source is completely biased
- The source shows how necessary the Night of the Long Knives was
- The source shows how easy the Night of the Long Knives was
- The source shows how Hitler struggled with these actions
- The source lies
- The source tells the truth

Now try answering the exam question:

What can Source A tell us about Goebbels' view of the Night Long Knives? Use the source and your own knowledge to support your answer. **(7 marks)**

6.4 The machinery of terror

The SS, led by Himmler, began as a small group but developed to be central in creating fear

- Originally the SS was a wing of the SA.
- In 1929, Heinrich Himmler became its leader and transformed it into an elite group with a reputation for **obedience** and commitment.
- The SS uniform was black and its logo was a double S that looked like two lightning bolts.
- After proving its worth in the Night of the Long Knives, it became an independent organisation.
- Over the next few years spies, police, courts and concentration camps all began to be controlled by the SS and Himmler.

> **Key point**
>
> Through the SS, the Nazis carefully monitored the public and any potential enemies were discovered and dealt with very harshly. This led the public to live in fear.

Through the Gestapo and informers the SS gathered intelligence on the people

- In order to monitor the public and stop resistance to Nazi rule, the SS developed an elaborate system of intelligence gathering.
- There were three main mechanisms for gathering intelligence and dealing with this information:

The SD (secret service)	Gestapo	Informants
• The main intelligence-gathering organisation • Focused on opposition to the party itself, particularly from the Church • It was led by Reinhard Heydrich and there were only a few hundred full-time agents	• The most famous organisation in the SS; its reputation was fierce • Focused on political opponents, Jews and homosexuals • Originally a branch of the Prussian police, it was never directly controlled by the party • Only 15,000 active officers at its height • It tapped phones and opened mail • Interrogation of potential enemies was ruthless, with torture techniques used	• Most intelligence was gathered from the public, people who **informed** the SS of potential enemies • All tip-offs were investigated by the SD or Gestapo • The Nazis also used the Block Leaders as informants. The Block Leader's job was to deliver news to the 40–60 houses in their area. They also spied on these people

The entire justice system, including police and courts, helped to destroy potential enemies

- The **Orpo** (ordinary police) and **Kripo** (criminal police) continued work as they did before Nazi rule but they also provided intelligence and rounded up potential enemies, including Jews.
- Judges had to swear an oath of loyalty to Hitler and sentences in the years of Nazi rule became far harsher.
- The number of crimes punishable by death rose from three in 1933 to 46 in 1943; 40,000 Germans were given the death sentence.
- The People's Court, which was directly run by the Nazis, was the most harsh type of court that dealt with political opponents.

A widely used punishment for those hunted down by the terror system was the concentration camp

- The aim of the concentration camp was to **concentrate** (keep together in one area) enemies of the state, not kill them (death camps would come later).

 Test yourself

1 Who was in charge of the Nazi machinery of terror?
2 How many active members of the Gestapo were there?
3 What was the purpose of the Block Leaders?

- Between 1933 and 1939, the Nazis mostly imprisoned political opponents (like the Communists) but by the end of the period the **work-shy**, religious opponents and Jews were also imprisoned.

- The SS developed the system to run the camps, led by their 'Death's Head Units'.

- In the camps there were strict rules, and even minor offences could result in harsh punishments including flogging or beatings.

- In 1937, Himmler declared that guards could not be sent to prison for their actions at camps and as a result the number of deaths in the camps rose dramatically.

- Prisoners were kept in barracks and made to do hard manual labour.

 ## Considering usefulness

In your exam you will be presented with interpretations and sources and asked how useful they are for studying a particular subject. Below are one interpretation and two sources related to the Gestapo. Your challenge is to complete the tasks below and then answer the question:

How useful are Interpretation A and Sources B and C for a historian studying the Gestapo between 1932 and 1939? In your answer, refer to the interpretation and the two sources as well as your own knowledge.

(15 marks)

Step 1: read each interpretation or source carefully.

Interpretation A	Source B	Source C
From The Gestapo *by historian Frank McDonough, 2015:* Nazi propaganda liked to give the impression that Gestapo officers were everywhere. Nothing could be further from the truth.	*Ernst Thaelmann was arrested by the Gestapo on 3 March 1933. This is his report of his interrogation:* It is nearly impossible to relate what happened for four and a half hours, from 5.00pm to 9.30pm in that interrogation room. Every conceivable cruel method of blackmail was used against me to obtain by force and at all costs confessions and statements both about comrades who had been arrested, and about political activities.	*Statistics from the Dusseldorf Gestapo cases showing where the Grestapo's information came from:* Of the 825 cases dealt with, information came from: • 26% general public • 17% regular police • 15% Gestapo • 13% other prisoners • 7% local government officials • 6% Nazi Party members (including block leaders).

Step 2: complete the table below.

	Interpretation A	Source B	Source C
Content: what exactly do we learn about the Gestapo from the interpretation and the sources?			
Context: when was the interpretation or source written? Who wrote it? Who was it written for? How might this affect how useful it is?			

Step 3: now answer the exam question. You need to focus on the 'useful to a historian' bit in particular. Use the details you have written in the table above and include some of your own knowledge about the Gestapo to support your answer.

6.5 Nazi propaganda

The **Nazis** needed to **win** the hearts and minds of the **people** through **carefully crafted propaganda**

- On 13 March 1933, the Ministry of Public Enlightenment and Propaganda was created.
- It was led by Joseph Goebbels, a highly intelligent and driven Nazi.
- Using a wide range of techniques, including modern technology, Goebbels aimed to persuade the German people of the Nazi mission.

> **Key point**
>
> Goebbels used a wide range of propaganda techniques to promote Nazi ideas to the German people.

The **different techniques** used meant the sophisticated Nazi propaganda would have been **difficult to avoid**

Technique	How the Nazis used it to spread their message
Newspapers	<ul><li>The Nazis controlled newspapers through the Reich Press Chamber</li><li>They closed down existing papers and by 1939 owned two-thirds of the newspapers</li><li>They published their own newspapers, like the very anti-Semitic *Der Stürmer*</li><li>Content in newspapers was tightly controlled and **censored**. Journalists and editors had to join the Reich Association of the Press and were told what they could and could not write about</li></ul>
Radio	<ul><li>All national and local radio stations were controlled by the Reich Radio Company</li><li>To ensure that people received their broadcasts the Nazis made cheap radio sets that everyone could afford – the People's Receiver</li><li>1.5 million People's Receivers were made in 1933 and by 1939 70 per cent of people had a radio in their home</li></ul>
Posters	<ul><li>The Nazis were masters of the visual image and posters were put up in all towns and villages</li><li>They often portrayed Hitler as god-like</li><li>Men and women nearly always had blond hair and blue eyes, emphasising their Aryan ideal</li></ul>
Rallies	<ul><li>The Nazis held large rallies to show their strength</li><li>They were like festivals with marches, speeches and parades</li><li>The annual rally at Nuremberg was the largest. In 1934, over 250,000 people attended. Lights around the field shot up into the sky and looked like a 'cathedral of light'</li></ul>
Culture	<ul><li>The Reich Culture Chamber supervised and regulated all culture, including art, theatre, literature and architecture</li><li>Culture that emphasised Aryan strength was promoted; abstract culture (for example, art that just used shapes) was deemed **degenerate** (meaning alien, wicked and undesirable)</li><li>Traditional German culture was seen as superior (for example, composers like Wagner); American popular culture like jazz was discouraged</li><li>There was even a preferred Nazi architectural style – pointed roofs were more Germanic!</li></ul>
Film	<ul><li>Film was the most modern type of media and the Nazis controlled it through the Reich Film Chamber</li><li>The Nazis tried to limit foreign films coming to Germany so that German films were shown in cinemas</li><li>By 1939, two-thirds of all films made were paid for by the state. They promoted films that showed Hitler to be great or that criticised Jews</li></ul>
Berlin Olympics	<ul><li>In 1936, the Olympic Games were held in Berlin and were used as an important piece of Nazi propaganda</li><li>Olympic flags and swastikas covered Berlin, including the new 100,000-seat stadium</li><li>Anti-Semitic signs were taken down and German newspapers toned down their stories</li><li>The Games promoted Aryan superiority and the nearly all-Aryan German team emerged victorious, winning the most medals</li><li>The notable exception was the African American athlete Jesse Owens, who won four gold medals</li></ul>

Mind map

Mind maps are a useful tool to help you organise information. You can use them to structure your notes, and also to plan answers to a particular question. Your challenge is to make a mind map about Nazi propaganda. Your mind map must have the following features:

- A branch for each of the seven propaganda techniques.
- In a different colour, each branch then must have fewer than four facts. Do not write whole sentences. Instead, limit each fact to fewer than five words. For example, for film, one fact might be 'controlled by Reich Chamber of Film'.
- In another colour, add one more sentence to each branch explaining why you think this might have been an effective technique. This can be a full sentence.
- Finally, rank the seven techniques by putting a large number next to each. Put a 1 next to what you think is the most effective, a 2 next to the second most effective and so on.

Link the source to the correct statement

In your exam you are going to need to analyse sources and think about what they are telling us, how they are limited and why they are useful to a historian. Below is a source about the power of radio, written by Joseph Goebbels (the Minister for Propaganda):

SOURCE D *A speech by Joseph Goebbels from August 1933.*

It would not have been possible for us to take power or to use it in the ways we have without the radio. ... It therefore does not need saying that the government ... cannot ignore the radio and its possibilities. To the contrary, it is resolved to use them to the fullest extent in the work of national construction that is before us, and in ensuring that this revolution can stand the test of history.

Below are lots of statements you could make about this source. Highlight the three that you think are most accurate.

- The source is limited as it is written by one of the Nazis
- The source is useful as Goebbels was the Minister for Propaganda
- The source shows the Nazis realised the power of modern technology
- The source is beneficial to a historian but is only one person's opinion
- The source shows how the Nazis used the radio

- The source is completely biased
- The source shows how necessary propaganda was
- The source shows how easy it was to indoctrinate the German people
- The source shows how Goebbels was decisive
- The source lies
- The source tells the truth

Now try answering the following exam question:

What can Source D tell us about Nazi propaganda? Use the source and your own knowledge to support your answer. (7 marks)

Test yourself

1 What message was often promoted in Nazi propaganda?
2 Who controlled the production of propaganda?
3 What modern technology did the Nazis use to help spread their propaganda message?

Challenge question

Given the context of the 1930s, which of the methods of propaganda do you think was most effective?

TIP

No one is expecting you to remember everything! With something like propaganda on this page, try to remember five methods and a clear and specific example to illustrate each one.

6.6 Opposition to Nazi rule, 1933–39

The most **active and persistent opposition** in the early years came from **Social Democrats** and **Communists**

- If these two groups had combined forces they would have provided effective opposition but they hated each other and refused to cooperate. As a result, their resistance was minimal.

Social Democrats	• After 1933, most SD leaders fled to Prague, leaving those that remained without clear leadership • Despite this, many formed into resistance groups who produced anti-Nazi leaflets and posters • Many were effectively hunted down by the Gestapo
Communists	• They were more visibly active than the SDs, with meetings, propaganda and newsletters • They produced 10,000 copies of their newsletter *The Red Flag* every month • Due to their visibility they were easy targets for the Gestapo

> **Key point**
>
> Opposition to Nazi rule came from lots of different sources but was not effective and was easily crushed.

Nazi interference in the **Church** and **Nazi ideology** led many **religious people** to resist

- The Church was the largest non-Nazi organisation in Germany. There were 22 million Catholics, 40 million Protestants and other smaller denominations at this time.
- Christian teaching about love and forgiveness was obviously opposite to Nazi ideas and so opposition was unsurprising.
- Initially, Hitler promised to not interfere with the Church.
- Hitler made an agreement with Pope Pius XI (a **Concordat**) to leave the Catholic Church alone.
- With the Protestants, a new **Reich Church** was set up and pastors had to sign an oath to Hitler.
- These promises were broken. In 1936, all Church youth groups were banned and by 1939 all Church schools had been closed. Priests who spoke out against this were arrested.

 **Test yourself**

1 Why was opposition from the Social Democrats and Communists ineffective?
2 Name two examples of Church leaders who opposed the Nazis.
3 Why did young people oppose the Nazis?

Religious opposition was **not that effective or widespread** but was **taken very seriously** by the Gestapo

Martin Niemöller
- Refusing to join the Reich Church, Niemöller founded an alternative, the non-Nazi **Confessional Church**. By 1934, 6000 pastors had joined, leaving only 2000 in the Reich Church
- Niemöller preached against Nazi racial policy and was arrested and sent to a concentration camp

Pope Pius XI
- He wrote a letter called *With Burning Anxiety* which was smuggled into Germany and read out in all Catholic churches on Palm Sunday
- The letter condemned Nazi beliefs and methods. The next day the Gestapo raided every Catholic church, seizing all copies of the letter

Examples of the most significant religious resistance

Jehovah's Witnesses
- Due to the rules of their faith, they refused to give the Hitler salute and refused compulsory military service
- They began writing anti-Nazi leaflets. A special Gestapo unit to combat them was created and 6000 were imprisoned in concentration camps

Youth opposition groups emerged all over Germany for a **variety of reasons**

- Young people often question authority and this was no different in Nazi Germany, although there was not a single national movement, but lots of small groups.
- Young people opposed the Nazis for a variety of reasons. Some did not agree with Nazi politics.

Some were angry about religious interference. Some were frustrated at enforced Nazi youth groups.

- The one similarity of all these groups was their refusal to conform to the **Nazi ideal** as promoted by the Hitler Youth.

The **main** youth opposition **groups resisted** the Nazis in **very different ways**

Group	Why did they resist the Nazis?	How did they resist the Nazis?
Young Communists	Politically they were opposed to Nazi ideology, like their adult counterparts	Joined into gangs or *meuten* (one gang in Leipzig was 1500 strong) Dressed differently, in leather shorts and bright scarfs Wrote anti-Nazi flyers
Christian Youth	There were 2.5 million members of Christian youth organisations in 1933. When these organisations were banned this angered some	Illegal **pilgrimages**
Swing Kids	Angry at the Nazis imposing German culture and banning American culture	Listened to American jazz music Grew long hair and wore baggy trousers
Edelweiss Pirates	In the Rhine region these young people were opposed to Nazi politics and the enforced Hitler Youth groups	Went on excursions and hikes Wore a white edelweiss flower or white pin badge as a sign of resistance Picked fights with the Hitler Youth

 Make revision cards

In your exam you will need to use precise, relevant and detailed information in your answers. Revision cards can help to make the details stick. Use the headings below to help you create some revision cards about the different individuals and groups who opposed the Nazis. You should create one card for each of the following:

- Social Democrats
- Communists
- Martin Niemöller
- Pope Pius XI
- Jehovah's Witnesses
- Young Communists
- Edelweiss Pirates
- Swing Kids
- Christian Youth

Put the title of the person or group at the top of the card and then split it into two. In the first half add detail about why they opposed the Nazis in one colour. In the second half add detail about how they opposed the Nazis in another colour. Limit the number of words in each half to fewer than ten. Finally, once you have made all the cards order them in terms of the threat they posed to the Nazis and number them from 1 for the greatest threat to 9 to the smallest threat.

Here is an example:

Edelweiss Pirates
WHY? They didn't want to be part of the Hitler Youth.
HOW? Went on hikes, wore white flowers and beat up Hitler Youth.
3/9 THREAT

Once you have made your cards you should test yourself, or work with a friend to test each other, on the key details.

6.7 The impact of Nazi policies on workers and women

Despite aiming to help **craftsmen and peasants**, the **Nazis** had **little impact**

- In 1933, the Law to Protect Retail Trade was passed which increased the taxes on large stores to protect the *Mittelstand* or craftsmen.
- The law had little impact and between 1936 and 1939 the number of artisans fell from 1.6 million to 1.5 million.
- Similarly, in the countryside, the Nazis passed the Reich Entailed Farm Law in May 1933, which aimed to force farm owners to pass the land on to their eldest sons rather than divide it or sell it to large-scale landowners.
- The negative impact of this was that peasants were tied to the land, which stopped innovation and the peasant population dropped from 21 per cent to 18 per cent.

> **Key point**
>
> The Nazis had grand plans to change life for workers and women but in reality little changed.

Although **wages rose** for **industrial workers**, they were **worse off** under the **Nazis**

- The Nazi obsession with **rearmament** made industrial jobs plentiful.
- However, wages were frozen at 1933 levels and rising prices meant that they were still not enough to easily feed a family.
- Welfare support had been cut by the Nazis and they replaced it with the **Winter Relief collection**, which provided soup kitchens.
- Donations to the collection were voluntary but constant pressure from the SA meant on average three per cent of all income was donated.

The **Deutsche Arbeitsfront** was designed to **organise** all aspects of a **worker's life**

- The **Deutsche Arbeitsfront**, meaning German Labour Front, filled the gap left by the trade unions.
- Led by Robert Ley, it had 29 million members by 1939, who all paid to join.
- It had three main branches:

Strength Through Joy	• Created to organise workers' leisure time, it offered subsidised tickets for holidays, theatre and gyms, to name a few. This was very popular • All activities involved ideological content
Beauty of Labour	• Aimed to improve the workplace by building new toilets, showers and facilities
Reich Labour Service	• Set up to tackle unemployment; all men aged 18–25 had to serve six months • They worked on big state projects like building motorways

The **Nazis** had an **incredibly traditional** view of **women**

Not smoke · Not wear make-up · Dress in traditional German clothes · The Nazis believed the ideal German woman should ... · Not be thin but 'physically robust' and ready for childbirth · Be in the kitchen. Once a month she should take part in **One Pot Sunday** and use up leftovers · Be a member of the National Socialist Women's League

Quick quizzes and answers at **www.hoddereducation.co.uk/myrevisionnotesdownloads**

The Nazis' main priority for women was to encourage motherhood but this was not successful

The Nazis wanted women ...	Impact on the German people
To get married and have more children: • Loans of up to 1000 Reichsmarks were offered to Aryan couples. The loan was reduced by a quarter for every child the couple had. In 1934, 250,000 loans were issued • The Honour Cross of the German Mother was issued to women who had large families. Bronze for four or five children, silver for six or seven and gold for eight or more • Divorce was made easier	• Marriages increased from 516,000 in 1932 to 772,000 in 1939 • Births rose in the early 1930s but by 1939 the rate had declined again. The average number of children per couple in 1932 had been 3.6 and by 1939 it had dropped to 3.3
To stay at home and not go to work: • They encouraged women to stay at home. The loans above were only given if the woman gave up her job • However, by 1937 this requirement was removed as they realised it was proving difficult	• The number of women in employment actually increased between 1933 and 1939 • In agriculture, 4.6 million women were employed in 1933; by 1939 this had increased to 4.9 million • In industry, the figure rose from 2.7 million to 3.3 million
To not be involved in higher education: • Female enrolment at university was limited to ten per cent of all students	• The number of women in higher education fell dramatically • The lack of qualified women during the war years became a problem

 Spot the second-order concept

Second-order concepts are the things that historians use to make sense of the past. They include: cause, consequence, change, continuity, significance and diversity. In the exam you will gain marks for using second-order concepts in your answers, but don't feel that you have to use the names.

This extract from an exam answer contains several examples of second-order concepts. Highlight where they occur and note the second-order concept in the margin.

'The Nazis had little impact on workers and women'. How far do you agree with this view of Germany between 1933 and 1939?

(18 marks)

> The Nazis had many policies and ideas aimed at changing the lives of German women. Their aim was to turn German women into traditional housewives who would stay at home, cook, clean and produce babies. In order to do this they gave women loans of up to 1000 marks if they married an Aryan! The loan was then reduced by 25 per cent every time the couple had a child. The results and outcomes of this push were mixed. Marriages did increase between 1933 and 1939, which showed that the Nazi policies were having the intended consequences. However, births were not so spectacular. Although the number of children born did rise in the early 1930s this had fallen again by the end of the decade, showing that the Nazis were not entirely successful and did in fact have quite a limited impact.

 Test yourself

1 What was the name of the law that aimed to help German farmers?
2 What were the three main branches of the Deutsche Arbeitsfront?
3 How did the Nazis try to encourage women to have more children?

Challenge question

Which group of people most benefited from Nazi rule?

6.8 The lives of young people in Nazi Germany

The **Nazis** realised that the first step in **controlling education** was to **control the teachers**

- In 1933, **politically unreliable** teachers were forced to resign.
- Jewish teachers were banned from teaching in non-Jewish schools.
- A National Socialist (Nazi) Teachers League was established which ran 'political education'

courses where teachers had to do military-style exercises and learn Nazi ideology.

- If teachers stepped out of line, they faced the Nazi **machinery of terror**. They were in constant fear of pupils acting as classroom spies.

The **Nazis** also set up their own **specialist schools** to create **future leaders**

- Napola or military cadet schools were set up and run by SS and SA officers teaching a military education.
- Adolf Hitler Schools were run by the leaders of the Hitler Youth and were designed to create future leaders of the party with a focus on physical and military education.

- Neither were very successful, and by 1939 only 6173 pupils were schooled at the sixteen Napola and ten Adolf Hitler Schools.

Old textbooks were **thrown out**. Teachers had to follow a **strict curriculum** that emphasised **Nazi ideology**

Subject	What was taught?
History	The struggle between nations and the superiority of Germany and the Aryan race
Geography	Pride in Germany and the need for *lebensraum* (living space)
Physics	The science of firearms, aerodynamics and radio communications
Mathematics	Often taught in the form of 'social arithmetic'. For example, they might be asked to work out the cost of keeping a mentally ill patient alive in an asylum
German	How the language had developed from a specific Aryan background
PE	Fifteen per cent of all lesson time was PE as the Nazis believed it was crucial to keep fit and ready for a war
Biology	*Rassenkunde*, the study of race

Young people's leisure time was also controlled by **Nazi youth organisations**

- The **Hitler Youth** was set up in the late 1920s and had four parts. There were different sections for girls and boys, with juniors aged between ten and fourteen and seniors aged fourteen to eighteen.

- At first, membership of Hitler Youth was voluntary. After 1936 it was made compulsory to join and after 1939 it was compulsory to attend meetings.
- The Nazis also shut down other youth groups and, after 1936, the Hitler Youth was the only way to access sports facilities and activities.

The purpose of the **Hitler Youth** was to provide **indoctrination (brainwashing) and physical activity**

- Hitler Youth members sang political songs, read Nazi books and paraded through towns.
- Boys' activities were often focused on preparation for the military, for example Morse code tests, map reading and firing rifles.

- Girls' groups concentrated on domestic duties.
- Both boys' and girls' groups had the possibility of going on holiday camps, which were very popular with the working classes.

Despite the Nazis' efforts **not every young person** was **convinced** by their **propaganda**

- Many young people were bored by or resentful of the Hitler Youth meetings, especially those who did not enjoy physical activities.
- Others enjoyed the activities but really hated the political messages.

Write an introduction

Below are introductions to two answers to the following question:

'The Nazis totally controlled the lives of young people.' How far do you agree with this view of Germany between 1933 and 1945? (18 marks)

Read through the introductions and annotate them to show their strengths and weaknesses. Which do you think is the stronger introduction?

Write your own introduction to the question. Make sure you begin with a clear statement of your overall judgement to answer the question 'How far … ?' then outline your main points.

ANSWER A

The Nazis definitely controlled the lives of German young people. They ran their own Nazi schools called the Adolf Hitler Schools. They got rid of teachers who criticised the Nazis and sacked them. In all schools they told teachers what to teach. The Nazi curriculum made all subjects spread the Nazi message. For example, in Maths they had to solve equations about the number of mentally ill people in Germany. Youth groups also controlled children. The Hitler Youth and the League of German Maidens provided cheap holidays, ran hikes and sang songs about Hitler.

ANSWER B

The Nazis did successfully control the lives of German young people. First they did this in school, controlling teachers and the curriculum. By doing this they successfully controlled the minds of the youth by indoctrinating them about Nazi ideology. Over time this made children learn to love the Nazis and follow them without question. The Nazi regime also controlled the leisure time of young children. Through organisations like the Hitler Youth the Nazis ensured that indoctrination went on at home as well as in school. This effectively brainwashed children and some even informed on their parents to the Gestapo.

TIP

Knowing your stuff is key. For each double-page spread of this book, try to remember five really important facts that cover all the different points.

Challenge question

If you were a historian of youth in Nazi Germany, how would you investigate the success of the Nazi Youth programme?

6.9 Jewish persecution, 1933–39

The Nazis were obsessed with race, believing Aryans were superior and other races were sub-human

- The Nazis believed that Aryans, the people of northern and western Europe, were the strongest (*Übermenschen*).
- Nazi scientists taught that there were distinct types of Aryan with specific features (like nose shape and hair colour). **Nordic** Aryans with blond hair and blue eyes were the most superior.
- *Untermenschen* ('sub-humans') included **Gypsies**, black people and **Slavs** (the people of eastern Europe), but the most vicious hatred was reserved for the Jews.
- The Nuremberg Laws of 1935 defined anyone with three or four Jewish grandparents as a Jew even if they did not have any belief in the Jewish faith. Those people with one or two Jewish grandparents were *Mischling* or half-Jews.
- The Nazis believed that Jews had distinct features including large noses.

> **Key point**
>
> Jewish persecution grew increasingly worse through the period as the Nazis used propaganda, laws and eventually violence to harass a group whom they saw as racially inferior.

The Nazis hated the Jews for many reasons, which were inaccurate myths

Nazi myth	Reality
Jews owned all the big businesses and profited from the economic crisis in the 1920s and 1930s	Some Jews owned big businesses but they were few in number. They had suffered during the crisis like everyone
The defeat in the First World War was the fault of the Jews	Jews had fought in the German army like other citizens
Jews were **Communists**	Some Jews were Communists but they belonged to all political parties
Jews controlled Germany	Jews were less than one per cent of the population and their influence was very limited

Persecution of the Jews grew through the 1930s as they were socially excluded and humiliated

- **Social exclusion** increased, with signs saying 'Jews not wanted here' becoming common.
- Although **physical persecution** was not as common as during the war years, Jews were often humiliated in the streets by the SA or police.
- Publications portrayed Jews as money-grabbers and Communists who were intent on destroying Germany. Nazi newspapers like *Der Stürmer* printed the worst of this anti-Semitic material.

Anti-Semitic laws grew more intense through the 1930s and excluded Jews from all aspects of society

- 1933: Jews were excluded from all legal professions.
- 1935: the Nuremberg Laws made marriage and sex between Germans and Jews punishable with prison.
- 1938: Jews had to have a J printed on their passports and had to add the middle name Israel or Sarah to their name.
- 1938: Jewish children were banned from non-Jewish schools.
- 1939: Jewish emigrants were not allowed to take valuables with them. Jews had to hand over all gold, jewellery and valuables to the state.

Kristallnacht (Night of the Broken Glass) was a turning point: **anti-Semitism** became **increasingly violent**

- On 7 November 1938, a Polish Jew, Herschel Grynszpan, assassinated a German embassy official, Ernst vom Rath, causing widespread anger against Jews.

- On 9 November, the Nazi decided they would not directly respond but if attacks on Jews happened they should not be stopped.

- Many local Nazi parties and many SA and Hitler Youth took this as an official invitation to unleash violence.

- On 9 November and into the next day, 267 synagogues were destroyed and 7500 Jewish-owned establishments had their windows smashed and contents looted. At least 91 Jews were murdered.

- At the same time, the SS and Gestapo arrested up to 30,000 Jewish men and sent most to concentration camps.

- The German public did not speak out against this and nor did the wider world.

Link the source

Link the parts of the source to the correct statement around the image. Once you have done this, explain why the Nazis would have included that element in the picture. Remember to use the facts you have learned from these two pages to do this. One has been done for you.

SOURCE E *A poster from a 1937 Nazi exhibition called 'The Eternal Jew'.*

A stereotyped big nose

The Nazis have included this as they believed that Jews were rich and owned all the big businesses in Germany. They believed they profited from the Great Depression

Gold coins

A map of the world with a hammer and sickle, the symbol of Communism and Soviet Russia.

A whip

Now you have linked the statements to the source and annotated them, you should be able to complete an exam question:

What can Source E tell us about Nazi views about Jewish people? Use the source and your own knowledge to support your answer. **(7 marks)**

Test yourself

1. Which groups of people were seen as *Untermenschen* (sub-humans)?
2. Can you name three examples of anti-Semitic legislation from 1933 to 1939?
3. When was *Kristallnacht*?
4. Why did the Nazis hate the Jews?

> **Challenge question**
>
> How and why did the Nazi persecution of the Jews evolve from 1933 to 1939?

6.10 Germany at war, 1939–42

In **December 1939**, Hitler announced that all of Germany would become a **war economy**

- All industries focused on supporting the war effort and had targets for production.
- **Military expenditure** rose dramatically. In 1939, 23 per cent of the goods produced in German factories were related to the military; by 1941 this had risen to 47 per cent.
- By 1941, 55 per cent of the German workforce was in war-related work.
- Despite this effort, production struggled. For example, in 1939, 8290 aircraft were produced, but this had only risen to 10,780 in 1941.
- Inefficiency and a lack of central control stifled innovation.

Key point

As the war progressed, the people of Germany faced an increasingly difficult situation. They were being used to fuel the war economy and faced great shortages.

Speer's appointment in **February 1942** led to an **improvement in the economy**

- In February 1942, Albert Speer was made Minister of Armaments and War Production.
- Speer's plan was to give factories independence ('industrial self-responsibility'), but at the same time ensure central control (through the Central Planning Board).
- His efforts increased production and made the economy successful. He did this by:
  - focusing factories on producing a single product
  - employing more women in factories
  - using concentration camp prisoners as workers
  - excluding skilled workers from compulsory military service.

During these **early war years**, the German people suffered **shortages and hardships**

- The war economy led to shortages of goods and **rationing** was introduced. Foods, clothing, shoes and coal were strictly controlled.
- The rationing system was very complex. People were allocated points according to their ages and occupations, and were given colour-coded ration cards for different products.
- Rationing ensured that most people were adequately fed during the war, but German civilians spent much time queuing and the quality of products was reduced.

The **war years** began to **change the role of women** as more joined the **workforce**

- Women were never **conscripted** into factories (as in Britain) as the Nazi leadership was split over their role.
- However, more did join the workforce. In 1939, 760,000 women worked in war industries and this had risen to 1.5 million by 1941. But out of a total of 30 million women this number was still small.
- With the restrictions on marriage loans lifted for people in work, more women entered the workforce.
- From 1939, women aged under 25 had to complete six months' Labour Service before being allowed to enter full employment.

 Test yourself

1 What new job was Albert Speer given in 1942?
2 How did war change the role of women?
3 What was the impact of war on German children?

Challenge question

Who suffered the most as a result of the war: workers, women or children?

German cities were heavily bombed and children were evacuated to escape the worst horrors

- In the spring of 1940, the RAF began bombing campaigns in Germany. By autumn, most cities faced air raids three or four nights a week.

- The government began a programme of building air raid shelters.

- In September 1940, the child evacuation programme known as *Kinderlandverschickung* began.

- All children below the age of fourteen were eligible for a six-month stay in a rural area.

- Those below the age of ten were placed in families and could be accompanied by their mothers.

- Older children were placed in 'camps', which were run by the Hitler Youth.

- Conditions in the camps were very strict. As a result, not many wanted to send their children. Of the 260,000 eligible children in Berlin, only 40,000 participated.

Link the source

On the right is a Nazi propaganda poster. In 1940, posters like this encouraged the German people to donate any unused metal that could then be melted down to make weapons and ammunition for the war.

In your exam you will be given sources like this and asked to explain what the source can tell you. In this case:

What can Source F tell us about the impact of the war on the German people? Use the source and your own knowledge to support your answer. (7 marks)

The last bit of this question, *'and your own knowledge'*, is really important. Next to the source we have given you some inferences you can make from this particular source. Your job is to find a piece of evidence from this page to support each inference. Write the evidence you find next to each box.

> This source shows us that the war years were difficult for the German people and they faced shortages

> This source shows us that women were an important part of the German war effort

> This source shows us that the German people were all expected to contribute to the war economy

SOURCE F *A propaganda poster from Germany in 1940. The text says 'I also help the Führer. Metal donation for the German people on 20 April 1940'.*

Auch ich
helfe
dem
Führer

Metallspende des Deutschen Volkes zum 20. April 1940

6.11 Wartime opposition

> **Key point**
>
> Opposition increased as the war went on, and ranged from assassination attempts to the simple act of writing anti-Nazi leaflets.

The **July Bomb Plot of 1944,** by disgruntled army soldiers, was **almost successful** in **assassinating Hitler**

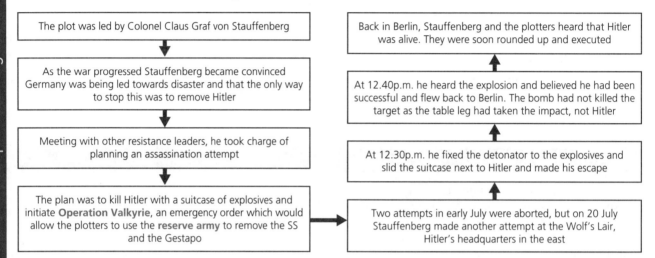

The plot was led by Colonel Claus Graf von Stauffenberg

↓

As the war progressed Stauffenberg became convinced Germany was being led towards disaster and that the only way to stop this was to remove Hitler

↓

Meeting with other resistance leaders, he took charge of planning an assassination attempt

↓

The plan was to kill Hitler with a suitcase of explosives and initiate **Operation Valkyrie**, an emergency order which would allow the plotters to use the **reserve army** to remove the SS and the Gestapo

→

Two attempts in early July were aborted, but on 20 July Stauffenberg made another attempt at the Wolf's Lair, Hitler's headquarters in the east

↑

At 12.30p.m. he fixed the detonator to the explosives and slid the suitcase next to Hitler and made his escape

↑

At 12.40p.m. he heard the explosion and believed he had been successful and flew back to Berlin. The bomb had not killed the target as the table leg had taken the impact, not Hitler

↑

Back in Berlin, Stauffenberg and the plotters heard that Hitler was alive. They were soon rounded up and executed

Despite the risks involved, some brave individuals **publicly criticised the Nazis** as the war progressed

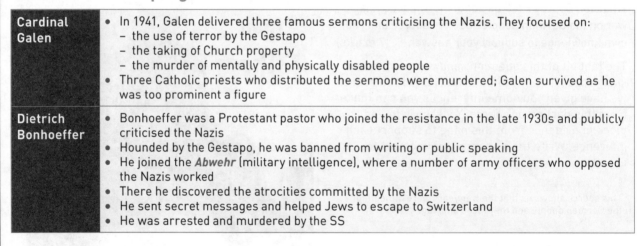

Cardinal Galen	• In 1941, Galen delivered three famous sermons criticising the Nazis. They focused on:
	  – the use of terror by the Gestapo
	  – the taking of Church property
	  – the murder of mentally and physically disabled people
	• Three Catholic priests who distributed the sermons were murdered; Galen survived as he was too prominent a figure

Dietrich Bonhoeffer	• Bonhoeffer was a Protestant pastor who joined the resistance in the late 1930s and publicly criticised the Nazis • Hounded by the Gestapo, he was banned from writing or public speaking • He joined the *Abwehr* (military intelligence), where a number of army officers who opposed the Nazis worked • There he discovered the atrocities committed by the Nazis • He sent secret messages and helped Jews to escape to Switzerland • He was arrested and murdered by the SS

Others like the **White Rose** chose to **criticise** the Nazis in **secretly distributed leaflets**

- The White Rose was a group at Munich University centred around Hans and Sophie Scholl.
- Influenced by Galen and what they had seen fighting on the Eastern Front, the group wrote anti-Nazi leaflets.
- The first four leaflets were produced between June and July 1942 and were distributed locally.
- The fifth was entitled 'An Appeal to All Germans' and 6000–9000 copies were distributed to nine German cities.
- After the Nazi defeat at Stalingrad, a sixth leaflet was produced in February 1943 but the Scholls were caught distributing them. All the members of the group were executed for their actions.

Passive resistance also increased during the war years although it is difficult to know by how much

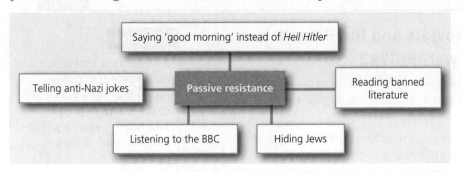

Test yourself

1 Who was Colonel von Stauffenberg?
2 How many leaflets did the White Rose Group produce?
3 What did Cardinal Galen's sermons criticise?
4 How did people passively resist the Nazis?

Although opposition increased during the war, it was still only a minority of the population

- Most people did not know of the Nazi atrocities so did not oppose them.
- Many people lived in fear of the SS and Gestapo and would not dare step out of line.
- Nazi propaganda was highly effective in winning over people.
- The Nazis were initially very successful in the war and as a result lots of people supported them.

Make revision cards

Use the headings below to help you create some revision cards about the different individuals and groups who opposed the Nazis. Create one card for each of the following:

- the July Bomb Plot
- Cardinal Galen
- Dietrich Bonhoeffer
- White Rose Group
- passive resistance.

Put the title of the person or group at the top of the card and then split it into two. In the first half add detail about why they opposed the Nazis in one colour. In the second half add detail about how they opposed the Nazis in another colour. Limit the number of words in each half to fewer than ten.

Spot the mistakes

This paragraph attempts to answer a question about opposition to the Nazi regime during the Second World War. However, there are some mistakes in the paragraph. Find them and correct them.

During the war years, opposition to the Nazi regime decreased. Lots of different groups opposed the Nazis for a vast number of reasons. Probably the most serious threat to the Nazi regime came during July 1943 when a plot led by Colonel Stauffenberg nearly assassinated Hitler with a bomb. The navy backed a plot aimed to kill Hitler at the Hound's Lair in the west. The bomb did explode but the chair took the impact of the blast and only injured the Führer. Serious opposition also came from Church leaders. Cardinal Galen wrote six sermons against the Nazis as he was opposed to the extermination of disabled and mentally ill people in Germany. Dietrich Bonhoeffer was a Catholic priest who joined the secret service and helped Jews to escape from Germany. Youth groups also opposed the Nazis. The most notable example is the Black Carnation Group which was led by Hans and Sophie Scholl who distributed leaflets in London.

6.12 The impact of total war on the German people, 1943–45

Facing defeat by the Soviets and the British, the Nazis moved to 'total war' in 1943

- On 18 February 1943, Goebbels addressed the German public at the Sportpalast Berlin and asked them to do anything they could to achieve victory.
- **Total war** (where everyone is enlisted to support the war effort) had numerous impacts on the German people:

Nazi total war policy	Impact
Women were mobilised into the war effort	Three million women between the ages of 17 and 45 were called to work. Only 1 million actually took up the call
Anything that did not contribute to the war effort was eliminated	Professional sport was ended, magazines were closed and non-essential businesses were shut down
Shortages became even worse	In August 1943, clothes rationing was suspended as the production of civilian clothes ended
An increase in propaganda	People were encouraged to embrace the idea of total war

Key point

As Germany increasingly faced defeat in the war, more and more was asked of the German people. The Nazis began a policy of 'total war', affecting all ages and classes of society.

Although Allied air raids on German cities had begun in 1940, they intensified after 1943

- In late July 1943, the Allies bombed Hamburg. Half the city was destroyed and 40,000 people were killed.
- In November 1943, the Allies began an intensive attack on Berlin with 750 planes; 500,000 people were made homeless and nearly 100,000 injured.
- In February 1945, Dresden was bombed by 727 British planes and 527 American planes. Their bombs caused a **firestorm** that destroyed 1600 acres of Dresden and led to the deaths of around 25,000 people.

Nazi leaders became more paranoid and increased their use of terror against the German people

- The huge number of refugees from those countries now occupied by the Soviet Union added to the pressures on fuel and food in Germany.
- The shock of the **July Bomb Plot** led to a surge in Hitler's popularity and an increase in arrests and executions.
- The Gestapo and SS arrested over 7000 people that they managed to connect to the plot and executed 5000 of them.

✎ Test yourself

1 What were the major changes introduced as a result of total war?
2 When did the Allied bombing raids intensify?
3 What was the *Volkssturm*?
4 Give three examples of the negative impact of war for the German people, 1943–45.

Challenge question

Does the fact that the Germans fought to the bitter end show that they were fully indoctrinated by the Nazis by 1943?

Goebbels as Reich Trustee for Total War (July 1944) ensured that every aspect of German society was focused on the war

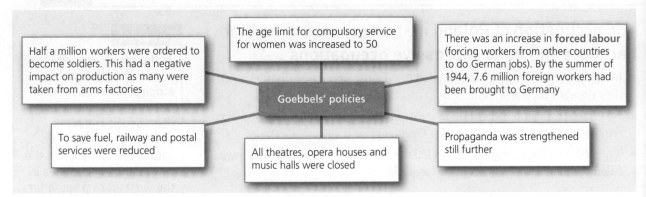

Half a million workers were ordered to become soldiers. This had a negative impact on production as many were taken from arms factories

The age limit for compulsory service for women was increased to 50

There was an increase in **forced labour** (forcing workers from other countries to do German jobs). By the summer of 1944, 7.6 million foreign workers had been brought to Germany

Goebbels' policies

To save fuel, railway and postal services were reduced

All theatres, opera houses and music halls were closed

Propaganda was strengthened still further

In October 1944, as the military situation worsened, Hitler ordered the creation of the *Volkssturm*

- All males between the ages of 16 and 60 who were not already in military service were forced to join the *Volkssturm* ('people's storm', a militia of the old and young).

- They received just four days' training.
- There were no uniforms and they were issued with old rifles and captured foreign weapons.
- All in all, the *Volkssturm* was ineffective.

By April 1945, all that remained of the Nazi Reich was in central Berlin. Germany surrendered on 2 May

- The Germans fought until the bitter end for a variety of reasons:
  - terror of the SS and Gestapo
  - loyalty and faith in Hitler
  - effective propaganda.

 Develop the detail

Each of the following statements could be used to support points made in an exam answer about the impact of war on Germany, 1943–45. However, the statements are vague and general. Add further details to show that you understand the general point being made.

Once you have done this, write a better version of each statement using the details that you have added.

Statement	Further detail
The Nazis changed their tactics and moved to total war towards the middle of the war	
The impact of this was vast	
The most notable example of this is that women were put into work	
Additionally, the Nazis stopped doing things which had no impact on the war	
Finally, to get the people behind this idea, propaganda really increased	
At the same time though, there were negative impacts of the war on Germany	
Bombing began in German cities and wrecked many town centres	
After someone tried to kill Hitler, the Nazis really increased their terror over the German people, who then lived in fear	
After this, Goebbels took over the war effort and made a lot of changes	

6.13 The contrasting nature of Nazi rule in eastern and western Europe

The **occupation of Poland** in the east was one of the **harshest and most repressive occupations**

- In September 1939, the Nazis invaded to take the *lebensraum* (living space) they thought they deserved.
- By October, Poland had ceased to exist and was split into five regions. Four regions would be incorporated into Germany.
- The fifth and largest region was called the **General Government** and was ruled by Hans Frank as Governor General.

The Nazis' plan to **remove Polish culture and people** was successful, with **horrific consequences**

Removing culture	Removing Slavic Poles	Removing other Poles	Removing Jewish Poles
In May 1940, Polish culture, education (schools and universities) and leadership were all systemically destroyed. Around 30,000 of the most talented Poles were arrested	Slavic Poles were considered racially inferior and 1.9 million non-Jewish citizens were murdered by the SS and *Wehrmacht* (German army)	Between 1939 and 1945, 1.5 million other Poles were sent to do forced labour in Germany. The Polish Decrees established rules for these workers, paying them less and humiliating them (for example, they had to wear a P arm band)	The worst fate was experienced by the Polish Jews. The 3.5 million population was ghettoised and 3 million would be murdered in the death camps

Facing such extreme occupation, the **Polish people** formed one of the **largest resistance groups in Europe**

- The Polish government, which had escaped to London in 1939, helped to establish **Delegatura**, a secret state within Poland.
- In August 1944, the Poles staged an uprising in Warsaw, a bitter struggle against Nazi rule that lasted for two months. The Nazis brutally crushed this, with 200,000 killed.

The **Netherlands** was invaded in May 1940. This was a very different **occupation** from that of **Poland**

- The Dutch were seen as having the same ethnic background as the Germans so were treated more as equals.
- Civil servants were allowed to continue working if they chose to, although 30 per cent of town mayors stepped down.
- The Dutch education system was not changed.
- A Dutch brigade of SS soldiers was created.
- On 29 June 1940, many Dutch people wore a white carnation, the flower of their now exiled royal family, but no one was punished.

> **Key point**
>
> At the height of their power, the Nazis ruled an empire from the Atlantic Ocean to the outskirts of Moscow. The Nazi occupation varied from country to country. On the whole, those countries in the west were treated far better than in the east but everywhere occupation brought suffering on the inhabitants of the country.

> **Test yourself**
>
> 1 Who was the governor of the General Government?
> 2 Why were the Dutch treated more favourably than the Polish?
> 3 Identify three policies introduced in Nazi-occupied Netherlands.

Dutch resistance increased in 1941: the Nazis realised they had to change their tactics

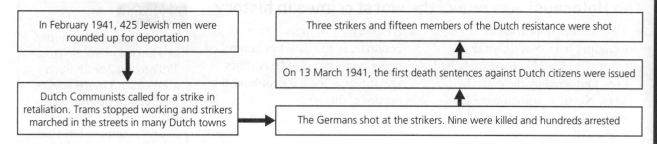

In February 1941, 425 Jewish men were rounded up for deportation

↓

Dutch Communists called for a strike in retaliation. Trams stopped working and strikers marched in the streets in many Dutch towns

→

The Germans shot at the strikers. Nine were killed and hundreds arrested

↑

On 13 March 1941, the first death sentences against Dutch citizens were issued

↑

Three strikers and fifteen members of the Dutch resistance were shot

In 1943, the Nazis abandoned trying to win over the Dutch and switched to intimidation and violence

- In April 1942, all Jews had to wear the Star of David.
- In 1943, the Nazis began deporting Jews to extermination camps. 107,000 Jews (76 per cent of the total Jewish population) were deported.
- With German men fighting on the front lines it was decided that Dutch men would be used as forced labour. By 1944, all men between the ages of 16 and 60 had to report for forced labour. 500,000 ended up working in Germany, a third of all eligible men.

- Dutch resistance grew as a result of this. They hid 300,000 men from forced labour and illegally published anti-Nazi leaflets.
- 20,000 resistance members were arrested. Most were sent to the four Dutch concentration camps.
- Living conditions had slowly worsened through the war but in the winter of 1944–45 food shortages became severe. 20,000 Dutch people died of starvation.
- On 5 May 1945, the Netherlands was liberated by Canadian soldiers.

 Support or challenge?

Below are a sample 18-mark question and a table giving examples that could support or challenge the statement given. Use the information on this spread and your own knowledge to make a decision by ticking the appropriate column. When you have done this, add three more examples and show whether they support or challenge the statement.

'German occupation in the Second World War was, in general, far harsher in eastern Europe than in western Europe.' How far do you agree with this view? (18 marks)

Example	Supports	Challenges
1.9 million non-Jewish Polish citizens were murdered by the SS and *Wehrmacht*		
After invasion Poland ceased to exist. It was split into five regions		
3.5 million Poles were ghettoised and 3 million of these were murdered in the Nazi death camps		
Living conditions in the Netherlands in 1944–45 were so bad that 20,000 died of starvation		
76 per cent of the Dutch Jewish population was murdered by the Nazis in the death camps, one of the highest percentages of any country in Europe		
The Dutch were seen as Aryan and as a result were treated fairly		
Around 30,000 of the most talented Polish intellectuals and artists were arrested. Most were murdered		
A Dutch brigade of SS soldiers was established		

6.14 The Holocaust

The **Holocaust** was one of the **worst crimes in history**

- Eleven million individuals, including Jews, Slavs, Gypsies, Communists and homosexuals, had been murdered by the Nazis by 1945. Nearly 6 million were Jews whom the Nazis systematically eradicated.

- As the Nazis occupied more countries in the east they controlled larger populations of Jews. They saw this as a '**Jewish problem**' that needed a solution.

> **Key point**
>
> The Holocaust developed in a series of steps from 1939 to 1942, with each step getting more severe. This ended up with mass extermination of Jews in death camps, the sole purpose of which was murder.

A **new solution** was needed to eliminate the **large numbers of Jews: concentration in ghettos** (1939–41)

- With 3.5 million Jews in Poland, forced emigration would not work.

- The Nazis decided they would move the Jews of Europe to a new reservation (an area of the Soviet Union was discussed) but in 1939 they did not have the land to do this.

- As a first step towards this they concentrated the Jews into **ghettos** (enclosed districts in most towns) so they would be ready for deportation.

- Ghettos varied in size and there were hundreds in German-occupied Poland alone.

- The largest ghetto was in Warsaw. Completed in May 1940, by March 1941 the ghetto had 445,000 Jewish inhabitants. A third of the Warsaw population lived in 2.4 per cent of its area.

- Overcrowding led to disease and death, particularly in the young and old. In its three-year existence, over 140,000 died.

The **mass murder of Jews** began with the **Nazi invasion of the Soviet Union** (June 1941)

- The *Einsatzgruppen* were mobile killing units of SS men, police and auxiliary units recruited from the local population.

- Four *Einsatzgruppen* (A, B, C and D), each consisting of 500–1000 men, followed the *Wehrmacht* as they invaded the Soviet Union.

- As they reached villages and towns, Jews and Communists were rounded up. Taken to a secluded area, often in woodland, the victims were forced to dig a large pit, then lined up and shot.

- In the winter of 1941, 90 per cent of the victims were Jews, around 1 million people.

- One of the worst crimes was at Babi Yar in Ukraine where 33,000 Jews were murdered in a single day.

While the **Jews on the Eastern Front** were killed by **bullets**, the **Jews of occupied Poland** were **murdered by gas**

- With no reservation found, in the autumn of 1941, the Nazis decided they would exterminate the Jews in the General Government (this is known as **Operation Reinhard**).

- This began at Chelmno, where Jews were gassed to death in vans by exhaust fumes.

- New extermination or death camps were created, the sole purpose of which was to murder. By 1942, Belzec (March), Sobibor (May) and Treblinka (July) were all operational.

- Each of the camps was kept in great secrecy. Managed by only 20–35 officers, the camps were all in wooded areas away from large towns.

- Jews were deported from the ghettos and would arrive at what appeared to be a train station. They were then stripped of their clothing and possessions before being gassed in chambers, which had been made to look like showers.

- By the end of the war, 1.7 million Polish Jews had been murdered in the camps.

A **plan** was formed in **January 1942** to **murder all Jews in Europe**

- In January 1942, in a 90-minute meeting at Wannsee, Reinhard Heydrich introduced the plan.
- The Jews of occupied Europe would be removed from their home countries and transported in trains to the General Government, where they would be murdered by gassing.
- Adolf Eichmann, a senior SS officer who was at the meeting, was put in charge of organising this mass murder.

Auschwitz II–Birkenau was the most famous extermination camp where **over one million Jews were murdered**

- Four gas chambers and **crematoria** (where the bodies would be burned) were designed and built to kill and dispose of thousands of Jews at the same time.
- Jews from across Europe were transported to the site in cattle trucks, packed in like animals, with no water or toilet facilities.
- When the trains arrived, the prisoners formed two lines of men and women. SS guards and doctors then began a selection process.
- The fit and able were sent to the right to work as slaves in the factories connected to the site. Everyone else (about 75 per cent of those who arrived) was sent to the left to be gassed immediately.
- The gas chambers were designed to look like showers. Zyklon B pellets were dropped in through the roof. The victims were dead within twenty minutes.
- *Sonderkommandos* (groups of Jews forced to work for the Nazis) would then enter the chambers, wearing gas masks, and remove the bodies to be burned in the giant ovens.
- Up to 12,000 individuals were murdered per day.

 Test yourself

1 What was the name of the organisation that followed the *Wehrmacht* and murdered Jews?
2 Where was the largest ghetto in Poland?
3 What was a *Sonderkommando*?
4 Name three extermination camps.

Challenge question

Was the Holocaust inevitable?

 Getting from A to B

The chain of events that led the Nazis to systematically murder nearly 6 million Jewish people is a complex story. It has a start, the invasion of Poland, and a clear end, with the mass extermination of Jews at Auschwitz II–Birkenau. The question is: how do we get from A to B?

You are not going to remember all the details of this story so you must select the most important parts. Four of the boxes below are empty. Your challenge is to decide what are the four most important steps that lead from A to B. Complete the empty boxes.

A The invasion of Poland				B Mass extermination of Jews in death camps

6.15 Responses to Nazi rule: collaboration, accommodation and resistance

In every **occupied country** the inhabitants had to decide how to **respond to Nazi rule**

Collaborate	Work with or for the Nazis, actively helping them in their occupation
Accommodate	Tolerate or put up with Nazi occupiers but do nothing to actively help this
Resist	Work against the Nazis, actively resisting their occupation. This stretched from very small to large acts of terrorism

Key point

People responded to Nazi occupation in a variety of ways, from helping the Nazis to actively working against them. Each individual's actions were driven by a large number of factors.

France was **split** into two zones, a **northern occupied zone** and a **southern 'free' zone**

- The 'southern zone', known as **Vichy France**, was ruled by the 84-year-old, right-wing French nationalist Philippe Pétain. The northern zone was directly ruled by the Nazis.
- Both zones suffered hardships. Hundreds of thousands of French men were sent to Germany as forced labourers. Over 70,000 French Jews were deported to death camps.
- Some people joined the **French Resistance**, who fought against Nazi rule by passing intelligence to the Allies or sabotaging Nazi rule.
- Other people took part in more minor resistance like listening to the BBC on the radio.

 Test yourself

1 How would you define collaboration, accommodation and resistance?
2 How did André Trocmé resist the Nazis?
3 Who were the Bielski partisans?
4 Why did some people choose to tolerate the Nazis and do nothing to resist or help them?

André Trocmé and Coco Chanel are good examples of resisters and collaborators to Nazi occupation in France

André Trocmé	• A Protestant pastor of the small village of Le Chambon-sur-Lignon in south-east France • When the authorities in Vichy France began putting foreign Jews into concentration camps, he felt that he had to act • Between December 1940 and September 1944, Trocmé arranged for 5000 Jews, mainly children, to be hidden around his parish • The local population worked together to place them in homes, hotels, farms and schools. They forged identification cards and ration cards, and in some cases led escapes to Switzerland • In February 1943, Trocmé was arrested. Eventually released after 28 days, he continued his work. But, in late 1943, he had to go into hiding himself for the rest of the war due to fear of further arrest
Coco Chanel	• In the 1930s, Chanel had established herself as a very famous fashion designer and perfume maker • After occupation, Chanel stayed in Paris and became friends with the Nazis • She began a romance with Baron Hans Günther von Dincklage, a military intelligence officer. Some historians think that she began working as a Nazi spy • In 1941, taking advantage of new anti-Semitic legislation, she tried to persuade the authorities to remove the Jewish directors of her perfume company. She was not successful in this

Across Europe there were many examples of **collaboration, accommodation and resistance**

Collaboration	Accommodation	Resistance
• In Belgium, the DeVlag movement had 50,000 members by 1943. They helped the Nazis to recruit members to the Waffen-SS • The Chetniks were a group of Serbian nationalists who agreed to work with the Nazi forces in Yugoslavia	• The Danish people were allowed to keep their government during the war in return for establishing good relations with the Germans • During the occupation of Greece, three Greek prime ministers, chosen and controlled by the Nazis, passed legislation demanded by the occupiers	• Significant numbers of Poles helped to rescue an estimated 450,000 Jews from certain death • The Bielski partisans numbered 1236. They were escapees from the Polish ghettos and lived in the forest completing sabotage missions against the Nazis

 Improve the answer

Below is an extract from an answer to the question:

'The Nazis were met with fierce resistance.' How far do you agree with this view of the reaction to Nazi occupation from 1939 to 1945? (18 marks)

Annotate the answer to show its strengths and weaknesses.

> In some ways the Nazis were met with resistance and in others they were not. The Nazis occupied a large number of countries in Europe and in each country people reacted in very different ways.
>
> In France, the people really hated the Nazis! They actively resisted the occupiers and did everything they could to undermine their rule. They plotted against them and tried to stop their laws from working. One man, André Trocmé, went as far as hiding Jews and helping them to escape. However, not everyone resisted the Nazis; some people liked them and helped them. The best example to prove this is Coco Chanel. She had a relationship with an SS officer and some people even think she gave away intelligence to the Nazis!
>
> In other countries across Europe there was a similar response, with some people resisting and others liking the Nazis. In Denmark, there is evidence that people just put up with the Nazis. The Nazis allowed them to keep their government so the people sort of went along with their rule.

Now write your own 18-mark answer to the question.

You can produce a strong answer and gain high marks by:

● starting with your own clear judgement in response to the question 'How far … ?'

● supporting your judgement with paragraphs that focus on different places or different responses to Nazi occupation

● including specific knowledge in each paragraph

● ending with a conclusion that summarises the main reasons for your judgement or a final paragraph that drives home your strongest reason for agreeing or disagreeing.

Notes

Quick quizzes and answers at www.hoddereducation.co.uk/myrevisionnotesdownloads

Acknowledgements

The Publishers would like to thank the following for permission to reproduce copyright material.

Photo credits: p67 National Geographic Creative/Alamy Stock Photo; **p75** Historic England/Mary Evans; **p107** ClassicStock/Alamy Stock Photo; **p111** Look and Learn; **p167** Granger Historical Picture Archive/Alamy Stock Photo; **p169** INTERFOTO/Alamy Stock Photo.

Acknowledgements: BBC History: 'English and Norman Society', www.bbc.co.uk/history/british/normans/society_01.shtml by Mike Ibeji, 2011. BBC Legacies (Cambridge): 'Awake the Hereward', www.bbc.co.uk/legacies/myths_legends/england/cambridgeshire/article_2.shtml by Emma Borley, 2014. BBC TV: *The Time Traveller's Guide to Elizabethan England*, written and presented by Ian Mortimer, 2013. California State University, Northridge: Family Life in Shakespeare's Time an online resource for American schools, 'The Ties That Bind: Family Life', www.csun.edu/~hflrc001/family.html by Joseph Papp and Elizabeth Kirkland, 2003. Coronet: *The Gestapo* by Frank McDonough, 2015. *Daily Mail*: 'Pirate who plundered Elizabeth's heart: How Walter Raleigh's silver tongue and broody looks bewitched the Virgin Queen', *Daily Mail*, 30 August by A.N. Wilson, 2011. Elizabethan Era, 'Elizabethan Theatre', www.elizabethan-era.org.uk/elizabethan-theatre.htm by Linda Alchin, retrieved July 2017. Encyclopedia Britannica: 'Sir Walter Raleigh', www.britannica.com/contributor/Agnes-MC-Latham/1690 by Agnes Latham, retrieved July 2017. History Extra: '7 things you (probably) didn't know about Elizabeth, www.historyextra.com/article/facts-elizabethi by Tracy Borman, 2015. *History Today*: 'William the Conqueror Reassessed' by Marc Morris, *History Today* Volume 66, Issue 10, 2016. Hodder Education: *Investigating History 1500–1750: Foundation Edition* by John D. Clare, 2004. Macmillan: *Foundation (History of England, vol. 1)* by Peter Ackroyd, 2011. Medievalists.Net: 'William of Normandy's Claim to the English Throne: Examining the Evidence', www.medievalists.net/2015/04/william-of-normandys-claim-to-the-english-throne-examining-the-evidence/by Jacob Deacon, 2015. OCR: mark scheme, © OCR 2018. Oxford University Press, *The Wealth of Anglo-Saxon England* by Peter Sawyer, 2013. Palgrave Macmillan: *Joseph Goebbels: Life and Death* by Toby Thacker, 2009. Transworld: *The Time Team Guide to the Archaeological Sites of Britain and Ireland* by Tim Taylor et al., 2005.

With thanks to OCR for permission to reproduce questions from the following exam papers:
OCR, GCE History B, J411/14 – sample question paper
OCR, GCE History B, J411/33 – sample question paper

Every effort has been made to trace all copyright holders, but if any have been inadvertently overlooked, the Publishers will be pleased to make the necessary arrangements at the first opportunity.

> **TIP**
>
> If you are looking for the glossary you'll find it here: www.hoddereducation.co.uk/myrevisionnotesdownloads. It defines all the key terms found in **purple** in this book.